We Flew Alone

SECOND EDITION

We Flew Alone

Men and Missions of the United States Navy's B-24 Liberator Squadrons Pacific Operations

February 1943–September 1944

SECOND EDITION

Alan C. Carey

Schiffer Military History
Atglen, PA

Acknowledgments

Many individuals spent considerable time providing me with information to make this book a true comprehensive history. Their dedication to preserving United States naval history is truly appreciated. Many of the veterans who aided with the original work have since joined their brothers in eternal peace. I especially thank Minoru Kamada for providing information on Imperial Japanese forces. Image and source credits are cited individually with the book. The following is the list of veterans, family members, and organizations that provided assistance throughout the years. I apologize to those I may have missed: Jack Authelet, Roy Balke, Randall Baylis, Ed Beasley, Frank Betz Family Collection, Harry Boche, John Bostick, John Dienst, Herb Donald, Richard M. Douglass, Howard Ells, Edith Falkenhagen, Mrs. Lillie Ann Flora (Baldwin), Gordon Fowler, Rex Hardy, Andy Halaz, Steve Hawley, Sterling Hays, Nate Hodge, Dianne Hunter, Bob Kirk, Joseph Komorowski Family Collection, Chris Longcrier, Al Marks, T. W. McCarthy, Davis McAlister, James McKay, Joseph Morgan, John H. Parker Jr., Ed Robinson, Kenneth Sanford, Harlan Scott, David Smith, Paul Stevens, Steve Surface, H. J. Thompson, Louise Thoman, Bill Thys, James Van Dyne, John Wagner, Danny Walters, Dick Webb, John Webster, George Winters, and Dick Webb.

Emil Buehler Library, National Museum of Naval Aviation
National Archive and Records Administration, College Park, Maryland
Navy Historical Center
San Diego Aerospace Museum
WFI Research Group

Library of Congress Control Number: 2017933337

Cover design by Molly Shields
Type set in Times New Roman

ISBN: 978-0-7643-5369-7
Printed in China

Published by Schiffer Publishing, Ltd.
4880 Lower Valley Road
Atglen, PA 19310
Phone: (610) 593-1777; Fax: (610) 593-2002
E-mail: Info@schifferbooks.com
Web: www.schifferbooks.com

Contents

Foreword

This is a revised and expanded second edition of *We Flew Alone* (first published in 2000) that includes additional historical information, corrected information, correspondence from veterans or their families, and images not available seventeen years ago. This work expands on the personal stories of those who served with Navy B-24 (PB4Y-1) Liberator squadrons, including the author's father. This work includes terms such as "Japs," which today many may find offensive, but were commonly used during the time. Included is an additional chapter investigating the loss of a combat air crew and subsequent execution of that crew's sole survivor.

This is the story of men who served in a little known aspect of WWII: United States Navy patrol bombing squadrons which flew the B-24 Liberator and the PB4Y-2 Privateer. This volume covers February 1943–September 1944—from the time of the first Navy heavy bombing (VB) squadron's arrival in the South Pacific, during the Solomon and the New Georgia Campaigns, to the final campaigns in the Central Pacific. The second volume covers the period from the liberation of the Philippines in October 1944 to the final days of the Pacific War, during which such units became known as Navy patrol and bombing squadrons (VPB). When possible each squadron's record is included, consisting of number of ships and aircraft damaged or destroyed. Additionally, the dates, names, and rank of men killed in action or in the line of duty are also included.

These men often flew alone on searches that extended 800–1,000 miles across an empty and unforgiving ocean. When a crew was lost, more often than not their fellow squadron members never knew what happened to them. The crews simply vanished without a trace, or every so often a passing plane would see dye marker spreading across the water where a plane had gone down. A temporary sign soon to disappear that there once was a plane with eleven men on board.

This book is not to glorify war, but simply an acknowledgment. This is for the men who served their country and never received the acclaim. They have told me stories of going back home and being asked what they did in the war. When they talked of what they did they were sometimes called liars. "The Navy didn't fly B-24s," was often the remark made to them when they replied. They did not argue, but went on with their lives.

After the war the men found jobs, got married, and had children. Over the years books were written and movies were made about the justified heroics of the Army Air Force, while those who served in Navy Liberator and Privateer squadrons went about their business living a life after WWII.

Their children often did not know their fathers' history, nor were they inclined to ask (as were many members of the "Baby Boom" generation). As the children of WWII veterans have grown older they have begun to pose questions to these men of the "Greatest Generation." Many of these children want to ask what their fathers did in the war. For some it is too late, and a few still do not want to talk about their experiences. For others, they have finally opened up and have begun to talk about their lives during the war.

It is sad to hear some of these men saying their kids could care less about the most dramatic experience in their lives, and even more so when they say to me, "I want you to have these photos or this log. My kids don't care." Most families do care about their father and his service to the United States. Therefore, I decided to write a comprehensive history of the men who flew with these squadrons.

Most people, then and now, do not know that "Swabs" flew the Liberator just as Army airmen did over Europe and the Pacific. They are the forgotten few that often flew alone on patrols that lasted up to twenty hours.

There are no graves to mark those men who were lost in the waters of the Pacific. The men who lived and fought with Navy Liberator and Privateer squadrons are the forgotten heroes of a great generation. This is dedicated to the young men who never returned home and for the families they left behind.

Glossary

United States Navy Enlisted Ranks
AMM: Aviation Machinist's Mate
PhoM: Photographer's Mate
AOM: Aviation Ordnanceman
ARM: Aviation Radioman
AOMB: Aviation Ordnanceman-Bombsight Mechanic
AOMT Aviation Ordnanceman-Aviation Turret Mechanic
S1c: Seaman First Class

Numbers following each rating
1c: First Class
2c: Second Class
3c: Third Class

Japanese Aircraft Engaged by PB4Y Aircraft
The Americans gave code-names to each model of Japanese aircraft:

American	**Model/Type**
Zeke:	Mitsubishi A6M/single-engine fighter
Hamp:	Variant of the A6M
Hap:	Variant of the A6M
Pete:	Mitsubishi F1M2/single-engine float-wing fighter
Rufe:	Nakajima A6M2-N/single-engine float-fighter
Kate:	Nakajima B5NS/single-engine Torpedo-bomber
Irving:	Nakajima Gekko J1N1-S/twin-engine night fighter
Betty:	Mitsubishi G4M/twin-engine bomber
Emily:	H8K/two-engine flying boat
Mavis:	Kawanishi H6K/four-engine reconnaissance flying boat
Nell:	Mitsubishi Type 96 G3M/torpedo bomber
Oscar:	Nakajima Ki-43/single-engine fighter
Tony:	Kawasaki Ki-61/single-engine fighter
Jill:	Nakajima B6N/single-engine Torpedo-bomber
Val:	Aichi D3A/ single-engine dive-bomber
Nick:	Kawasaki Ki-45/twin-engine fighter-bomber
Tess:	Two-engine transport
Topsy:	Mitsubishi Type 100 Ki-57 (L4M)/transport
Tojo:	Ki-44/single-engine fighter

Introduction: Formation of Land-Based Navy Bomber Squadrons

In summer 1942, the Navy needed long-range aircraft to patrol the vast reaches of the Pacific. Other Navy patrol aircraft, such as the PBY-5 Catalina, PBM, and the PB2Y, were too slow and lightly armed; a distinct disadvantage if they were to patrol close to enemy-held islands. Additionally, the PV-1 and PV-2 did not have the range. In July 1942, the Army agreed to the Navy receiving a quantity of B-24D Liberators, changing the designation to PB4Y-1 for patrol bomber four engine. A rumor still exists that the Army gave the Navy B-24s that failed their inspection—not good enough for the Army, but just right for the Navy.[1]

The Navy's use of the Liberator made it possible to cover wider search sectors than before, and more importantly, extensive photographic reconnaissance could be made before a major operation. The squadrons to be established would be designated VB for Navy Bombing until October 1944, when the designation was changed to VPB for Navy Patrol Bomber.

Reading over squadron after action reports, one might think they were in constant combat with the Japanese. However, the first function of a PB4Y crew was always reconnaissance. Enemy shipping or installations were secondary, and only authorized if it did not interfere with their primary mission. Patrols often lasted over twelve hours, hours looking at an empty ocean with hopes the boredom would be interrupted with the sighting of an enemy naval or merchant vessel. Being on the front line, some squadron commanders modified their squadron's purpose and took the offensive against the enemy.

The Navy Liberator had to be modified to suit the needs of long-range patrolling over the Pacific. The first Navy Liberators sent to the Pacific varied little from the Army B-24D, retaining the distinctive Plexiglas nose with free-hand machine guns mounted to protect against frontal attacks. This type of defensive armament would soon prove to be inadequate. Furthermore, a few of the earlier models were not equipped with the Sperry ball turret under the fuselage. Instead, they had twin .50-caliber tunnel guns that were manually fired by a crewman. This piece of equipment was all but useless, in part because it gave the gunner vertigo bending over the guns while firing. By summer 1944 the tunnel guns were gone.

The distinctive Navy version of the Liberator was introduced when most of the conventional B-24s were modified with the

PBY Catalina.

PB2Y Coronado.

PV-2 Harpoon.

Erco bow turret in the nose that extended the length of the aircraft by three feet. The bow turret had twin .50-caliber guns and carried twice the ammunition supply of other turrets—800 versus 400. It also had armor plating in front that gave the pilots additional protection. Some squadrons, such as VPB-111, received J, L, and M models with the Emerson nose turret. A total of 977 PB4Y-1 Liberators (the majority being D and J models) were received by the Navy before war's end.[2]

Unfortunately, there are no examples of the PB4Y-1 Liberator in aviation museums today. The only known example of this plane lies under the Pacific Ocean off Maui, Hawaii. Lost in 1944 and located in the 1980s, this aircraft has been visited by numerous sport divers.

A B-24/PB4Y Bomber being assembled, July 1943. The plane appears to have USAAF Serial Number 42-41109. ***Courtesy of the National Archives***

The second of 977 PB4Y-1s delivered to the Navy was Bureau Number 31937, accepted on 1 September 1942.

Cdr. E. C. Renfro's PB4Y-1 *Sugar* with the Erco Bow Turret. The Japanese in the Central Pacific felt her sting when she served with VB-108. *Courtesy of the National Archives*

Interior view of the cockpit in a B-24 (PB4Y-1) Liberator. *Courtesy of the San Diego Aerospace Museum*

How many B-24s went to Pacific-based squadrons has been difficult to ascertain. Several squadrons served in the European Theater (103, 105, 107, 110, 111, 112, 113, and 114), and there were three Marine Corps squadrons (VMB-154, 254, and 354).

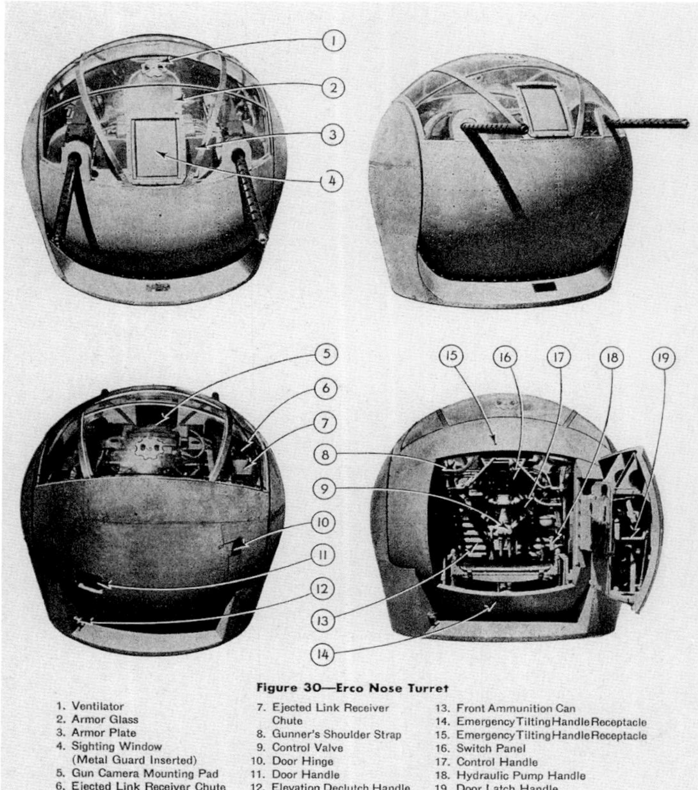

Views of the Erco Bow Turret from the PB4Y-2 Airplane General and Armament Manual produced by the Consolidated-Vultee Aircraft Company.

In the appendix I have tried to document every Liberator that served with Pacific-based Navy squadrons, including all squadron assignments, date of loss, and with nose art names provided. A full accounting of all aircraft has proven to be a complex undertaking for a couple reasons. First, some were assigned to several different squadrons at different periods, or "borrowed" from another squadron. Second, some squadrons failed to list the bureau numbers of Liberators assigned to them. Therefore, history cards of PB4Y-1s in the Navy's inventory were checked for squadron assignments, as were log books and personal recollections. Even with this information accurate assessment proved difficult.

PB4Y-1 Liberator Specifications

Length	67'3"
Wingspan	110'
Height	17'11"
Wing Area	1,048 sq. ft.
Empty Weight	36,950 lbs.
Gross weight	60,000 lbs.
Power Plant	R-1830-43/65
Armament	10 × .50-caliber
Bomb load	8,800 lbs.
Maximum speed	279 mph
Cruising Speed	200 mph
Service ceiling	31,800 ft.
Range	2,960 miles

1

VP–51Arrives in the Pacific January–March 1943

With the arrangement between the Army and Navy completed, the first PB4Y-1 Liberators were turned over for training at Camp Kearney, California. By October 1942, VP-51 had transitioned from the PBY-5A Catalina to the PB4Y-1 and would become the first such naval patrol squadron to conduct operations against Japanese forces; however, the distinction of being the first PB4Y-equipped unit stationed in the South Pacific went to a Marine Corps photographic squadron (discussed later in this book), which began missions a month earlier than VP-51.

Under the leadership of Cdr. William A. Moffett Jr., the men of VP-51 had already experienced war in the Pacific, with the squadron having the distinction of serving in three areas of operation at the same time. During spring and early summer 1942, sections of the squadron served at Midway, Fiji, and Dutch Harbor in Alaska. For those at Midway, they took part in the battle that changed the course of the war.

Cdr. Moffitt, US Naval Academy Class of 1930, was the son of Rear Adm. William A. Moffitt Sr., the architect of naval aviation and a recipient of the Medal of Honor. Moffitt Sr. drowned when the airship USS *Akron* (ZRS-4) crashed off the New Jersey coast on April 4, 1933, a year after his son qualified as a naval aviator. Training of PB4Y-1 crews took place at North Island Naval Air Station and Camp Kearney. The PB4Y crew consisted of ten to twelve men, and each trained to be an integral part of a team. Typically, but not always, the following represented a bomber crew: the pilot or patrol plane commander (PPC), co-pilot, navigator, plane captain, radio-radar operator, bombardier, bow gunner, top turret gunner, port waist gunner, starboard waist gunner, belly gunner, and tail gunner.[1]

All except the first three were enlisted personnel. An interesting aspect of the Navy Liberator crew, and later the Privateer crew, was the bombardier. The first Navy squadrons held to the Army Air Force tradition of using a commissioned officer as a bombardier. However, later squadrons, in stark contrast to Army Air Force crews, utilized an enlisted man.

Typically flight crews were taught the general characteristics of the aircraft and then sent to specialist training in their occupational fields: radiomen went to radio school, ordnance men went to ordnance class, mechanics went to mechanics class, and so on. Every enlisted man went to gunnery school for two weeks and learned how to fire the guns. Andy Halaz, a plane captain in VB-109, recalls going through such training during the fall of 1943:

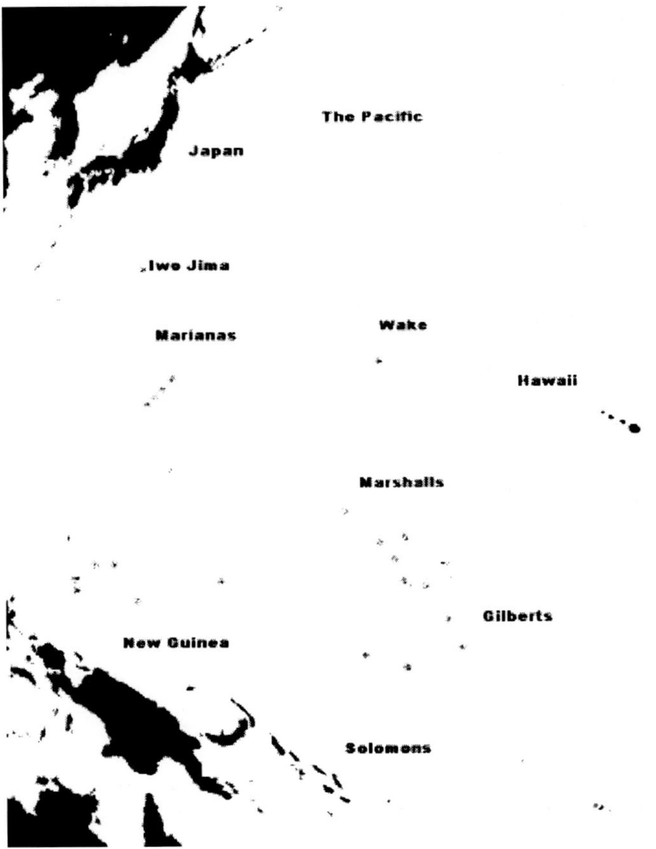

Right and Following Page: Area of Operations of PB4Y-1 Squadrons February 1943–September 1944.

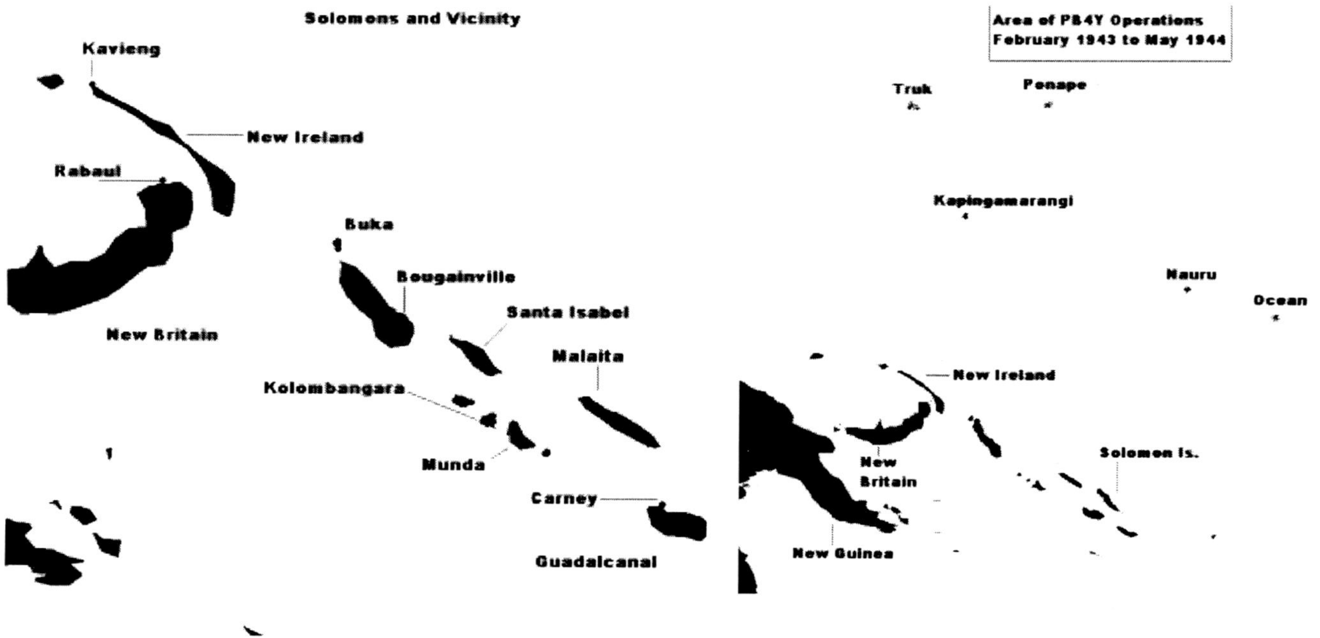

"Everybody had to learn to fire all gun positions—bow, top, waist, belly, and tail. All turrets had .50-caliber machine guns, but each was mounted differently. In addition, the waist guns did not have interrupters to prevent the gunner from hitting his own plane while firing at the enemy. Those gunners had to be particularly careful not to shoot off the plane's tail, or the engines (which did happen to a plane from VB-115).

We used mock-ups of the turrets in class. When we finished classroom training we trained on our planes. We practiced firing at sleeves towed by other aircraft and at targets in the Salton Sea."[2]

After training was completed in California, squadrons flew their aircraft to Hawaii (called TransPacs) for an additional two months of training. This time was spent on practice bombing, additional gunnery practice, and over sea and night navigation flights. Such was the training of PB4Y aircrews throughout WWII.

After getting familiar with the new aircraft in California, VP-51 flew to Hawaii for additional training in December 1942. Within weeks of their arrival Cdr. Moffett received orders to commence the transfer of men and planes to the South Pacific. On 15 January 1943, squadron planes began arriving at bomber strip number two at Espiritu Santo and were placed under Vice Adm. Fitch's Task Force 33, Air South Pacific.

Espiritu Santo, some 500 miles southeast of Guadalcanal, was the headquarters for Air South Pacific (AirSols). Here Adm. Fitch planned air search operations to cover every possible route Japanese forces could use to launch counterattacks against American and Australian forces operating in the Solomons and New Guinea.

The allies and the Japanese were exhausted after bitter fighting, and it would be another four months before there would be another push. For now, it was a time for the Japanese to rebuild their air forces and strengthen their positions in New Georgia,

A fully outfitted PB4Y-1 Liberator squadron. These are the men of VB-109 prior to their departure in late 1943.

Nine-plane formation of VP-51 (VB-101) dropping bombs on the *Hitachi Maru*, a 6,500-ton merchant vessel, on 14 February 1944. Photograph was taken from the waist position. Not long afterward the formation was jumped by Japanese fighters, resulting in the loss of two bombers. ***Courtesy of the National Archives***

the Bismarcks, and the Admiralties. For the Americans and their Australian and New Zealand allies, there would be continued fighting across New Guinea while naval planners outlined the next offensive toward liberating the Philippines.

The advance to the Philippines required that the Japanese base at Rabaul be either invaded or neutralized. To do so, the Americans needed advanced air and naval bases to launch such an attack. Therefore, the first step in the campaign was to take New Georgia.

Japanese forces occupying islands in the Bismarck Archipelago were formidable. One strategy for reducing enemy air and naval forces before amphibious landings involved continuous aerial reconnaissance to locate military build-ups and strong points and attack.[3]

VP-51 arrived as final plans were being made to launch a new offensive against Japanese forces in the Russell and Bismarck Islands as another stepping stone toward the Philippines. Moffett and his men would play a small role in this grand plan to conquer the Solomons.

From their new base the first Navy Liberator squadron flew seven special missions to the Solomons. One such mission involved a special anti-submarine patrol over the USS *Chicago* that had been torpedoed during the Battle of Rennell Island. After their watch was over the VP-51 Liberator was relieved from the duty by another patrol squadron. Later that day the *Chicago* was attacked again by thirteen Japanese torpedo bombers and sunk. The squadron stayed on Espiritu Santo less than a week, as new orders were issued sending them to Guadalcanal.

The 2,000-square mile island is mountainous, with heavy jungle forests. While VP-51 started training the Solomon Island Campaign in the South Pacific began. American troops landed on Guadalcanal in August 1942, with the objective of isolating Japan's major forward air and naval base at Rabaul, on the island of New Britain. The Japanese called it the Island of Death, and for over 30,000 it did become their last resting place. For the allies who finally took it some 7,000 men would never go home again.[4]

On 12 February, the squadron arrived at Henderson Field only a few days after the remaining Japanese survivors of the battle were evacuated. The airfield had been captured the first day of the battle and was a beehive of activity when the squadron arrived, as it was the only allied airfield in the Solomons. Named after Lofton Henderson, a Marine pilot who was killed at the Battle of Midway, the air base was home to hundreds of men who formed the "Cactus Air Force."

The squadron was introduced to life on the island. The stench of decaying corpses and vegetation, disease, and lack of maintenance facilities taxed man and machine, and would continue throughout their tour of duty. Food was K-rations, and personnel were given atribine tablets every day to prevent malaria. Poor maintenance facilities and the lack of spare parts were the rule for land-based air operations in the Pacific. Often parts had to be salvaged from Liberators that were beyond repair due to battle damage and operational accidents.

Moffett was lucky; his squadron brought ground maintenance personnel who had served with the Catalina squadron. These men kept the Liberators air worthy through perseverance and salvaged parts from Army Liberators that had crash-landed. In the seven months that Moffett's squadron served in the South Pacific there was not one operational loss of an aircraft or crew (non-combat related). The men of each unit had a special relationship built upon a common past that would not be repeated by any other Navy heavy bomber squadron during the Pacific War. Conversely, other squadrons would suffer a shortage of parts and a lack of maintenance facilities that would cost the lives of many Liberator crews.

Lt.Cdr. William A. Moffett Jr. (third from left) and his crew stand in front of 101-B-2 on Guadalcanal after the squadron designation was changed from VP-51. The only other individual identified is Sidney H. Wagner (kneeling far right). ***Courtesy of John Wagner***

Moffet's Liberators were early D models, featuring a greenhouse nose with up to four flexible-mounted .50-caliber machine guns operated by the bombardier. Crews quickly learned that array was highly inaccurate when defending frontal attacks by enemy fighters. The aircraft also lacked a belly turret, instead having a pair of manually operated .50-caliber machine guns; months would pass before naval PB4Y squadrons either retrofitted nose and belly turrets on available aircraft or upgraded models arrived to the forward areas.

The St. Valentine's Massacre

Two days after their arrival the Navy Liberators took part in their first of many bombing missions, and would find out the Solomons was a meat grinder for both sides. The squadron received a report of a Japanese ship off the Southern coast of Bougainville. Nine of Moffett's PB4Y-1s, each carrying 1,000-pound bombs in their bellies, were sent out on a daylight strike to search for their quarry, and in the process got tangled up in an aerial battle that was to be called the "Saint Valentines Day Massacre."

The Liberators flew to the Buin, Bouganville, and Shortland Island area. Climbing to 22,000 feet, the bombers were joined by a fighter escort of ten Army Air Force P-38G Lockheed fighters of the 339th Fighter Squadron flying top cover and a dozen F4U-1 Corsairs of Marine Fighter Squadron 124 (VMF-124)—the first combat appearance of the gull-wing fighter—flying low cover. While the fighters kept a lookout for Japanese fighters the Liberators dropped a string of bombs, hitting several enemy cargo ships, including the *Hitachi Maru*, a 6,500-ton merchantman. The Japanese sent up heavy and accurate anti-aircraft and several of the PB4Ys suffered damage.[5]

The Japanese quickly learned American tactics and knew that two to four P-38 fighters would conduct high altitude reconnaissance flights over the area approximately one to two hours prior to the major attacking force. This was verified when a P-38 appeared over Ballale at 0520 and headquarters for the 11th *Kokusental* warned all bases to prepare for an

ARM1c Frank Betz and the rest of his crew aboard a VP-51 Liberator piloted by Lt. Jay D. Bacon Jr. were killed in action during the "St. Valentine's Day Massacre" of 14 February 1943. ***Courtesy of the Frank Betz Family***

Carney Field on Guadalcanal. ***Courtesy of the National Archives***

A "Short Snorter" is a bank note signed by individuals flying together. This one, dated 20 January 1943, belonged to Frank Betz and bares his name, along with some of his crew and other passengers. Those identified as members of his crew are J. D. Brown, E. J. Kolazyk, O. K. Ward, and E. F. Adams. The other names are G. E. Welch, J. D. Lancaster, D. Ramasco, M. A. Bolock (sp), and two unrecognizable. ***Courtesy of the Frank Betz Family***

Wearing bulky flight clothes and an oxygen mask, an aerial photographer of VD-1 at work during a high altitude mapping run. ***Courtesy of the National Archives***

Two unidentified waist gunners smile for the camera aboard Lt.Cdr. Moffett's PB4Y-1. The blue cotton shirt and denim jeans were typical garb for enlisted naval combat air crewmen serving in the Pacific. ***Courtesy of John Wagner, son of Sidney Wagner***

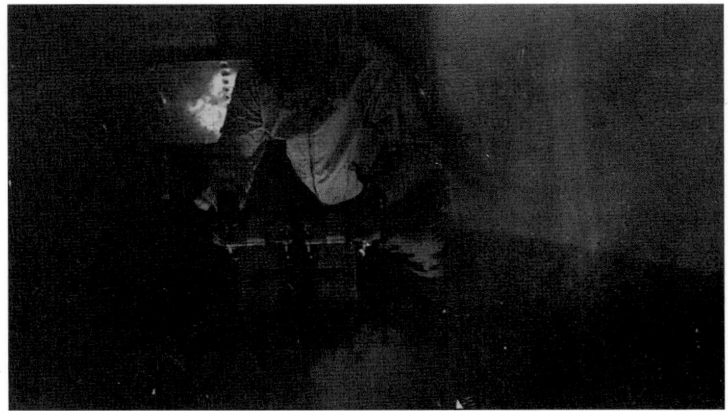

The early Consolidated B-24D Liberators provided to the Navy lacked a belly turret and were equipped with a single hand-held machine gun at the forward camera hatch. A gunner aboard Lt.Cdr. Moffett's aircraft is operating an improvised twin-tunnel machine gun arrangement. ***Courtesy of John Wagner***

attack. At 0931, four A6M Zero (Zeke) fighters of the 252 Ku based at Ballale intercepted and shot down an F-5A Lightning—a photographic reconnaissance variant of the P-38—flown by Lt. Ardell A. Nord, 17th Photographic Reconnaissance Squadron. Lt. Nord was probably killed in action.

At 0945, a pair of F1M2 Pete bi-wing floatplanes from the tender *Kunika-wa Maru* departed for combat air patrol (CAP) and intercepted the American force at 1020 hours, approximately the same time as eighteen A6M Zeros of the 252 Ku and thirteen Zeros from 204 Ku from Buin (Kahili) joined the attack. Previous sources written about the battle stated forty-five to sixty Japanese fighters participated, consisting of approximately thirty Zeros and fifteen A6M2-N Rufe fighters (a floatplane variant of the Zero).

Lee Baldwin was a twenty-year-old aerial gunner when his plane was shot down on 5 March 1943, during a night bombing mission of Japanese airfields. ***Courtesy of Lillie Ann Baldwin Flora, sister of Lee Balwin***

It became a one-sided battle, as the Japanese fighters, at a higher altitude than the P-38s, dove and tore into the formation, making head-on attacks on VP-51's bombers and singling out B-3 and B-4 (the in-squadron codex usually located on the forward fuselage behind the nose), apparently damaged by flak. The two crews lost that day were commanded by Lt. Jay D. Bacon Jr. and Lt. Stuart T. Cooper. Jack W. Cook, an air gunner aboard Lt. Davis' plane, wrote in his flight log, "I've never shot so much in my life and was so scared." Cook further adds he saw Lt. Bacon's plane go down:

"I'll never forget how Atkins [Aviation Ordnanceman Second Class (AOM2C) Frank E. Atkins] waved at me as they went down or what Baldwin looked like, or what was left of him, in the top turret."[6]

Cook's last statement about Baldwin is incorrect, as the latter was killed on 5 March 1943, which adds to the confusion that follows, specifically the bureau numbers of the PB4Y-1s lost during this mission.

The Japanese fighters pummeled the Americans in the "St. Valentine's Day Massacre," shooting down six of the escorting American fighters along with the PB4Y-1s at the cost of one plane and pilot of the 252 Ku. The Japanese claimed destruction of three B-24s, five P-38s, three F4Us, and two P-39 Airacobras. The Americans claimed fourteen Zekes and one Pete. Six escorting fighters were lost. The 339th FS lost four planes and three pilots: Lt. John R. Mulvey Jr. ditched his damaged plane near the Russell Islands and was rescued, while Joseph Finkenstein and 1st Lt. Donald G. White were MIA, and 2nd Lt. William H. Huey was captured and briefly held at Kahili Airfield before being transferred to Rabaul, where he and other allied POWs were executed.

VMF-124 lost two planes and their pilots were listed MIA. First Lt. Gordon L. Lyon Jr. had the unfortunate distinction of having the only confirmed enemy aircraft destroyed that day when a Zero collided with his Corsair; both he and the Japanese pilot, Petty Officer Second Class (PO2c) Yoshio Yoshida, were lost. Second Lt. Harold R. Stewart's Corsair was raked by machine gun fire, and with fuel exhausted, he descended toward the water to make a ditching while Japanese fighters followed, shooting at the American fighter. Stewart ditched and appeared to have exited the plane while the Zeros continued strafing and he was not seen again.[7]

VB-101's Lt. Davis and his crew on Guadalcanal standing by their early model Liberator. These aircraft were highly vulnerable to frontal attacks and those coming from under the aircraft, since both areas lacked power turrets. Jack W.Cook (third from right) was a member of Lt. Davis' crew. *Courtesy of Randall Baylis*

Confusion concerning which bureau numbers (serial numbers) belonged to B-3 and B-4 remains unresolved. An official document generated by the Navy and utilized for the first edition of the author's work *We Flew Alone* shows 31948 and 31970 lost that day, but does not list the assigned codex. Since initial publication, PB4Y-1 31948 appears in the log books of VP-51's Aviation Machinist Mate Second Class (AMM2c) James J. Curry and Aviation Radioman Third Class (ARM3c) Lee Baldwin after 14 February 1943. The last entry for both are dated 3 March, and shows 31948 (codex 51-P-11) on a bombing mission with Lt. Frank Moore Fisler as PPC.

The loss of two bombers identified one serious flaw of the B-24D: the lack of defensive armament in the nose. Moffett and the Navy learned a valuable lesson that day and went on to solve the problem by installing nose turrets in the bombers. It would be several months before the first such Liberator was made available to VP-51. After the air battle AirSols decided it was too risky to send out Liberators in the day and Moffett's squadron decided to change tactics and strike only at dawn and dusk.

While Moffett and his squadron were licking their wounds, the Navy made a small forward push toward New Georgia with landings on Russell Island. Some 9,000 men under the command of Richard K. Turner made an unopposed landing on 21 February to establish a naval base for a push on Munda scheduled for June 1943.[8]

Change in Squadron Designation

The end of February 1943 brought a new designation to VP-51, as the Navy reclassified land-based patrol units operating the PB4Y-1 Liberator heavy bomber or Lockheed PV-1 Ventura medium bomber as Navy Bombing (VB) squadrons, while units operating amphibious aircraft, such as the PBY Catalina and PBM Mariner, retained the original VP designator.

The next two months brought a series of strikes by AirSols to neutralize Japanese air bases and reduce enemy reinforcements and supplies in the Solomons. The occupation of the Russell Islands had been a minor forward movement and further allied landings in the Solomons and New Guinea were still a few months away. The job of VB-101 and B-24s of the 13th Air Force—also based at Henderson—was neutralizing the Japanese airfields of Kahili, on the southern end of Bougainville; Ballale, named after the island and part of the Shortland's group; Villa, on the southern coast of Kolomangara Island; and Munda, on New Georgia Island.

Munda was one of the most important airfields for the Japanese. At Munda Point, the airfield was a staging point for Japanese bombers coming in from Rabaul to refuel and bomb Henderson Field. The Japanese wanted to keep it operational as a means of preventing the Americans from advancing farther than the Russells. The Americans knew it and began sending army and navy bombers against the airstrip almost nightly, but the Japanese troops would crawl out of their underground shelters and repair the damage.

Subsequent attacks over the next weeks and months were from high altitude, consisting of three to nine Liberators, and were designed to catch planes on the ground and anti-aircraft gunners asleep. The tactic usually worked. AirSol's heavy bomber squadrons continued to pattern their strikes based on the high altitude missions over Europe, with multiple formations and fighter escort, making them susceptible to enemy radar, fighters, and anti-aircraft fire; the tactic of low level attacks by Navy Liberators was still some months away.

March 1943 was a rerun of the previous month, with high and medium altitude bombing of enemy airfields. One night Moffett sent out nine PB4Ys on a medium altitude mission against enemy airfields at Kahili, Ballale, and Villa. The planes took off between one and one-thirty in the morning and arrived over the targets two hours later.

All nine of the planes reached their objective and proceeded through blinding searchlights and anti-aircraft fire to drop their payloads of 500-pound bombs, hitting dispersal areas and runways. Two of the bombers were lost to intense anti-aircraft fire. Aboard bomber 31948 was twenty-year-old Lee Baldwin from Iowa, a peacetime enlistee who joined the Navy on 22 July 1941; he turned nineteen two days before. He was a young man with ambition, according to letters he wrote to his family:

"June 1, 1942. I am a qualified aerial gunner now. As soon as possible I will take my flight physical and try to get some pilot training. My ambition is to become a fighter pilot. It is a short, fast, and exciting life, with plenty of contact with the enemy."[9]

In a letter to his younger sister Lillie Flora that he started on November 27, 1942, and completed on December 2, 1942, he discusses his postwar plans:

"Tonight I just finished working on my course for my next advancement in rating, which I expect to make the first of January or soon thereafter. I have learned an awful lot about radio already. When I get out of the Navy I will go to college and become a Radio Engineer, if I can save enough money."[10]

Lee Baldwin was lost with his crew aboard bureau number 31948. Ens. Donald H. Lehman, previously an enlisted chief naval aviation pilot (NAP), piloted the other PB4Y-1 lost during the mission. Fate played a role that night, as a co-pilot from another crew asked Lehman's regular co-pilot, Chief NAP George Webster, if he could take his place and the latter agreed, but with the approval of Lehman, who in turn granted the change, thus saving Webster from certain death.[11]

Another plane from the squadron sighted a large fire with pieces falling off around 1,200 feet between Cape Esperance and Russell Island that may have been one of the missing aircraft. Two days later Moffett led eight other Liberators for a repeat performance on the airfields with the additional target of Munda, but only six reached their objective after one suffered mechanical problems, while another encountered severe weather and returned to Henderson.

A letter sent by Cdr. Moffitt to Lafayette L. Baldwin, father of Lee Baldwin, dated March 21, 1943, was one of nearly four dozen he wrote between February and August 1943 to the families of men under his command who had been killed:

"My dear Mr. Baldwin

"This letter is an attempt to give you more information regarding the circumstances under which your son became missing in action.

"I regret that rules of censorship prevent giving you exact details.

"Your son Lee was reported missing after the completion of a very successful attack on the enemy. He had participated in more than one such mission. His performance of duty was at all times in keeping with the highest tradition of the service. Such men cannot be replaced. His memory is an inspiration to each and every officer and me of this command.

"I would not endeavor to hint to you that there is hope for his recovery. There is however definitely that possibility and join you in [unreadable word] fervent hope that such happiness may come to pass."[12]

For any person in command writing such letters is difficult, and due to censors lacked specific details, often containing generic phrases such as, "...in keeping with the highest tradition of the service." Families typically received specific information of the missing or killed within two years after the war; for some longer, and for others a final conclusion was never reached, especially since many combat aircrews in the Pacific crashed at sea and bodies were unrecoverable. The services issued Certificate of Death for presumption of death along with a detailed letter if possible discussing circumstances surrounding the loss. An excerpt of a letter from the secretary of the Navy to Lee Baldwin's father dated 4 January 1946 provides such details about the mission in which Baldwin and twenty-three other men lost their lives.

Mr. Baldwin must have endured great pain, losing not just Lee, but three other sons who passed away at birth or soon afterward; his wife Leta Mae Rankin Baldwin died in childbirth along with a newborn son—her thirteenth child—in 1936. Lee's younger sister Lillie cherishes the memories of her older brother Lee:

"Several years ago I had a conversation with a former navy pilot about my brother's service and death in 1943. He wanted me to know that the Distinguished Flying Cross was a very special award to be given. He made me realize how much my 'hero big brother' in this kid sister's eyes was a true hero in every sense of the word. That made me sadder, and yet prouder. He had so much potential, but was never able to realize all the ability that was in him. How sad! Yet those outstanding innate qualities of leadership came through in those few short months of service."[13] By month's end the squadron left Henderson for Carney Field, an air base some five miles from their old home. The new airfield, consisting of two airstrips—bomber one and two—was a grass strip covered by marston mat constructed by the 14th Navy Construction Battalion (NCB) at Koli Point. The squadron continued to send out single-plane searches during the day to track enemy surface units while still engaging in nighttime bombing of Japanese airfields. In mid-April, Lt. Peter Kooy was sent out on one such mission and found a convoy of four enemy light cruisers and two destroyers some 640 miles from Henderson, northwest of New Ireland, and was lucky to get away.

Flying at 2,200 feet Kooy closed in; when the Liberator was three miles from the warships the Japanese opened fire with their main batteries. Four shots fell behind the bomber while two others burst in the air above it. In response Kooy dove the PB4Y down toward the water as five more shots hit around the plane. Changing course, he gained altitude and flew out of range as the warships continued firing.

Kooy could not let a chance of attacking six warships get away, but he also knew he could not risk attacking at low altitude. He decided to leave the area and let things die down a little. An hour later he came back and dropped four 350-pound bombs from 10,000 feet. Below the cruisers and destroyers fired back and took evasive action at thirty-five knots. The bombs did not come close to hitting any of the targets and Kooy and his crew flew home as the warships continued firing at the retreating bomber.

Arrival of USMC and USN Photographic Squadrons

In late April, the navy's first photographic squadron equipped with B-24s arrived on Espiritu Santo. Led by Lt.Cdr. Howell Dyson, VD-1 immediately began photographic patrols throughout the Solomons area from Suramuni Cove, around Villa Point, and Kuigi Point. The full name for this type of squadron was Fleet Air Photographic Reconnaissance Squadron, which was shortened to VD. The squadron was formed in spring 1942 and was equipped with the Liberator.

B-24 aircraft assigned to such squadrons were designated PB4Y-1P because of modifications made to the aircraft. Photographic planes were equipped with two four-hundred gallon fuel tanks in the forward bomb bays and one of the two rear bays was equipped with four mapping cameras, while the remaining bay could carry bombs. Besides the usual complement of flight personnel, photographic squadrons carried a navigator/bombardier who would use the Norden bombsight to direct the flying of mapping lines. Two of the enlisted men acted as photographers and gunners. Dyson's men ran a fully self-sufficient camp. They built it along the Malimbu River, with tents serving as their first quarters until Quonset huts were built. The squadron maintained a fully staffed photo lab and a large group of photo interpreters.

The Marine Corps operated three such PB4Y-1P Liberator units in the Pacific, designated Marine Photographic Reconnaissance Squadrons (VMD) VMD-154, 254, and 354. VMD-154, nicknamed "The Pathfinders," was actually the first PB4Y-1P reconnaissance squadron to operate in the Pacific (November 1942–December 1943) at Carney Field, Guadalcanal, under the command of Col. Elliot Bard. The squadron lost two aircraft and crews during its deployment: one through enemy action and the other an operational accident. Nine Zeros of the 204 Ku intercepted and shot down 2nd Lt. Gorden E. Gray and crew aboard 31940 near Munda on 29 December 1943—there were no survivors. The second loss occurred when 31958 crashed in the water shortly after take-off from Espiritu Santo. The bodies of the twelve men aboard—eleven crewmen and 1st Lt. Harold W. Ervin, USAAF—were not recovered. VMD-254 replaced -154 in February 1944.

Arrival of Second Bombing Squadron VB-102

After two months of being the lonely Navy stepchild of AirSols, 101 celebrated the arrival of VB-102, led by Lt.Cdr. Bruce Van Voorhis.

The navy addressed Moffett's concern for adequate firepower on the bow and belly of the PB4Y-1and began modifying the aircraft back in San Diego by installing Consolidated, Emerson, or Erco nose turrets. VB-102, the second Pacific-bound Navy Liberator squadron, removed the tail turrets from PB2Y Coronado flying boats and installed them in the noses of Liberators; however, they still lacked a belly turret. In the months to come 102 would earn quite a reputation for itself, and for the commanding officer a posthumous Congressional Medal of Honor—the only one to be awarded to a Navy PB4Y pilot.

Like 101, Van Voorhis' group were old Catalina men who utilized the entire personnel and material of VP-14 and traded in their PBY5-As. VP-14 had already proven itself in combat, beginning with their baptism of fire at Pearl Harbor to reconnaissance missions in the Solomons. At Pearl Harbor one of the men, Lt. William Finn, was awarded the Medal of Honor for his actions on the darkest day in American history.[14]

The men of 102 had already felt the loss of an entire crew before their arrival in the Pacific during advanced training in Hawaii. On 8 April 1943, Lt. (jg) Sidney H. Bonn took off in plane 31989 for a routine night navigation mission from Kaneohe. A few minutes later witnesses saw the bomber crash into the water eight miles off the coast, killing the entire crew.

VB-102 completed its deployment on 1 May and began joint operations with her sister squadron. Both would join with the Army Air Force in bombing strikes against Japanese airfields. Between such missions the squadrons of Moffett and Van Voorhis sent out planes to search for elusive Japanese naval and land forces.

2

The New Georgia Campaign
June–July 1943

On 21 June, Operation Toenails—the invasion of New Georgia—began with the first landing at Segi Point. The landing force met only light opposition, and within a week the Sea Bees were building a new airstrip. To keep pressure on the Japanese by preventing their aircraft from interfering with the landings Army and Navy B-24 squadrons continued pounding away.[1]

Three days after the landings, Van Voorhis sent out three of his planes to Ballale on an early morning bombing run. VB-101 and -102 now operated as the Special Search and Strike Command under CTF-33, and later as Navy Search Group operating under the 13th AAF Bomber Command. ComAirGuadal, ComFair Wing One, took operational control in October as VB-101, and -102 prepared to be relieved by VB-104 and 106. Each plane carried twenty 120-pound fragmentation cluster bombs—nasty explosive devices used to produce maximum damage on aircraft and personnel. The Liberators flew singly in a staggered formation, at altitudes of 11,000, 14,000, and 15,000 feet. Coming over Nusave Island in the Solomons, the first bomber was immediately picked up by a searchlight that was soon followed by inaccurate anti-aircraft fire. Mistaking Nusave for the primary target, the bombardier let go a string across the island. The other two bombers did not make the same mistake. They flew a couple dry runs to get their bearings and let loose a string of bombs across Ballale from one end of the island to the other.

Moffett's followed suit on 27 June, sending three of his Liberators to bomb Ballale airfield. From 10,000 feet Lt. Hall's bombardier dropped a string of fragmentation cluster bombs that ran from one end of the airfield to the other, destroying revetments and aircraft and damaging the runway. On 30 June, the Army's 43rd Infantry Division landed on Rendova Island, just five miles across a channel from Munda. By the time Munda was secured there would be some 1,100 American casualties. After two months of flying medium and high altitude missions Navy Liberators began to seek prey from lower heights.[2]

As the army was slogging ashore on Rendova, 102's Lt. Burton Albrecht became the squadron's first killer of coastal vessels when he found nine diesel-powered vessels off the St. Matthias Group.

The ships managed to mount a weak and ineffective defensive fire with light machine guns as the bomber came in for the kill. Carrying four 325-pound depth bombs for anti-submarine duty, he dropped two of them at 3,000 feet and the last two from 2,000 feet, each time scoring near misses and causing one coastal to start listing badly. Out of depth bombs,

Lt.Cdr. Bruce Van Voorhis, the commanding officer of VB-102 and the only PB4Y pilot to be awarded the Congressional Medal of Honor. *Courtesy of Navy Squadrons 102/14 Association*

On the right is Gordon Fowler, commanding officer of VB-102. Sitting next to him is Kurt Vossler, executive officer. ***Courtesy of Navy Squadrons 102/14 Association***

he dove the Liberator down to fifty feet, where his gunners hit the ships again and again, causing two of them to burn and causing several casualties among the ships' crew.

Throughout June and July, the two squadrons went after enemy shipping and airfields, with VB-102 alone encountering forty-three Japanese ships and fifty-one aircraft. On 4 July, Van Voorhis and crew were on a routine search when they sighted a large cargo ship being escorted by a destroyer and a destroyer escort.

The ships were cruising between eight to ten knots, probably ferrying fresh troops to New Georgia to reinforce the beleaguered garrison there. The destroyer began sending up inaccurate defensive fire as the bomber approached. The patrol plane commander dropped a string of 325-pound depth bombs from 13,000 feet that missed. Van Voorhis decided it was not worth going down and tangling with two warships with machine gun fire. Three days later the commanding officer of 102 would find himself and his crew in a more difficult situation, a situation he would not survive.

The Japanese were in desperate need to reinforce Munda and Villa and began sending troops and supplies via the "Tokyo Express." American destroyers picked up the movement, and on the evening of 6 July, the two opposing forces met at the Battle of Kula Gulf. During the night time engagement the Japanese lost the destroyers *Niizuki* and *Nagatsuki*, while the Americans lost the destroyer *Helena* when it was sunk by two long lance torpedoes. For the next few days army and navy search planes looked for the survivors of the *Helena* who were struggling to survive.[3]

Lt. Howard Nopper of VB-102, while on a special search for enemy surface units retiring from the naval battle along the Vella Lavella-Kolombangara area, saw other survivors of USS *Helena* and radioed it in. Continuing on patrol, a Japanese destroyer

Gordon Fowler and crew. ***Courtesy of Navy Squadrons 102/14 Association***

Jim Eggland and his crew from VB-102 standing next to *Demon Dilbert*. Courtesy of Navy Squadrons 102/14 Association

was spotted and Nopper started climbing to 10,000 feet for a bombing run. As the run began five Zekes appeared on a parallel heading, slightly above and to the right of the Liberator. Three more Zekes were soon sighted high and to the rear. The destroyer's air cover consisted of twenty-three fighters: five from the light carrier *Ryuho*, fourteen from the 251 Ku, and four from the 582 Ku. Nopper probably would not have conducted such a dangerous move if he had known the bomber was vastly outnumbered, but the run continued as the fighters engaged.[4]

The first attack damaged the bomb sight and killed top turret gunner William Bartek; the second knocked out the number-two engine. The pilot realized they were in serious trouble and dove the Liberator at full speed toward the water before leveling off at about 350 feet. There was no place to hide as cloud cover was too sparse. Fighters peeled off and attacked in pairs, one on each bow, while others conducted individual runs on the bomber's tail. For the next twenty-five minutes Nopper kept maneuvering his plane to keep the gunners targeted on the incoming fighters.

The fighters continued coming in, dealing damaging blows to the Liberator and its crew. Bullets and cannon fire tore into the fuselage, damaging the right aileron, the leading edge of the left vertical stabilizer, and shattering the cockpit's Plexiglas. Nopper coaxed the damaged bomber back to base and made a successful landing despite a bullet-punctured tire that went flat upon contact with the airstrip. His gunners claimed the destruction of two fighters and one damaged during the encounter, but Japanese records list no losses, with their fighters landing at Buin between 0900 and 0930.

The Loss of Van Voorhris' Crew

The morning of 6 July 1943, Lt.Cdr. Voorhis volunteered for a reconnaissance mission to Greenwich Island (Kolombangara) to check reported enemy movements of surface vessels. He reached the objective after a nearly 800-mile journey. There was no element of surprise, as the PB4Y-1 Liberator fought a relentless battle under fierce anti-aircraft fire and aerial opposition.

Although forced lower and lower by pursuing planes, he was able to conduct six ground attacks and demolish the radio station on Hare Island; according to American records he shot down one fighter plane in the air and destroyed three floatplanes on the water. According to Japanese records three F1M2 Petes of the 902 Ku were preparing to take off when the PB4Y began the attack and the rear gunners in the floatplanes returned fire. The records are incomplete and do not discuss any losses, but if Van

The *Galloping Ghost*. She was piloted by 102's Don Butler.

Don Shiley and crew. ***Courtesy of Navy Squadrons 102/14 Association***

Voorhis' crew did destroy four aircraft, were they A6M2-N Rufe or Aichi E13A Jake floatplanes, since the Petes actually became airborne during the attack and returned safely twenty-five minutes afterward. The Japanese expended 120 rounds of 20 mm and forty rounds of 7.7 mm ammunition, but do not identify whether they came from ground positions or aircraft.

Whether brought down by anti-aircraft fire or caught in its own bomb blast, the Liberator crashed into the lagoon some 700 meters from the beach, killing everyone on board. For his actions Van Voorhis was awarded the Medal of Honor, the only pilot of a Navy Liberator or Privateer to receive such an honor. The aircraft was found after the war lying in scattered pieces in approximately twenty to thirty feet of water and the remains of the crew were recovered and returned to the US.

Gordon Fowler Assumes Command

Commander Gordon Fowler, only twenty-eight years old at the time, assumed command. The death of their commanding officer, although a morale buster, did not stop regular strikes against the enemy. Three days later two 102 bombers executed a night attack on several Japanese warships—two light cruisers and four destroyers—operating in and near Kula Gulf. The warships were probably Rear Adm. Shungi's light cruiser *Jintsu* and several destroyers coming from Rabaul to land troops at Villa.[5]

Aided by illumination flares dropped by Lt. John W. Erhard's PBY *Black Cat* of VP-54, Lt. (jg) Burton dropped a string of 500-pound bombs on one of the light cruisers and scored two direct hits. Next came in three Liberators from 101 that had been alerted.

The first Liberator, flown by Lt. Beswick, could not find the ships, instead salvoing his bombs on Villa Airfield. Lt. Clark was the first to reach the targets a little after 0500 and contacted the patrolling PBY *Black Cat* which led him, dropping flares to illuminate the warships for the attacking bomber.

The ships were now twenty-five miles off Kolombangara as Clark began his bombing run from 7,000 feet. Three 500-pound bombs were released, with one a near miss on one of the destroyers. An hour later Lt.Cdr. Heywood arrived, and with the help of *Black Cat* dropped eight 500-pound bombs from 2,000 feet. Again all missed, with the closest hitting 200 yards from one of the destroyers.

The *Jintsu's* luck did not last long. During the evening of 12–13 July the two navies met again at the Battle of Kolombangara, and during the engagement the *Jintsu* was lost at the expense of the American destroyer *Gwin*.[6]

Bill Paulin's ***Lil Nell. Courtesy of Navy Squadrons 102/14 Association***

Thurlow Doyle's *Spirit of 76. Courtesy of Navy Squadrons 102/14 Association*

Lt.Cdr. Heywood was given another chance to attack an enemy warship five days later, when he was engaged in a routine 800-mile search off of New Ireland. At noon Heywood sighted a ship on the horizon and went to investigate. Through binoculars he saw it was a large single-stack gunboat with turrets fore and aft. The ship saw the Liberator and began evasive action as its guns began firing at the patrol bomber. Heywood kept coming in, and at 6,500 feet his bombardier dropped six 325-pound depth bombs. The bombs fell in a string across the warships' stern, with one of them a direct hit. As the Liberator departed the ship continued at eighteen knots, trailing oil as its guns continued to fire at the PB4Y-1 that tried to sink her.

Engaging Enemy Fighters

Army and Navy bombers continued the job of neutralizing enemy airfields during the next several weeks. On the seventeenth in a pre-dawn attack, two PB4Ys from VB-102 and three from 101 dropped cluster bombs from 12,000 feet over Kahili Field, Bougainville, hitting the runway area. On the return leg the Liberators from 102 were jumped by Irving night fighters from the 251st Air Group.[7]

In the ensuing engagement a night fighter piloted by Shigeru Okado, with observer Masao Onuma, targeted a PB4Y-1 (31952) piloted by John B. Haskett. Lt. (Jg) Frazier, commanding a VB-101 Liberator, noticed tracer fire over Buin, followed by a small ball of fire at 11,000 feet. Lt. Haskett's bomber received mortal damage inflicted by the night fighter, and a moment later his aircraft became engulfed in flames as the Liberator and its occupants plunged into the water.

After the two naval engagements against the Americans the Japanese found it nearly impossible to re-supply their troops in and around New Georgia because of constant harassment by allied aircraft. The two Navy Liberator squadrons on Guadalcanal added to the enemy's problems. A much needed supply of aircraft for Japanese forces never made its destination on 20 July, when a lone plane from 102 searching near Bougainville dropped a string of six depth bombs from 3,000 feet on two cargo ships from New Ireland. Three wide misses and two near misses caused a small fire forward of one of the ship's deck cargo hatches. The Liberator received intense small caliber anti-aircraft fire from positions along the deck and superstructure. Before a strafing attack could be carried out three enemy fighters began interception, forcing the PB4Y-1's withdrawal.

With the New Georgia campaign winding down, Fowler and Moffett's group began prowling deeper into enemy territory in search of shipping. On 26 July, VB-102's Robert E. Nadeau was at the end of his search sector, flying at 200 feet near the coast of Bougainville, and was setting course to go home when eight Zekes were sighted about four miles distant, coming in from 2 o'clock from 6,000 feet. Nadeau decided not to tangle with them so he turned east, away from land and out to sea, but found seven more Zekes coming in from 8 o'clock at 5,000 feet.

The Liberator was in some serious trouble, but due to the skill of the pilot the bomber reached cloud cover at 2,000 feet just as the first fighters jockeyed into a loose formation to port and starboard. Lt. Nadeau increased power and flew between clouds, slightly altering speed and course in an attempt to shake off the pursuing fighters.

The strategy of hide-and-seek succeeded in upsetting enemy timing but did not stop the fighters from attacking. The Zekes kept out of range on either side of the bomber before coming in on simultaneous runs from each side of Nadaeu's plane. The Japanese pilots were relatively unskilled in tactics and not aggressive enough to continue a combined attack and knock the PB4Y-1 out of the sky. The PB4Y took a hit from a 20 mm round in the aft section and two more

Lt.Cdr. Gordon Fowler's PB4Y-1 bureau number 31995 with the Emerson nose turret fitted to VB-102 Liberators prior to and during the squadron's deployment. Fowler was executive officer of VB-102 and became commanding officer on the death of Bruce Van Voorhis. ***Courtesy of Frank Ziberna***

machine gun bullets hit the bow turret. Fortunately, due to the turret's armor plate, the gunner was not injured.

The Liberator's starboard waist gunner riddled one of the fighters and it fell to the water in a mass of flames. Another Zeke was caught in the crossfire of the top and bow turrets; apparently killing the pilot, the fighter spun into the water. After fighting off the Zekes for thirty minutes by shooting down two and damaging a couple more, the remaining Japanese fighters decided the expense was not worth losing more planes and broke off the attack.

A combat air crew of VD-1 experienced what Prussian military analyst Carl von Clausewitz eluded to as the "fog of war," in which, in one example, operations are jeopardized by incomplete or inaccurate intelligence. A failure in aircraft recognition resulted in the downing of an allied aircraft and the disappearance of its crew when the crew of PB4Y-1 bureau number 31982 *Satan's Wagon* misidentified a Royal Australian Air Force (RAAF) Beaufort A9-225, with a four-man crew piloted by Flying Officer (FO) J. C. Davis, as a Japanese Mitsubishi G4M Betty bomber.

During a routine search on 12 July 1943 near Buka Passage, the Liberator, piloted by Lt. (jg) W. C. Corbett, spotted a twin-engine aircraft low over the water flying in the opposite direction and dove from 1,000 feet to intercept; meanwhile, the Beaufort, probably seeing the aircraft coming from astern, made a turn toward the PB4Y-1. At approximately 100 feet off the deck both aircraft fired at each other; a waist gunner and the tail turret gunner claimed to have seen splashes in the water indicating the other aircraft was firing.

The Liberator's bow and top turret opened fire, scoring hits as the Beaufort made a sharp right turn at some 500 feet and began to pull away out of range. Lt. Corbett continued the pursuit for another ten minutes when one of the Beaufort's engines began smoking and caught fire. FO Davis conducted a ninety-degree turn and made a controlled water landing. Circling the downed aircraft, the Liberator's crew realized their huge mistake when they saw two white men in the water clinging to a wing. Corbett's men dropped a life raft and life jackets, followed by food rations, water, a first aid kit, fishing gear, a very pistol, and a smoke grenade attached to another pair of jackets. The unknown members of the Beaufort climbed into the raft and collected the rations. Corbett's radioman reported the location of the incident to base operations but did not receive a reply. Low on fuel, the Liberator departed the area.

Subsequent efforts to rescue the men failed, as inclement weather scrubbed air operations on the thirteenth and RAAF Australian Beauforts failed to locate the men on the fourteenth. The raft, reportedly carrying three men, was seen again on 1 August by land-based aircraft and one last time five days later on 6 August. It is presumed they perished during a storm on the night of 6–7 August. Lost along with Davis were Flight Sgt. G. R. Emmett (observer), Sgt. G. Collins, and W. T. Brain (air gunners).[8]

Nose art became standard to all land-based B-24 Navy squadrons in all theaters. Lt.Cdr. Fowler's aircraft displays the nose art *HELL'S ANGEL*. ***Courtesy of Frank Ziberna***

3

Commander Sears and His Buccaneers August 1943

August 1943 brought an end to major ground operations of the New Georgia campaign, but it was a costly endeavor, with American casualties reaching approximately 5,000 killed or wounded; the battles of Vella Gulf, Vella Lavella, and Lae would follow in the coming weeks. Adm. William F. Halsey, as commander of Allied operations, contemplated the next move of capturing Kolombangara; however, in light of casualties suffered on New Georgia, along with the estimated 10,000 Japanese defending that island, Vella Lavella was selected, and thus began the strategy of "island hopping."

Early Navy Liberator squadrons continued using the US Army Air Force tactic of high altitude bombing following the disastrous St. Valentine's Day Massacre of 14 February 1943; useful and somewhat accurate when bombing ground targets, but significantly ineffective when attempting to hit a moving target, such as a ship. Medium altitude runs against shipping between 5–8 August were ineffective, as described in an after action report dated 7 August against a 12,000-ton freighter and its escorting destroyer off New Ireland. A pair of VB-102 Liberators attacked independently forty-five minutes apart at 10,000 feet, each dropping five 500-pound bombs. The freighter's captain easily maneuvered away from the plunging bombs by conducting radical turns every time the PB4Ys came in for an attack. The destroyer attempted to interfere with the bombing run by placing herself between the Liberator and the merchantman. Heavy clouds at 3,000 feet interfered with the ship's fire against the plane's attack, but also interfered with the bombing run. The accuracy of the defensive fire caused the bombers to take evasive action and all bombs fell wide; no hits or near misses were scored.

The Japanese were good at avoiding bombs dropped from higher altitudes, with the freighter's captain making radical turns every time PB4Ys came in for an attack.

At Carney Field, the long-range search group was formed and doubled in size when Lt.Cdr. Harry E. Sears arrived with advance elements of VB-104 on 19 August. Sears' squadron, nicknamed the Buccaneers—like 101 and 102—was formed from a PBY Catalina squadron (VP-71), and many of the men of 104 were "old salts" of the Solomon Island Campaign and conducted the first bombing missions against the Japanese based in Guadalcanal before the invasion. A 1928 Naval Academy graduate, Sears was admired and respected by

Harry Sears, commanding officer of VB-104. ***Courtesy of Nate Hodge***

A silver cigarette case given by the officers of VB-101 to Lt.Cdr. Moffett engraved with a map of the Solomon Islands and his name. This artifact was inherited by his son William A. Moffett III. ***Courtesy of William A. Moffett III. Lt. Col. USMCR (ret)***

officers and enlisted personnel under his command. He found the living conditions comparable to what Cdr. Moffett had found eight months earlier.

Moffett's squadron departed Guadalcanal to conduct operations, albeit briefly, from Owi Island, part of the Schouten Island Group off New Guinea. Lt. H. Peter Kooy conducted one of VB-101's last searches on 22 August. Taking off at 6:00 a.m. in *Moonlight Madonna*, Kooy climbed out of Carney Field for an 800-mile search along Bougainville and New Ireland. Not long after leaving the field crew chief Bill Green smelled gas fumes in the bomb bay, and not wanting to risk an explosion Kooy returned to base and borrowed a PB4Y-1 from VB-102.

Resuming patrol in the borrowed plane, Kooy spotted an enemy convoy consisting of a cruiser and three destroyers some sixty miles from the Japanese airfield of Kahili. Moments after sending out a contact report seven Zekes appeared, diving from a higher level toward the Liberator. Kooy, seeing the predicament, nosed the bomber toward the water while instructing the gunners to open fire when the fighters came in range.

The fighters came in from the rear and Kooy jinked the bomber in steep turns to throw off the enemy's timing. The firepower from every gun on board the PB4Y kept the attackers at bay for a while. Kooy now had the Liberator just 100 feet off the water as one of the more aggressive fighter pilots came in head-on, firing his machine guns and 20 mm cannon and flying over the Liberator not more than ten feet above the cockpit. Suddenly, for some unknown reason, the fighters broke off the engagement and headed toward their base, one of them trailing a thin line of black smoke.

The crew, conducting an in-flight check of the bomber's interior after the attack, counted twenty bullet holes in the aircraft; after landing they found a 20 mm shell had torn a hole through the wing, while another had lodged in the fuel cell without exploding. If it had exploded, it would have sent the PB4Y-1 down in a massive fireball. Shortly after Kooy's patrol VB-101 headed back to the United States for reformation; less than a year later the squadron would return to the Southwest Pacific under a new commander.[1]

VB-104 Combat Ready

During the first week of VB-104's arrival it was breaking-in time, getting a feel of the operational area with 102 helping the new guys out. VB-104 sent four crews flying 800-mile sectors and wound up making their first contact with the enemy a few days after their arrival. The night 25 August, three Japanese destroyers began evacuating the Japanese sea plane base at Rekata Bay.

The first of the Buccaneers to hit the Japanese was Lt. H. L. Donald in his Liberator *Donald's Duck*. After climbing out from Carney they flew over Santa Isabel Island, near Rekata Bay, and climbed to 8,000 feet. Off the coast of Santa Isabel, Bill Knudsen (bow turret) and C. M. Osiecki (port waist gunner) sighted the three destroyers making twenty-five knots, heading northwest.

Seeing the destroyers were so close to Guadalcanal and might be friendly Donald decided to challenge them by flashing a blinker signal for the date and time. The warships responded with flashes of their own—flashes from their five-inch anti-aircraft guns blasting away at his plane. The enemy gunners were quite good, with three rounds exploding near the bomber: the first exploded off the starboard wing, the second off the

Officer's quarters at Carney Field. ***Courtesy of Herb Donald***

port—both at their altitude—and the third exploded in the middle, but *Donald's Duck* was in a hard right diving turn.

Donald continued circling the ships for some thirty minutes, closing in on them until they opened fire and then turning away out of range. Then the Liberator crew noticed seven to nine enemy fighters below flying combat air patrol (CAP) over the warships. The starboard waist gunner reported a Nakajima B5N torpedo bomber (nicknamed "Kate") coming in, but the enemy plane began what appeared to be a half-hearted attack. Instead of taking up a defensive posture against such an attack, Donald turned the PB4Y-1 toward the "attacker." Probably not used to seeing a heavy four-engined bomber coming after him, the Kate's pilot broke off and turned away toward the destroyers for protection. Soon after Donald received a radio message from base telling him to continue on patrol and he left the area.[2]

An hour later, Lt. A. E. Anderson spotted the ships five miles from his position while flying at 4,000 feet. Getting closer, the patrol bomber began drawing anti-aircraft fire. Reversing course, he spotted the enemy CAP coming for the snooping patrol plane and reversed course again, only to receive gunfire from the destroyers. After thirty minutes of this Anderson decided to send in a contact report and get the hell out of the area.

The next search planes to pay the enemy a visit were flown by Lts. F. L. Feind and R. W. Stoppleman, who noticed the ships were now without air cover. Feind, in *Saints and Sinners*, set up a bombing run from 5,000 feet, while Stoppleman, in *The Schooner*, flew cover at 10,000 feet. For Feind the anti-aircraft fire was inaccurate, but for *The Schooner* the defensive fire was highly accurate, with the bomber taking numerous hits. Feind's bombardier Ens. Nolan Weller set his sights on the lead destroyer and released two 500-pound bombs.

A burning Japanese vessel under attack by a PB4Y-1. ***Courtesy of the National Archives***

The living area of VB-102 improved over time from tents to semi-permanent screened-in structures with wood floors. It kept the men dry from rain and mud, however, the humidity and heat of Guadalcanal kept it from being comfortable. ***Courtesy of Frank Ziberna***

As the bombs sailed down the warships began making violent turns to get out of the path of the incoming explosives. Two of the destroyers turned hard to starboard while the other turned to port. For the last ship the move almost proved fatal, as one of Feind's bombs hit the water seventy-five feet away. No hits were observed, and with heavy anti-aircraft fire continuing and Stoppleman flying a damaged plane the Liberators headed home.

An hour earlier, after hearing the contact reports coming in, Sears decided to launch a more serious campaign against the destroyers, taking eight Liberators—five from 104 and three from 102. Each plane carried eight 500-pound bombs. Leading in his plane *Sears Steers*, they headed out to meet the enemy warships. On the way *Red's Devils*, flown by Lt. Van Benschoten, had to return to base after suffering mechanical problems, leaving Sears with seven PB4Y-1s for the strike. After rendezvousing at 2,000 feet the formation climbed to 15,000 feet, turned north, and headed for the destroyers, reaching them a half hour after Stoppleman and Fiend had left. The warships were back in a V formation and steaming at twenty-five to thirty knots some ninety miles northeast of Buka Passage.

Old Tactics, Same Results

For thirty minutes—an eternity if you are being shot at—Sears led the formation in fake bombing runs on the ships, trying to set up the best possible run. Each time the destroyers would take evasive action and send up heavy anti-aircraft fire, with one burst hitting a bomber from 104, causing minor damage. Sears decided to end the fake runs and go in for real. Coming in from the sun, he released his four 500-pound bombs. A flash of smoke and an explosion indicated a direct hit on a destroyer's bridge section, with the three others scoring near misses. The destroyer stopped dead in the water for a few minutes as her sister ships stood by to assist. After a few minutes the damaged warship was back under way, leaving a trail of oil behind her.[3]

Sears exemplified the role of a Navy Liberator squadron commander by leading his men into battle with ferocity and tenacity that would not be rivaled until a man named Norman "Bus" Miller arrived in the Central Pacific the following year. The Buccaneers of 104 would become the model for future Navy heavy bombing squadrons by embracing the tactic and would develop the art of low-level attacks.

A couple days after the attack on the destroyers Lt. John Alley and his crew from the Buccaneers were the first to destroy an enemy plane in the air. Around half past noon they sighted a four-engined Mavis flying boat in the distance heading for Rabaul.

Alley's plane *Open Bottom* quickly closed the distance on the flying boat, and at a range of 500 yards his gunners opened fire. A. J. Lymenstull (AMM2c), in the bow turret, was the first to open up with four short bursts. The first burst hit the Kawanishi HK6 Mavis' number four engine, while the second found the number two engine. The flying boat's wing dropped and Lyme poured two more bursts into the engines on the port wing. Losing speed, it banked sharply, plunging into the water.[4]

Why didn't those first Navy Liberator squadrons get down to minimum altitude as B-25s from the 5th Air Force were doing around New Guinea? Before the arrival of delayed fuses for bombs, the first Liberator squadrons had to use instantaneous fuses that prevented them from bombing enemy ships from an altitude lower than 500 feet. Dropping this type of ordinance from a lower altitude could be hazardous to a crew's health. Cdr. Whitney Wright found out how dangerous dropping a particular type of munitions could be while attacking an enemy gunboat.

Flying near the end of his sector on the shipping lane between Truk and Kavieng, and just an hour after Alley shot down the Mavis, Wright and his crew sighted what was later identified as a gunboat. Nearing the target that was now putting up anti-aircraft fire, he decided to reduce the ship's defenses by letting his gunners work over the target for twenty-five minutes.

After his gunners had reduced defensive fire Wright dove his bomber *Whit's Shits* down to 500 feet and released a couple 500-pound bombs with contact fuses. The explosions lifted the big bomber up and shrapnel punctured the bomber in several places. In the bombardier's compartment a 7.7 mm bullet entered the bow at the bombsight and struck Tom Dempster in the mouth, causing such a severe wound that he spent the rest of the tour in the hospital.[5]

Whitney and company left the gunboat sinking and a little wiser about dropping bombs with contact fuses from low altitude. It would be another two months before delayed fuses would arrive and search planes could venture down closer to their intended targets and thus changing the tactics of Pacific-based PB4Y-1 units.

While *Whit's Shits* was being patched up, on the last day of August Lt. D. M. L. Hager and crew caught five Rufe float planes on the water at Kapingamarangi Island; some 400 miles south of Truk, the island held a seaplane base. In only one fly-by strafing attack his gunners in *Vulnerable Virgin* left the float planes burning.[6]

Bombing Missions Continue

During September, the two squadrons continued their 800- to 1,000-mile patrols with a couple large bombing missions mixed with attacks on small shipping and encounters with enemy planes. Navy Liberators continued to team up with B-24s from the Air Force for bombing runs on Kahili and Ballale. For some reason only known to the those who planned the mission, the Navy bombers were often at the rear or "tail end Charlie" position of the 13th Air Force formation; a sometimes very dangerous place to be after Japanese gunners found the range of incoming bombers.

Sears led his nine-plane bunch toward the target after meeting up with the Army bombers and fighter escort and climbed to 21,000 feet. The formation reached the target a little after four in the afternoon and dropped almost 80,000 pounds of bombs on the airfield. Anti-aircraft fire from Kahili and Ballale was heavy, and by the time the formation's "Tail end Charlie" section came over the Japanese had found the range and peppered the sky around the Navy Liberators.[7]

Encounters with enemy aircraft intensified, with Cdr. Fowler's crew engaging a pair of Bettys near Choiseul Island on 8 September. The Betty's pilot obviously saw he was being pursued and dived toward the ocean, skimming across the waves and trying to get away from the attacker. The Liberator's bow and top turrets opened up while the Japanese plane returned fire with its tail and waist guns. The Betty took hits, went into a dive before leveling off near the water, and headed

Downing of Mavis by Lt. C. J. Alley of VB-104 on 28 August 1943.
Courtesy of the National Archives

toward Kahili with smoke coming from its engines. Fowler turned the PB4Y-1 around and went after a second Betty; the Japanese pilot, possibly seeing he was out-gunned, banked away, increased power, and fled the scene.

Navy Liberators were fully loaded with bombs and fuel for the typical 800- to 1,000-mile patrol; losing an engine on take-off often led to a catastrophic disaster. Taking off was the most dangerous part of flying the four-engined bomber. Typically, to keep as much weight out of the tail as possible, the crewmembers stationed in the rear of the plane would stand in the bomb bay—not a very safe place to be if a take-off was aborted. Lt. Searls and crew of VB-104 survived such an ordeal on 10 September 1943.

Searls borrowed the commander's plane *Sear's Steers* for a routine patrol, and just as the wheels of the Liberator cleared the field the number one port engine died. He banked right to come around for an emergency landing still carrying a full load of gas and bombs. As the bomber was about to land another plane turned on to the runway and started its takeoff. Searls aborted the landing and came back for another try but turned into the dead engine, causing the plane to lose altitude. He managed to straighten out on final but was too low and tried to make a no-flaps landing. The bomber came down like a steer falling to the ground in a rodeo. Halfway down the runway the landing gear hit the ground, but the bomber was still going too fast. The Liberator raced down the runway and hit a pile of sandbags; the right landing gear collapsed and the bomber spun around before finally coming to a stop at the end of the runway—scratch one commanding officer's Liberator. Searls and crew survived that ordeal, but most of them would later perish on another mission.[8]

The following evening nine Liberators of VB-102, with one of the planes carrying a photographer from VD-1, went on a high altitude bombing against Kahili airfield, installations, and dispersal areas with the intent of dropping a total of 21,000 pounds of fragmentation cluster bombs. The formation met up with its escort of F4Us at 19,000 feet and headed toward the target via Cape Esperance, passing east of Fauro Island before turning into the target from the northwest.

The target was clearly visible, with some two dozen planes parked on the field below as the bombs were released. The anti-aircraft batteries did not open up until the bombs were away and it was heavy and intense, with some of the bombers in the rear taking some hits. For some reason a flight of Japanese fighters flying at a lower altitude did not come in to attack, instead watching as their airfield was destroyed. Flashes of bombs impacting were seen as the field and the surrounding area were thoroughly saturated, and as the bombers turned toward home they left a thick cloud of black smoke drifting up from the airfield.

4

Against the Odds
September–October 1943

Flying in the Pacific was no easy task; in fact, planes and crews were lost daily due to other factors besides the Japanese. The difficulty in maintaining a formation at night, in bad weather, over water, and without getting lost rested largely on the capability of the navigator. Lt. H. J. Thompson, first pilot and navigator on Lt. Claggett's crew, was on a mission to Nauru Island and recalls one such mission. (Claggett's crew flew *Pistol Packin Mama*, named after the title to a popular song of the time.)

On the evening of 18 September, twelve Liberators took off on a bombing strike against Nauru, each plane carrying twenty 100-pound bombs in their bellies. By the time the aircraft rendezvoused at 3,000 feet over Carney there were ten left to complete the mission, two having mechanical problems shortly after take-off. Thompson relates his story of trying to find the rest of the formation and the target:

"After takeoff I sat at the navigation table for a short while and noticed we were heading south in our climb. I stood, leaned into the cockpit, and found Page [Lt. Page Clagett] and Jock [Lt. (jg) Jock Sutherland] trying to catch up with a white light they saw occasionally and assumed to be a tail light of a PB4Y-1. I pointed out to Page that the light was a star, and he was heading south and would soon hit the mountains of Guadalcanal. Page turned 180 degrees to port and headed north.

"We soon lost sight of the other planes, presumably when all planes turned off their navigation lights as scheduled. I was now busy navigating, getting a departure from Malaita. I tracked Page as he swung back and forth on headings generally east of north as he looked for other planes. After about one hour Page realized we would not join other planes, so we continued our mission as a single plane. We did not see another plane until the end of our flight at Carney Field.

Unidentified men of a VB-104 crew at an unknown location cleaning their machine guns prior to a patrol. VB-104 was the third South Pacific-based PB4Y-1 squadron, relieving VB-101. *Courtesy of the B-24 Club*

Herb Donald and crew of VB-104.

"Page asked for a course to Nauru, and I told him to just hold the course. We were now at 9,000 feet at standard cruise. I began serious navigation, passing the bubble octant up to Jock so he could shoot stars on our beam. I worked out the sights, and when one was plotted I gave Jock the octant for another sight on the same star, or another star on our beam. Jock shot every navigation star that would give us a course line. I ignored speed and had Page hold the same magnetic heading. The numerous star sights that we took during our second and third hours of flight gave us our track line that was taking us to the west of Nauru.

"About three hours after takeoff we switched from shooting stars on our beam to shooting stars ahead and astern. As before, Jock worked the bubble octant and I pushed the pencil. Several lines across our track gave us our speed and a determination of wind speed and direction at our altitude. Page was as nervous as a pregnant bride, because he wanted to head directly toward the island. I finally worked out a time to turn to a heading that would take us over the island. Page was so eager to get to Nauru and blast the destroyer that he turned early. In a few minutes I gave him a corrected heading."[1]

Pistol Packin Mama's crew found Nauru and soon bombs were away. On the same mission Herb Donald recalls a similar experience as he piloted another Liberator:

"I decided to get some rest before the predawn attack. I turned the flying over to co-pilot Bill Goodman, telling him to fly on the port light of the plane that was leading us and laid down on the flight deck for a few minutes. On returning to the cockpit Bill pointed to the red light he was following. To my dismay I realized it was Venus rising on the horizon!

"We then began a futile attempt to locate the rest of the formation. Not a single plane could be found. Our leader had aborted the flight without breaking radio silence. We then took up our own navigating for Nauru. At the expected ETA, with no radar contact, we took several courses for a radar search. As I was about to give up and turn back Art Felice, our second radioman, got a blip on the radar screen and we started to attack.

"As we started our bombing run down the runway the bomb bay door crept closed just enough to cause the safety switch to prevent the bombs from releasing; however, we bombed them with a case of beer bottles dropped from the tunnel hatch by Plane Captain Rolland. The crew had wired razor blades to the bottles that were supposed to cause whistling prior to plopping on the runway.

"The crew agreed that they wanted to finish the job. Rolland jammed a screwdriver in the bomb bay mechanism, I made a quick 270-degree turn, and we dropped twenty bombs a second apart across the runway and into a barracks area. By that time the Japs were awake and the anti-aircraft shells and searchlights were lighting up the cockpit and bouncing the plane."[2]

One must truly praise the skill of such navigators and pilots as Thompson and Donald to get a four-engined bomber to its target at night, across an empty ocean broken up only by tiny specks of land. Such skills involved pinpoint accuracy

The Vulnerable Virgin undergoing refueling. ***Courtesy of Nate Hodge***

and faith in the capabilities of such men; without it, a bomber crew could have easily gotten lost over the Pacific. It was an era of sextants and charts, navigating by the stars, and long before little black boxes which tell a pilot their exact position just by pushing a button.

Encountering Enemy Aircraft

The number of aerial engagements with Japanese aircraft by VB-102 and 104 increased during the last few months of 1943, with well-trained PB4Y-1 aircrews typically being victorious even when confronted with the enemy's best fighters. Indeed, during the war a few crews would actually engage and score five or more aerial victories, thus reaching "ace" status.

Both squadrons continued to tangle with Japanese fliers, with the former coming out ahead nine out of ten times during such aerial battles. Contacts with the enemy were almost a daily occurrence. The PB4Y-1 Liberator would become one of the Navy's more successful fighters—a mission it was not designed for, but was utilized in such a manner by patrol plane commanders and aerial gunners.

VB-104's executive officer Whitney Wright damaged a Betty near Nauru on 8 September, and eluded seven Zeke fighters by diving the bomber down to twenty feet, pushing the aircraft at full power while his gunners provided accurate defensive fire. The fighters stayed with Wright's aircraft for forty minutes before they disengaged, but not before putting some 120 holes into the PB4Y-1.

The following day Cdr. Sears caught a twin-engine Mitsubishi G3M Nell bomber about one hundred miles west of Kapingamarangi flying at 12,000 feet toward Buka. Increasing power, the PB4Y-1 caught up to the unsuspecting quarry, and positioning his aircraft 150 yards below the Nell, Sears' bow turret (AMM2c H. L. Colclasure), top turret (ARM2c X. F. Yuzapavich), and starboard waist gunner (either ACMM L. J. Cole or AOM1c L. D. Little) opened fire. The Nell's port wing burst into flames and a moment later the plane exploded;

pieces of the wreckage hit the bomber, with one creating a one-foot square hole in the right aileron.[3]

Nearly three weeks passed before another successful aerial interception was conducted; meanwhile, the Navy Search Group continued routine reconnaissance flights mixed with high and medium altitude strikes against shore installations and shipping with little success. One interesting respite from the mind-numbing patrols occurred on 13 September, when Cdr. Sears flew down to Espiritu Santu in PB4Y-1 *Open Bottom* (32075) in preparation to fly First Lady Eleanor Roosevelt back to Guadalcanal to visit the sick and wounded. *Open Bottom* featured a nude woman and the aforementioned name, and the powers that be decided the woman could stay, but the name was deemed unsavory and thus painted over. The goodwill trip was uneventful, with Mrs. Roosevelt touring Henderson Field on 17 September and then departing in Sears' plane the following day; however, in his log book Sears noted that the First Lady flew "Open Bottom" during the return flight for two hours.[4]

Quite a few times the Navy crews were on the receiving end of some vicious aerial engagements, and it took the skill of the patrol plane commander to get out of it. VB-102's Gordon Fowler found himself in such a predicament on September 27, as did Lt. (jg) Albrecht a day later.

Fowler was approaching Nauru at 200 feet to inspect shipping when one solitary enemy fighter identified as a Zeke was spotted about five miles ahead at several thousand feet directly over Nauru. Several others were taking off as Fowler made a 180-degree turn and climbed toward cloud cover at 2,500 feet. Within five minutes four Zekes were making individual runs, while a fifth one kept on a parallel course to the PB4Y-1. The attacks came from such angles that Fowler could not get any of his guns to bear on the fighters except for the belly and port waist guns.

During the next twenty-five minutes the patrol bomber dodged from cloud to cloud with the port waist and belly gunners scoring hits on at least two fighters, one of which exploded and disintegrated when it was hit at the wing root by the belly gunner. In all, the fighters made twelve runs on Fowler, pressing attacks to within 300 feet of the Liberator before giving up and going home. Again, the Japanese pilots failed to be aggressive and push their attacks. If they had, VB-102 would in all likelihood have lost an aircraft. A day later it was Burton Albrecht's turn to tangle with Japanese fighters after spotting eight enemy warships heading for Buka Straits.

He sighted three destroyers about three miles ahead at 2,000 feet. Climbing to 9,000 feet to get a better look, he sighted five additional destroyers on a similar course scattered across the water for some ten to twenty miles. The warships spotted the American plane and started sending up a heavy curtain of anti-aircraft fire. The Liberator then became the focus of enemy fighters flying CAP as two Zekes appeared, followed by approximately a dozen more for what the Japanese pilots probably assumed would be a short, quick kill of one American bomber.

The odds were rapidly turning against the Liberator as the fighters began individual runs; however, Albrecht's bow and top turret gunners targeted a fighter which apparently went into a climbing stall more than 500 feet ahead. The combined firepower of the bow and top turrets tore into the enemy plane, causing it to explode and disintegrate into hundreds of flaming pieces; a Zeke met a similar fate seconds later through the efforts of the starboard waist gunner.

Albrecht put the PB4Y-1 into shallow turns while using cloud cover to dodge the relentless pursuers, and his gunners continued providing heavy defensive fire. The bomber's firepower was reduced when a waist gun jammed, followed

The Crew of *Vulnerable Virgin*. *Courtesy of Nate Hodge*

by the tail turret becoming inoperable when a cartridge ruptured inside one gun and the solenoid of the other went out. Gunner A. H. Rose managed to replace the solenoid and resumed firing with one gun.

One fighter, varying the attack, started a diving run from the rear and slightly above and was hit in succession from 500 yards by the top turret, tail turret, and belly turret, blowing its tail off as it burst into flames and then spun down out of sight. Another Hap withdrew smoking but under control. Seeing cloud cover, the pilot of the PB4Y-1 raced into the clouds and contact was broken. After fifteen minutes of combat the fighters withdrew. The only damage to the Liberator was one 7.7 mm bullet hole in the starboard horizontal stabilizer. Credit for the destruction of the Zeke went to starboard waist gunner F. H. Dotson, while the destruction of the Haps went to tail gunner A. H. Rose, top gunner W. J. Cooper, belly gunner W. G. Williams, and bow turret gunner J. L. Jenkins.

VB-102 closed out September 1943 with Lt. Clagett's crew, while on a routine patrol in a sector that included Nauru Island, coming under attack by nine enemy fighters—an encounter that varied in altitude from 2,500 feet down to the deck. For the next forty minutes the planes slugged it out, with Clagett attempting to take the bomber into a thick cloud bank as the pursuers conducted some forty runs on the Liberator. The starboard waist gunner caught one fighter at 250 yards as it made a nearly vertical climb before breaking away. The fighter exposed its belly and the gunner's rounds hit, catching the engine on fire. The plane was last seen entering a thin cloud below in an inverted spin.

The Liberator was not immune to the fighter's guns, as it began taking hits, with one 20 mm shell hitting the port elevator before passing through the vertical stabilizer. Another shell entered the starboard side of the fuselage in the rear and exploded, leaving six holes in the port and starboard sides. A third 20 mm entered the bottom of the bomb bay, exploded, and made fourteen holes, severing the hydraulic flap control line. Clagett finally found sufficient cover to hide in and the attack was broken. Throughout the encounter not one crewmember was wounded at the cost of one destroyed Zeke and another two probables.[5]

On 29 September, a VB-104 downed the last Japanese plane of the month, as Lt. Humphrey was at it again with attacks on Japanese Bettys. It was a very hazy morning as the Liberator cruised at 5,000 feet some ten miles off Empress Augusta Bay when they spotted the Betty five miles away and flying at 2,500 feet, heading for Kahili. Humphrey pointed the Liberator's nose down and dived until the air speed indicator read 275 miles per hour, only fifteen miles per hour under the aircraft's top rated speed.

The PB4Y closed rapidly, and when it was some 500 yards from the Japanese aircraft the bow, belly, and top turrets opened fire. The Betty pilot increased speed, trying to get away from its pursuer while his tail and top turret gunners fired back with their 7.7 mm and 20 mm guns. The Liberator's gunners were better shots and rounds began hitting the twin-engine bomber. A fire broke out on the Betty's starboard wing; it began to lose altitude rapidly until it hit the water and exploded.

By the first week of October 1943, the Japanese had completed the evacuation of New Georgia and prepared to defend their remaining bases in the Solomon Group, especially Bougainville. Meanwhile, the Americans completed the invasion plan for Bougainville (Operation Cherry Blossom), and in preparation for the operation slated for 1 November, allied air forces began a massive campaign to neutralize the Japanese base at Rabaul, while strikes against enemy airfields on Bougainville continued. The Japanese, anticipating further allied landings, increased long-range aerial reconnaissance to locate the American fleet and the G4M Betty was pressed into providing such work. Reducing the aircraft's weight, it could patrol wide search sectors, and it was believed at the time could outdistance any allied aircraft except for the fastest fighters. Between 5 and 8 October, the Japanese would lose four bombers (one per day) to Liberators of the Navy Search Group.

Cdr. Gordon Fowler's Crew One became the first Navy Liberator crew to engage one of the Bettys while patrolling off New Britain at high noon on 5 October. At 1,200 feet and emerging from a rain squall, he spotted the plane flown possibly by either Petty Officer Second Class Yukio Ogawa or Petty Officer First Class Yukio Koyama of the 751Ku about half a mile distant on a converging course at 500 feet. (Note: members of the crew were PO2 Kenji Tsuji [observer]; PO2 Kenzo Nakahara [radioman]; Leading Seaman [LS] Shinji [o] Kawakami; LS Goichi [o] Sakamoto; and LS Takeo Fujii [flight mechanic].)[6]

He was able to close to 700 yards and maintained altitude advantage before the Betty's crew apparently detected the approach. The twin-engine bomber dropped to one hundred feet and increased speed, trying to outrun the approaching American plane. The Liberator, now in a power glide, closed to about 500 yards and Fowler's gunners opened fire. Accurate bursts scored numerous hits and set the port engine on fire. The Betty immediately lost speed and the PB4Y-1 overtook her rapidly, strafing thoroughly with little return fire. According to Robert E. Jacques, one of the gunners, he aimed for the cockpit and he, "could see the cockpit glass breaking and the pilot jumping in his seat as he shot him." According to Jacques' nephew, some forty years later he confided that it was very disturbing and that he felt sorry for the pilot.[7]

The Japanese pilot conducted a perfect water landing, but Fowler's men were not finished, as they repeatedly strafed the stricken plane, leaving no visible survivors. Such was the brutality of the Pacific War; appalling to many who read such accounts, but at the time justified by many bomber crews who participated in such attacks. They believed, as did this writer's father, survivors could be encountered again and become the ones that would kill you or fellow squadron members—a means of improving the odds to survive a tour of duty.

Earlier in the morning of 5 October, Cdr. Dyson led three Liberators of VD-1 to Choiseul Island. Cloud cover obscured the target so the formation broke up, with Dyson heading for the Treasury Islands and another Liberator headed back to Carney. Lt.Cdr. Eady, in the third Liberator, decided to fly one flight across Choiseul from 25,000 feet. During the run two enemy fighters were spotted flying 8,000 feet below and headed for the photographic plane. Eady nosed the bomber over and headed for Vella Lavella.

The Liberator's airspeed indicated 250 miles per hour as its pilot nosed the bomber down toward the attackers. The two fighters were then joined by four more Zekes and Tonys. Pressing in their attacks to 400 yards of the fleeing Liberator, the fighters were met with the combined firepower of Eady's bow, top, tail, and waist guns. The bomber's top turret and waist gunners scored hits on one fighter, sending it down in a mass of flames. The aircraft were down to 6,000 feet as the Japanese fighters came around for one last attack. Eady turned towards them and the top turret gunner hit another fighter, sending it down toward the ocean. The Liberator had taken no hits from the attacking planes.

Lt. Burton Albrecht with VB-102 engaged another Betty from the 751KU piloted by Petty Officer Second Class Osamu Shinoda the following day (6 October) off Choiseul Island. Three miles behind the intended victim Albrecht approached undetected while increasing the PB4Y-1's altitude from 1,800 to 4,000 feet. When the Liberator was 800 yards from its quarry the Betty's pilot, seeing he was being pursued, increased his plane's speed and started a power glide toward the water. The maneuver came too late, as Albrecht's guns began firing at a range of 500 yards and continued to do so as the distance closed to within 200 yards. Withering fire demolished the Betty's top turret, riddled the fuselage, and set fire to the starboard engine. The Japanese tail gunner managed to return fire with one of his 20 mm cannon rounds, hitting and knocking out the Liberator's number four engine. The mortally wounded Betty began a long death glide before striking the water and disintegrating into pieces.

The other half of the Navy Search Group encountered patrolling Bettys as well, with VB-104's Crew 16, commanded by Lt. Anderson, the next to shoot down a Betty the following morning. He was cruising along at 8,000 feet when he saw the bomber five miles ahead being pursued by another Navy Liberator—probably Lt. Humphrey of VB-104, who lost contact soon thereafter. From his point at 6,000 feet Anderson saw the Japanese aircraft now flying at 200 feet, five miles from his position. Anderson jettisoned his bombs, went down after the other bomber, and closed in for the kill. The Betty saw he was again being pursued and opened fire with his tail cannon. Closing to 500 yards, the Liberator's gunners began riddling the Betty with rounds, destroying the tail gun position, top turret, and the cockpit. The Betty's starboard engine caught fire and it soon spread to the rest of the aircraft. It slowed enough to where Anderson closed in and flew alongside the other aircraft's port wing. At point blank range his gunners continued to pour rounds into it. The bomber could no longer take the punishment and plunged into the ocean, exploding on impact. The impact sent one of the unfortunate plane's crew hurtling some 200 feet across the water.[8]

Lt. H. L. Donald led Crew 8 of VB-104 in the fourth downing of a Betty in as many days near the end of a nine-hour patrol on 8 October, some twenty miles off Ontong Java Atoll. The Betty and Liberator headed toward each other, with the former a mile ahead and approximately 1,000 feet below the latter. Donald throttled back, conducting shallow diving turns to maneuver behind the enemy, and at maximum range his bow, top, and belly turret gunners opened fire. The Japanese top, tail, and waist gunners immediately began returning fire, and for the next twenty-five minutes the two bombers battled it out over the Pacific.

R. L. Hammond (AOM2c), in the belly turret, aimed for the Betty's 20 mm tail cannon gunner. When the belly turret started firing waist gunners C. M. Osiecki (AMM2c) and A. E. Rolland (AMM1c) knew they were in range and joined in, followed by Bill Knudsen (AMM2c) in the bow turret. Rolland

Gordon Fowler's gunners continue to strafe a Japanese aircraft they had just downed. ***Courtesy of Navy Squadrons 102/14 Association***

fired so many rounds at the Betty that he had to go back to the bomb bay to bring back additional ammunition.

The Japanese gunners began scoring hits on the PB4Y-1 as a 20 mm shell exploded inside the bomb bay, while 7.7 mm rounds struck the cockpit, shattering the glass above co-pilot Ens. L. R. Bauer's head. According to Lt. Donald, "One bullet passed through my intercom and under my seat six inches from my butt." The top turret was hit as well, wounding gunner Bill Sams (ARM1c) in the chest and face.

The Donald's gunners were firing so rapidly that the barrels in the bow and belly turrets burned out and stopped functioning for a moment. Seeing his gunfire drastically reduced, Donald maneuvered the Liberator to get his waist gunners in position to fire. The waist guns managed to fire long enough for the barrels in the two turrets to cool off before they started firing again. Smoke began pouring from the Betty's engines and there was no more return fire.

It went down gracefully and made a perfect landing on the water as the Liberator overshot the downed plane. Below, four of the Betty's crew scrambled out of the wreck and dived into the water just as the Liberator came back around. There was no escape for the men in the water, as the PB4Y-1's gunners concentrated their machine gun fire on plane and crew, leaving at least one of them dead and floating on the surface and the plane burning.[9]

Nerves frayed from incessant enemy air or naval attacks conducted primarily at night caused many shore and sea-based American anti-aircraft gunners to become trigger happy. Such was the case when a PB4Y-1 flown by the commanding officer of VB-104 nearly became a victim of anxious gunners the night of 13 October 1943. After carrying a Marine officer to inspect Empress Augusta Bay, Sears and his crew were approaching Carney Field. They made all the proper recognition signals and turned toward Carney with wheels down, preparing to land. On their approach one friendly cargo ship began shooting at the bomber, immediately followed by additional ships opening up on the aircraft.

Hundreds of tracers converged on the hapless Liberator and her crew, with rounds passing around and through the aircraft. Then searchlights came on, blinding pilot and crew. Somehow, by God's intervention, luck, or bad shooting, Sears managed to get through the curtain of fire and made a safe landing. Inspection the following day showed the plane had been hit by several 20 mm shells in the starboard wing and the number one engine. In all, the American gunners had put 124 holes in Sears' aircraft.[10]

5

Unsung Valor

Nathan Hodge, who served as a bow gunner with VB-104, remarked, "We didn't get a damn thing!" a sentiment he and others shared while serving with PB4Y-1 Liberator squadrons in the Pacific between 1942 and 1944. They felt their contribution to the war effort was largely ignored, especially with issuing, or lack thereof, of military decorations to personnel other than the patrol plane commander. The first reported low-level anti-shipping mission conducted by a PB4Y-1 Liberator crew provides a case in point. October 17, 1943, marked the first successful masthead height bombing of an enemy ship by a Navy Liberator. After three months in combat, the Buccaneers received delayed action fuses for their bombs. This device allowed aircraft to attack shipping at minimum altitude, typically releasing bombs between fifty to one hundred feet off the ship's port or starboard sides and crossing over the ship as the ordnance detonated, with accuracy increasing exponentially. VB-104's Lt.Cdr. Whitney Wright, borrowing Lt. M. V. Montgomery's Crew 4, conducted a search off Kavieng and Emirau with his plane armed with five 300-pound bombs with delayed action fuses.

Whitney Wright and crew next to *Whit's Shits* (bureau number 32081) fitted with the Erco bow turret. He was VB-104's executive officer, and he and his crew were the first PB4Y-1 squadron to conduct a low-level anti-shipping attack armed with bombs with delayed action fuses. *Courtesy of the B-24 Club*

Some ten minutes before noon, Wright spotted a three-ship convoy consisting of 8,000- and 4,000-ton troop transports escorted by a destroyer. The largest of the three ships became the focus of the attack as the plane came in at masthead height, his gunners providing suppressing fire against the vessel's gun positions. Conducting such a strike precluded the use of the Norden bomb sight, thus the pilot used a device called a pickle—a tubular device about the size of a dill pickle with a switch or button called a toggle. Wright pressed the pickle but nothing happened; the bombs did not drop. He turned the plane around for another attempt, and this time the bombs fell toward the ship, scoring a pair of direct hits on the transport's bow, while two others detonated alongside the ship. Heavy, billowing smoke poured from the holes created by the explosions and the transport began settling by the bow. Wright retired to the north, away from the fighter bases on Emirau and Kavieng.[1]

We Didn't get a Damn Thing!

The Navy command reportedly awarded only Whitney Wright with a medal and none of his crew. The Navy, whether formally or informally, had a tendency to be biased when it came to commending crew members servicing with patrol/bombing squadrons. Indeed, granting individual awards to enlisted crew members higher than a letter of commendation was almost unheard of during the first two years of VB operations in the Pacific. The commanding officers of VB-102 and -106 addressed the manner in which awards were granted. Lt.Cdr. Gordon Fowler, while addressing his squadron's tour of duty in an interview conducted by the Navy Air Intelligence Group on 14 March 1944, discussed the inconsistencies between how the Army Air Corps and Navy awarded pilots, stating, "An Army pilot operates in the South Pacific three months and come back with a DFC, Air Medal, and incidental oak leaf cluster. A Navy pilot engaged in the same operations gets nothing but a star on his theater ribbon."[2]

Nate Hodge of VB-104. ***Courtesy of Nate Hodge***

Fowler's testimony probably occurred prior to Wright being officially awarded the Navy Cross. The Air Intelligence Group interviewed Cdr. Hayward, commanding officer of VB-106, several months later on 23 June 1944. He also discussed the inconsistency, stating, ". . .it's bad on morale." He further added his disappointment, in that Cdr. Sears was recommended for the Navy Cross for sinking an enemy tanker at masthead height, but the award was reduced to a Distinguished Flying Cross.[3]

The often used quote that, "time heals all wounds," in the context of military awards may be true for many that felt slighted by the Navy, but for some, especially those who made the military a career, resentment lingered, since such decorations are an integral part of the promotion system. In the context of this work's subject, patrol plane commanders were rated a higher award for meritorious action. If the pilot was awarded the Distinguished Flying Cross, typically the rest of the crew received the Air Medal. Very rarely was an enlisted man awarded a higher medal than an officer. Indeed, controversy still surrounds such treatment, especially among air gunners.

Often the men manning such positions were not even mentioned in official after-action reports as being the agent responsible for bringing down an enemy aircraft. Instead, the only name mentioned was the pilot. Nate "Gremlin" Hodge, then a twenty-four-year-old crewmember of Lt. Hager's crew with VB-104, provided an example of such treatment while visiting Cdr. Sears soon after the war. His old skipper looked at the enlisted man's uniform and asked, "Where's all your medals?" Hodge replied, "What medals, sir?" Sears could not believe Hodge had not been awarded any medals for his service with VB-104. Nate Hodge added, "We didn't get a damn thing at the time. It took me eight years after the war to get the Purple Heart for wounds I suffered in 1944."[4]

A bomber crew was made up of men who relied on each other during an engagement. The pilot relied on his gunners to defend the aircraft from attack and the latter relied on the pilot's ability to command a four-engine bomber. They worked as a team, enlisted or not. To give a plane commander solitary credit for bringing down an enemy aircraft was a disservice to the gunners. Late in 1944, the Navy expanded the award system by adding the Strike/Flight criteria for the Air Medal and Distinguished Flying Cross for participation in sustained air operations. The traditional manner in which officers and sailors were awarded such medals for individual acts remained. However, those who returned earlier from a tour never knew of the change in regulations and the Navy made no effort to inform the veterans. It was not until 1996 that the author's father finally received a pair of Distinguished Flying Crosses and an additional eight Air Medals—thirty years after retiring from the military. He was grateful, but he remarked, "A little too late, isn't it?" referring to their significance in the possibility of retiring at a higher rank.[5]

The barrier, either formally or informally, of recognizing individual actions by enlisted personnel began to erode by late 1944, with a few men receiving such awards as the Navy Cross and the Silver Star Medal. Yet some men remained resentful they were underappreciated in their contribution, as it appeared unfair to many that served in the early PB4Y-1 squadrons while over-generous to others that came afterward. Another area of contention regarded the lack of official post-mission briefings of enlisted combat air crewmen, who were often excluded in such meetings, with only the pilot and co-pilot interviewed about a mission in terms of what happened, who did what, etc., whereas every member on a bomber crew in the Army Air Force were interviewed after a mission. Thus, the recollections of naval enlisted flight personnel often went unrecorded.

The participation of Navy Liberators in mass bombing missions against enemy land and naval shipping began to fade during the last months of 1944, as the Navy Air Groups began focusing on conducting armed reconnaissance flights. Some patrol plane commanders flew their assigned search sectors and never encountered the enemy, while others pursued a more aggressive role, seeking targets of opportunity on land and sea. Most squadron commanders left it to individual patrol plane commanders whether land installations would be hit in their search sector; however, enemy shipping or aircraft encountered during a routine search would be targeted. The pilot, co-pilot, and navigator would discuss specifics with the commanding officer and intelligence officer. Usually the pilot would then fill in the rest of the crew prior to departure.

Free Drinks for a Purple?

It is often said the only military commendation military personnel do not want to receive is the Purple Heart. The Purple Heart Medal is awarded to those wounded, killed, or missing in action and are universal among the service branches—an award that few if any seek to earn. Sometimes, after a period of "white cap" patrols, a Navy Liberator crew went out to search for trouble. Often a crew would attack an island or a ship and get away with relatively slight damage to the aircraft and no injuries to the crew—sometimes not.

On 23 October, VB-104's Lt. Searls went looking for trouble at Kapingamarangi in his Liberator *Wata-Honey*. There he found a small ship and dove down to attack it at 150 feet. During the second run his co-pilot, Ens. Harp Joslyn, was at the bomb sight when a 7.7 mm round went through the compartment and grazed his head, shattering his earphones. Fragments of the earphones hit another crewmember behind Joslyn. R. M DeGolia, a fellow crewman, remembers the incident.

"There was much blood and pain, but we were able to get Harp Joslyn home to the hospital. He was in great pain, so I gave him a morphine shot. Of course he liked that and wanted more. I learned later that you never administer morphine for a head injury."

Ens. Joslyn enjoyed showing everyone his Purple Heart Medal. Afterward, he said that the scar and medal would be good for free drinks when he got Stateside. He did not get a chance to test his theory, as he was killed in action along with Searls and most of the crew of *Wata-Honey* three weeks before the Buccaneers of VB-104 went home.[6]

Allied Advance to Bougainville

American forces began another series of amphibious assaults in the Treasury Islands and Bougainville. The job for Army and Navy Liberator squadrons was to reduce air opposition by bombing the enemy's airfields. A joint effort consisting of thirty-one Liberators, with Cdr. Sears leading seven aircraft from his squadron, struck Kahili on 26 October. Approaching the target at 21,000 feet from the southeast, the Japanese started sending up heavy anti-aircraft fire from shore batteries on Kahili, Ballale, and from ships in the harbor, with some of the aircraft receiving minor damage. The Liberators went down to 19,500 feet and released their payload, saturating the runway and revetment areas.[7]

Aboard PB4Y-1 *Donald's Duck*, the bombardier of Crew 8, Bill Goodman, could not get his bombs to drop in sequence, so he released all five 1,000-pound bombs in a cluster. A VD-1 photograph taken the next day showed a cluster of five craters in the runway alongside a control tower. Back at the officer's club on Guadalcanal, Australian flyers broke out in a song to the tune of "Bless Them All." It went like this: "They asked for the Navy to help bomb Kahili. The Navy said yes, they agreed. They sent every section a different direction. It looked like a cattle stampede. Bless them all. . . ."[8]

The air campaign against Japanese airfields continued, but it did not interfere with the Liberator squadrons' propensity to look for trouble elsewhere. Earlier in the day Curtis F. Vossler of VB-102 sighted and attacked three cargo ships outside Green Island Lagoon. Green Island is a small group of coral atolls some thirty-seven miles northwest of Buka and fifty-five miles east of New Ireland. Japanese troops based on the largest island Nissan sent barge and ship traffic to Rabaul and Buka. Elimination of such traffic would hamper the enemy's ability to send in reinforcements.

Enemy ships were underway and heading toward the lagoon in an effort to have the island's anti-aircraft protect them as the Liberator approached at 200 feet, but it was too late, as Vossler's gunners began strafing the vessels. Vossler pickled off bombs just as the ships changed course to successfully evade the falling ordnance. The patrol plane commander then swung the PB4Y around to allow his gunners to possibly inflict some damage on the enemy. However, the aircraft sustained some hits from anti-aircraft fire that cut a hydraulic line and wounded co-pilot Lt. Merle Lawrence. A damaged plane with a wounded man aboard forced Vossler to break off, but not before leaving one vessel burning and another afire and beached.

On October 28, 1943, the 2nd Marine Parachute Battalion made an unopposed landing on the Treasury Islands for the purpose of drawing Japanese forces away from Bougainville, and to build a staging point for the future offensive. November opened with the 3rd Marine Division landing at Empress Augusta Bay; by nightfall, over 14,000 troops were on the beach. The following evening American and Japanese ships engaged each other forty-five miles from Bougainville in the Battle of Empress Augusta Bay. An increase in Japanese shipping in the area improved the likelihood of American patrol aircraft spotting them, and such was the case when Navy Liberators of the Navy Search Group conducted anti-shipping strikes during 4–5 November 1943.

6

Intense to Routine Operations November–January 1944

The twenty-four hours covering the period 4–5 November 1943 saw the squadrons engaged in almost continuous combat against enemy shipping and aircraft, culminating in the last missions conducted by Fowler's VB-102. The day started with Lt. Humphrey taking *You Got It* to Kapingamarangi, where he almost "got it" from eight Rufes. A small seaplane tender was spotted in the harbor and Humphrey went down at masthead height.

During the first two attacks several fires were started on the vessel by the concentrated fire of the Liberator's gunners. *You Got It* came in for a third attack when enemy float planes came up to intervene. Diving down to the tops of the waves, Humphrey and his crew battled the Rufes for ten minutes, during which time two of the crew were wounded and the aileron cables were severed. After ten minutes the attack was broken off and Humphrey managed to nurse his damaged bomber 700 miles back to base.[1]

The strike on the seaplane base was just the beginning of a combined strike by VB-102 and 104 against Japanese shipping. American intelligence knew the Japanese would try to oppose the Bougainville landings, so special searches were sent to look for enemy surface units. Taking off an hour after Humphrey, Lt.Cdr. Sears went out and found a convoy 180 miles north of Kavieng.

Two large oil tankers, weighing some 11,000 tons, were spotted being escorted by two destroyers. The tankers were the *Nichiei Maru* and the *Nissho Maru*, and were bound for Rabaul to refuel heavy cruisers of the Japanese Second Fleet. Immediately after sending a contact report back to base Sears went down and began his attack. Going down to masthead height, his gunners delivered a deadly hail of machine gun fire as the squadron commander dropped two 300-pound bombs. Both bombs were near misses, but his gunners started several small fires on the vessel's deck. Meanwhile, the destroyers sent up a stream of anti-aircraft fire to no avail as the Liberator targeted the second tanker.

As Sears began his run, Lt. Anderson's Liberator arrived on the scene and began his own attack on the first ship. Coming in at only thirty-five feet, Anderson dropped his five 300-pound bombs and scored three direct hits. Coming out of his dive over the tanker, the bomber's vertical stabilizer snagged a ten-foot long piece of cable from the ship's radio antennae. They did not find out about it until they landed back at base.

The Buccaneer's skipper went in for the kill on his target and scored two direct hits on the tanker's stern. The explosions caused the ship to begin burning and sent up billowing clouds of smoke. With all bombs away Sears and Anderson went back to base.

Unfortunately for the first tanker crew their battle with American PB4Y-1 Liberators continued later that day, as Gordon Fowler caught up to it twenty miles from the location of Sears' attack.

A small Japanese cargo vessel is strafed by a Liberator of VB-106. ***Courtesy of the Naval History Center***

The ship had lost speed and was now being escorted by a Japanese destroyer. Fowler went in, braving intense defensive fire from both ships, and dropped six 300-pound bombs from masthead height across the tanker's starboard beam while his bow gunner fired bursts to discourage additional anti-aircraft fire.

One bomb hit amidships with another a near miss to starboard, causing a heavy underwater explosion. No burning, list, or other evidence of serious damage was observed. With anti-aircraft fire growing in intensity Fowler decided to leave. The two tankers, battered by the aerial attacks, were towed back to Truk after Adm. Kurita dispatched the cruiser *Chokai*.[2]

Early the following morning Sears dispatched Lts. Searls and Montgomery to track the enemy and two enemy convoys north of Kavieng were sighted; contact reports were sent back to Guadalcanal. Later Army Air Force Liberators found the light cruiser *Isuzu* escorting three troop-laden transports. The ensuing attack damaged two of the transports. In all, nineteen Japanese naval ships were reported in the area; it was obvious the Japanese were preparing to oppose the landings at Princess Augusta Bay.[3] To prevent it Adm. Halsey decided to hit Rabaul proper with all available carrier aircraft.

While American carrier forces were preparing to swing into action against Rabaul, VB-102's Lt. Thompson took on a Japanese seaplane tender attacked earlier in the day by Lt. Humphrey's crew, but Japanese float planes interfered with the former's plan. Thompson found a vessel at Kapingamarangi unloading in the harbor, but before he could attack eight float planes (seven Rufes and one Pete) came up after him.

The skipper of VB-106 Cdr. "Chick" Hayward and his crew. Front row (L to R): Ens. Walter Vogelsang; Cdr. John T. Hayward; and Ens. Jack More. Middle row (L to R): William P. Hikel, AMM1c; Thomas Boose Jr., AMM2c; Carl H. Swift, ARM1c; and R. Schreffler, ACRM. Back row (L to R): David M. Kelly, AOM2c; Ralph L. Gibson, AOM2c; Edward W. Brooks, AMM2c; and John F. Moe, ACMM. *Courtesy of Steve Surface*

There were successive single attacks from the fighters, with only two being made by two aircraft. The bomber took hits to the hydraulic system, the leading edge of the port wing, and the bomb bay. Every time the fighters would come in the Liberator pilot would turn in on them, thus breaking any type of coordinated run. Gunfire from the tail and port waist gunners sent one Rufe down in flames, while another was seriously damaged.

Japanese forces on Kapingamarangi continued to be the focus of Navy Liberator combat air crews. The crew of a lone VB-102 Navy Liberator decided to check on the Japanese at Kapingamarangi. Lt. B. F. Albrecht, on the return leg of his assigned search area, decided to approach the island just after dusk to check for any of the aircraft that had attacked Thompson. Approaching the island at 150 feet and using a line of rain squalls to hide, he spotted five Rufes and one Pete lined up along the inner shore wing tip to wing tip and two patrol boats anchored across the lagoon. The Liberator came in above the island at one hundred feet, dropping a string of bombs and strafing which immediately drew the response of a single enemy anti-aircraft gun on a vessel boat, followed by individual rifle fire.

The sound of gunfire alerted men working on the planes and most ran into the bushes. The pilot pickled off six 300-pound bombs while his gunners strafed, setting three Rufes on fire. Subsequent strafing runs at fifty feet set the other two Rufes afire while the waist gunners raked the other patrol craft in passing. On the fourth run a pilot attempted to climb into the cockpit of one of the Rufes, but was swept off the wing by .50-caliber fire as the plane was riddled. As Albrecht departed a huge explosion occurred among the planes.

Hayward's Hellions

While Marines were battling the Japanese on Bougainville and Navy Seabees were building a bomber strip on the island, Cdr. John D. "Chick" Hayward's Hellions of VB-106 joined

A VB-106 PB4Y-1 over the Southwest Pacific. *Courtesy of the Naval History Center*

the search and reconnaissance group, officially relieving VB-102. The attacks during 4 and 5 November marked the end of VB-102's tour of duty. In 102's place Cdr. Hayward's VB-106 would take over the duties of her sister squadron.

The new squadron had already seen over a month of combat while stationed in the Central Pacific, and in the months to come would become one of the best Navy Liberator squadrons of the war. Hayward's Hellions of VB-106 immediately began hitting Japanese shipping and installations.

A few days after 106's arrival, one of its pilots, Lt. Mitchell, damaged a small cargo ship in Kapingamarangi Lagoon. A single Rufe went up to oppose the attack and was quickly run off when Mitchell's top and bow turrets damaged it after firing 200 rounds. The real baptism of fire in the Solomons came on the seventh, when Lt. D. C. Davis spotted five ships consisting of one 6,000-ton and two 4,000-ton freighters being escorted by two gunboats while flying at 6,000 feet off Saint Matthias. As usual he reported the ships to base, and for the next twenty minutes dodged in and out of clouds, trying to identify the vessels.

The sharp eyes of the crew spotted two Petes below flying cover for the convoy at 2,000 feet. Either the enemy planes were not interested in the Liberator or they had not seen it. After an hour Davis got tired of waiting for any additional help and went in to attack alone.

The first bomb run was against the largest merchant ship, with two 300-pound bombs dropped from 3,700 feet. The first landed very short of the intended victim, with the second being a near miss seventy-five feet off the ship's port bow.

Seeing the convoy they were supposed to be protecting under attack one of the Petes came to intercept, jettisoning two bombs as he approached. The bi-winged float plane from another area of aviation history came in from nine o'clock, but turned off at about 800 yards as tracer rounds from the Liberator's waist positions flew around him.

It came back around and maneuvered in from 11 o'clock, slightly above the PB4Y-1. The enemy pilot began firing even though he was still out of range and continued firing as he came within 400 yards, only breaking off the attack as Davis' bow and top turrets poured fire into the plane. The Pete was injured, with a trail of smoke coming from it as it headed away from the Liberator—he had had enough.

PB4Y-1 *Chick's Chick* (bureau number 32238), named after the aircraft's pilot, Cdr. John "Chick" Haywood of VB-106. *Courtesy of the Billy Bran Acott ARM2c Family*

Safe for the time being from fighter attacks, Davis went down to 3,000 feet and flew over the ships, strafing the merchant ships and one of the gunboats. Davis was receiving small caliber gunfire from every ship, but he had enough gas and went in again. Coming in again for another run at the biggest target, he dropped two more 300-pound bombs from 5,500 feet, but they all missed. Hayward's Hellions were somewhat inexperienced and had never practiced low-level bombing. With time and practice they would find it easier to hit shipping at masthead height.

The battle was far from over, as the second Pete came up to intervene just after the Liberator's bombing run. The float plane managed two runs on the bomber. The first was stopped by concentrated fire from the belly and starboard waist guns. This pilot was aggressive—too much so—and probably inexperienced, as he made a second attack from seven o'clock from behind the bomber. This was his last duel with a Navy patrol bomber, as the Pete was hit hard by tail turret fire. Except for the strikes conducted on the fourth and fifth, the remainder of November was a time of routine searches, highlighted occasionally with strikes on minor shipping off New Ireland and Green Island.

Routine Searches

Allied efforts turned to reducing the offensive capabilities of Japanese forces at Rabaul. Throughout October and November 1943, the base was subjected to constant allied bombings. On 11 November, Lt. Gehlbach of VD-1 went out to photograph the results of one strike. While dodging enemy fighters and anti-aircraft fire the crew photographed the damage on shore and took notice of Japanese warships fleeing the harbor. Rabaul was on its way to being knocked out of the war. Some 100,000 of her defenders waited in vain for an allied invasion force that never materialized. They were left to wither on the vine.

For Sears' squadron, routine searches and strikes were interrupted by the loss of their second aircraft and crew. On 15 November, Lt. Honey and Crew 17 were lost while attacking Nauru. The Liberator they were flying was one that VB-102 had left behind, *Jungle Fever*. The loss of this crew would not be the last.

Thanksgiving Day saw the last Japanese offensive on Bougainville, with the 23rd Imperial Infantry waging an unsuccessful counterattack and being annihilated by Marines at the battle of Piva Forks. The same day American destroyers under the command of Capt. Arleigh Burke fought Japanese surface units trying to reinforce Buka at the battle of Cape St. George. The last month of 1943 saw continued efforts on the part of allied forces to neutralize Japanese forces. On 16 December, Arawe, on the southern coast of New Britain, was captured, followed by Cape Gloucester on the twenty-first.

Both proved useless to overall American strategy at the cost of a few hundred Marines.[4]

For the Navy Search Group, the focus was on increased searches for enemy shipping leaving Rabaul and Kavieng, with Cdr. Sears first to spot the exodus on 2 December, when he sighted twelve large freighters in Kavieng Harbor. Lt. Stoppleman spotted more ships in the harbor on the eighth. The same day Sears attacked seven small coastal vessels between Truk and Buka, sinking one and damaging another five.

Flying at tree top height as if a Liberator was a fighter a crew could sometimes find various targets of opportunity. Flying low over the southwest shore of New Ireland on 18 December, Lt. Donald's bow gunner eyed a truck and destroyed it with one long burst. A couple minutes later the starboard waist gunner poured rounds into another truck and then targeted the vehicle's driver fleeing from his burning vehicle. The Liberator's guns then shifted to a group of Japanese troops who were cut down while running toward their anti-aircraft guns.[5]

It had been a month since either squadron had suffered the loss of men or aircraft, but it would not last. On Christmas Day 1943, VB-106 suffered a tremendous loss when Ens. William Snead took off for a routine search, only to lose an engine and crash in the water 1,000 yards from shore, killing Snead and three others on board. Suffering from a broken leg, Joe J. Walker (ARM2c) dove under water and freed L. N. Briggs (AMM3c) from the sinking aircraft. On the surface Walker and Charles F. Thrasher (ARM2c) kept Briggs afloat until a rescue boat arrived. Briggs died en route to a hospital. Again, operational losses were as efficient killers as the enemy.

The end of 1943 was marked by a series of sightings of Japanese task forces between Kavieng and Truk. On 27 December, Lt. Donald spotted the battleship *Mutsu*, heavy cruiser *Aoba*, and two destroyers only one hundred miles from Truk. Later in the day an American submarine reported the battle force had reversed course and was heading full speed back toward Truk. On New Year's Eve the sighting was followed by Van Benschoten, who spotted the cruisers *Kumano* and *Suzuya*.

Pacific twilight. Maintenance personnel at work on one of VB-106's bombers. *Courtesy of the Naval History Center*

While Hayward's Hellions and Sears' Buccaneers were hitting the enemy when they could, the first Navy Liberator photographic squadron continued their job of aerial reconnaissance and mapping. For them 1944 started with a change in VD-1's compliment, with the original flight crews transferring back to the United States and replacement crews taking over; Cdr. McElroy assumed command.

Rotating crews while keeping the squadron in the war zone was a new concept for Navy Liberator squadrons. Typically, the squadrons served eight months duty on average and returned to the States for reforming. Every squadron but VD-1 held to this concept until late in the war, when VPB-116 became the first to begin rotating their crews in the Central Pacific. The squadron stayed in the combat zone and only the crews changed. The reasoning was that experienced crews could train new ones while out in the field. Sending an entire squadron back required up to seven additional months of retraining before they were able to return to the combat zone.

One of the first command decisions made by VD-1's Cdr. McElroy was to build an officer's club with the help of the Seabees, which boosted morale and raised him to almost god-like proportions. Operationally the squadron continued to cover Rabaul, Kavieng, New Ireland, Bougainville, and the Treasury Islands for future surface and aerial bombardments.

Executed

For the Buccaneers and the Hellions, most of January 1944 turned out to be a month of routine ten to twelve hour patrols with occasional glimpses of the enemy. Most of the patrol squadron's activities were reconnaissance missions to Kavieng and Nauru, along with token strikes against small shipping.

The Japanese were rapidly losing their hold on the area and would continue to do so, but the region could still be deadly, as the Buccaneers lost an entire crew on the eighth when Lt. H. E. Dvorachek borrowed Lt. Hager's Liberator *Vulnerable Virgin* and went on a routine search and never returned. No wreckage was ever found; like her sisters, she disappeared with the epitaph "failed to return." According to Nate Hodge—a close friend of one of the missing crew members—some of the crew were rescued by the Japanese, only to be executed shortly before the Japanese surrender.[6]

Throughout the war aviators unlucky enough to be shot down and "rescued" by the Japanese never made it home. Especially brutal toward allied air crews were the men living and barely surviving on bypassed islands, who did not have the food nor the means of taking care of their unwanted guests. For some death came quickly through beheading, while for others death would not come so easily; some were used for bayonet practice or simply starved to death. In a few instances,

Commander Sears' squadron attacks a Japanese cargo ship. ***Courtesy of the National Archives***

during the closing months of the conflict a small number of PB4Y crew members were taken prisoner and survived their ordeal; others were less fortunate. Hayward dropped out of high school and joined the Navy at sixteen, was accepted to attend Annapolis, and graduated two years later in 1930.

While searching for their fallen friends the Buccaneers continued chasing enemy bombers, with Lt. Anderson cornering a Betty on the eleventh and shooting it down. VB-104 suffered an operational loss of a plane and a crewman on the twenty-ninth. Because his own aircraft *Vulnerable Virgin* was lost with Lt. Dvorachek on the eighth, Lt. Hager borrowed *Donald's Duck* from Lt. Donald and was testing new instrumentation installed in the plane.

Sitting in the bow turret was Nathan "Gremlin" Hodge. Gremlin liked sitting in the turret on landings; it was fascinating to watch from the front seat as the big bomber came in for a touchdown. Orphaned as a child, he only knew the Navy as a family and had decided to make it his life. This time it would not be a typical landing.

Coming in to an airfield in the Russell Islands the bomber began weaving, and before the pilot had a chance to make a correction it crashed. Tail gunner William R. Farr Jr. was killed, and Hodge, still in the turret, was catapulted from the aircraft, rolling 150 feet down the runway. The circular turret rolled to a stop, and as witnesses to the crash watched, Hodge climbed out, his face a bloody mass of torn skin from hitting the turret's gun sight.

Evacuated to the United States, he needed quite a bit of patching up, including a steel plate in his nose. After his release from the hospital the Navy planned to discharge the sailor. The physical scars were healing, but there was still a psychological scar. A man who enjoyed flying no longer wanted to step inside an aircraft.

Seeing his career slipping away, he spoke with Cdr. Sears, who, knowing the young man and his past, ordered him to fly in a small single-engine aircraft to remove his phobia. It worked, and no longer scarred, Hodge continued his career in the Navy, retiring in 1960.[7]

7

Rest, Relax, Resume Missions February–March 1944

By late 1943 and early 1944, it was obvious the men needed some time away from the combat zone to ward off combat fatigue, so Cdrs. Sears and Hayward established a rest and relaxation (R&R) program that ferried individual crews on a rotational basis to places such as Auckland, New Zealand, and Sydney, Australia. To ferry the men, a non-combatant Liberator *Fat Cat* was utilized. Loaded down with bargaining items, such as cartons of cigarettes and war souvenirs, the men boarded the plane for a week's vacation that included warm beds, hot baths, and women.

Those on the trip were expected and obliged to bring back beer and whiskey for the men on the island. The system was highly successful with very few cases of combat fatigue, in stark contrast to the Navy Liberator squadrons that served in the Central Pacific. Such squadrons rarely, if at all, had such a system, and consequently, they had a higher number of combat fatigue cases. For those stationed on islands such as Apamama, Eniwetok, and Kwajalein, swimming and shell gathering comprised most of their leisure activities.

An activity that VB-106 participated in was indirectly related to R&R. One of the squadron's search sectors included the Stewart Islands, where the light-skinned female natives looked like Dorothy Lamour. Passing patrol planes would fly low and throw out their flight lunches to the waving women and children on the beach. After a few more visits the women would take their grass skirts off and wave at the plane.

The sector soon became a very popular area to fly. One 106 crew decided they wanted to go to the Stewart Islands for R&R instead of Australia or New Zealand. When Cdr. Sears presented this option to the admiral the response was a deafening, "No! If they don't want to go to Auckland, put 'em to work and be damn sure they work!" Hayward's Hellions decided Sydney was a better option.

The establishment of R&R tours alleviated some of the stress from combat and boredom often associated with living on a remote island; however, the commanding officer of 106 had also experienced a slight problem among his non-pilot navigators often referred to as the "third pilot." Cdr. Hayward remarked during an interview with the Air Intelligence Group, "The third pilot didn't care about navigation; all he wanted to do was fly."[2] The commander of 106 had also been his non-pilot

VB-106 crew of *Unapproachable*. *Courtesy of the Naval History Center*

One of VB-106's PB4Y-1 bombers being stripped after it crash-landed. ***Courtesy of the Naval History Center***

navigators. By February, some of the men were making friendly reminders that their tour was about up and they were ready to head back to the United States for flight training. Hayward began referring to the navigators as his "agitators."[1]

The Agitators

Many of the non-navigators believed they would not be going home until the squadron's tour of duty ended, which was slated for June, but fortune shined upon the men. Cdr. Hayward invited one of his "agitators," Ens. Art Hacker, on an administrative flight to Espiritu Santos.

During a brief stop on Guadalcanal, Hacker got into a conversation with, as he put it, "An obvious new jungle arrival." It seemed the man, Ens. Richard P. Goldthwait, was looking for a PB4Y squadron named VB-106. He and several others had been sent to replace some navigators who were being ordered back to flight school. For the next two weeks Hayward's agitators became model officers. Either referred to by Cdr. Hayward as his "agitators" or by other men as the "Terrible Thirteen," Goldthwait was one of them.

Munda Operations

There were originally fourteen assigned to be shipped out, but the last (number 14) missed the boat and has become immortally named "Lucky." Soon after their arrival Ens. Roland P. Therrien was killed when he was loaned out to VB-104. Three others—Ens. Marvin R. Denzig, W. C. Mathews, and Fox—were killed in action when the squadron returned to the combat zone later in the war.[3]

The next step toward the Philippines was the occupation of the Admiralties as additional advance bases. American possession of this island group would also mean air superiority all the way to Truk. Before this major offensive began Adm. Halsey decided an additional airfield and naval base was needed to keep Rabaul and Truk further isolated. On 15 February, the 3rd New Zealand Division invaded the Green Islands. The twelve-man garrison on Nissan was quickly dispatched, and by early March an airfield became operational. The invasion of the Admiralties followed, with the two largest islands of the group, Manus and Los Negros, targeted for occupation. The Japanese had constructed an airfield at Momote, on Los Negros, and another at Seedler Harbor, on Manus. The invasion of Los Negros began on 29 February, with Manus following on 15 March. By the end of the following month

The crew of 106's *Mitzi-Bishi. Courtesy of the Naval History Center*

Aerial Reconnaissance photo of Japanese facilities at Truk, taken by Marine Corps PB4Y-1 Squadron VMB-254 on 4 February 1944. Dublon Island is at bottom left, and Fefan Island is in lower right. In center is the Eten Island airbase. Two aircraft carriers are visible at right, and several other warships and merchant vessels are present. ***Courtesy of the National Archives***

American forces had completed their occupation, thus placing two additional airfields in operation.[4]

Meanwhile, February 1944 marked the one-year anniversary of Navy Liberator operations in the Pacific. VP-51/VB-101 arrived in the Solomon Islands during a lull in offensive operations, with future amphibious assaults still months away. A year later, Sears' Buccaneers and Hayward's Hellions were taking part in a massive campaign to dislodge the Japanese from New Guinea, the Admiralties, and the Bismarcks. For the Navy Liberator squadrons February was a routine month, except for one thing: in early February advanced echelons of 104 and 106 moved to Munda, a move that extended patrol sectors a little less than 200 miles.

Munda airfield was carved out of the jungle after its capture. The runway was coral-paved, smooth, hard, and easily repairable; a vast improvement over Carney's Marston matting. The move also allowed Hayward's squadron to venture a little farther into Japanese-held territory.

For Hayward's Hellions the month was a heavy operational period, with bombing and photographic reconnaissance missions in conjunction with VD-1. On the third, Lt. Alan L. Seaman spotted a convoy of two transports and two destroyers north of Kavieng. Seaman and his crew were perhaps the most aggressive crew in the squadron. For him, the war started in the Philippines at the outbreak of the war. During that time he was shot down over Manila Bay and fought on the ground with the beleaguered American and Filipino forces on Bataan. After the fall he managed to escape, and now found himself a patrol plane commander of a Liberator. Now he was attacking a convoy of ships.

The ships had air cover, and before Seaman knew it four Zekes jumped him. The Liberator's gunners managed to shoot one down and damaged two others before escaping into the clouds. The Liberator's number four engine was shot out during the engagement and Seaman knew he could not make it back to base; he had to find the closest airfield. This turned out to be Cape Glouchester, New Britain, which he successfully reached and thus became the first four-engined bomber to land at the airfield. His battle with enemy aircraft was repeated several times during the month by both squadrons, including successful interceptions of Betty bombers on 9, 14, and 17 February by crews from 104.

Lt. Van Benschoten's Crew 11 was the first to score when they shot down one of the twin-engine bombers 500 miles off of Munda. The crew were on the return leg of an 800-mile patrol flying at 9,000 feet when the Betty was spotted below, above the water, at an estimated height of 500–1,000 feet. The Liberator's pilot turned on a parallel course while decreasing altitude for an interception. One of the Betty's crew must have spotted the approaching American plane as it jettisoned its bomb load and increased speed, although maintaining the same heading. Van Benschoten likewise dropped the PB4Y-1's bomb load and increased speed. The Liberator closed in for the kill after a six-minute chase, and at a distance of 2,000 feet the bow turret, belly turret, and port waist gunners opened fire. There was no return fire as the Betty made a shallow dive to port and crashed into the water. The Liberator's gunners continued firing at the partially submerged wreck until one of its wings exploded. Two unfortunate crewmen who survived the crash did not survive the hail of gunfire unleashed upon them by Van Benschoten's gunners.[5]

For Humphrey, a routine 800-mile patrol on the fourteenth turned out to be a running battle with two Bettys north of Munda. Flying at a leisurely pace at 8,000 feet, they were halfway through their outbound search when a Betty was spotted ahead of the Liberator cruising along at 500 feet. A safe altitude for a lone patrol plane to fly as a means of hiding from American fighters, Humphrey jettisoned his bombs to increase power and went down to intercept.

Munda airfield. ***Courtesy of the National Archives***

As the Liberator descended the Betty began to turn and lose altitude; Humphrey had been spotted and there would be no surprise today. The Betty descended to wave-top level—ten feet from the water—as Humphrey increased power and intercepted. When the PB4Y was 600 yards behind the aircraft four of the patrol bomber's gunner positions opened up.

Flashes from rounds tore into the Betty as the Japanese gunners responded weakly toward their attacker. The pursued aircraft slowed for Humphrey to catch up as his gunners poured more .50-caliber fire into it. The plane made a slight bank to port and the propeller grazed the water as the pilot fought to recover. Billy Lofton, in the belly turret, blasted the Betty's cockpit to shreds from point blank range, and in an instant the Betty exploded in mid-air, parts of it fluttering to the water before the rest of it plunged into the sea.

After the destruction of the enemy aircraft Humphrey resumed his normal patrol, and three hours later he encountered another Betty only forty miles away from the first engagement. This time Humphrey could barely keep up with the Liberator's nemesis, and in a long chase managed to severely damage the second one before his gunners ran out of ammunition. From the damage inflicted it was very doubtful the Betty made it back to base.[6]

Searls and his men were the next crew of 104 to hunt down a Betty three days later. After leaving Carney Field in the morning they went on a routine 800-mile search and saw nothing but empty water. They were more than halfway home, flying at 10,000 feet, when the vague outline of another aircraft was spotted flying at 1,000 feet. It was a Betty. The alert crew of the enemy plane spotted the Liberator as it approached within 5,000 feet and it began turning away from its pursuer.

Searls continued to close, and when his plane *Wata-Honey* was 600 yards away the bow, belly, and starboard waist guns began firing. The Betty responded with 20 mm fire from its tail gun. The Liberator had the speed and advantage as it closed within 100 yards—point blank range for the gunners. The Betty's pilot knew he was in deep trouble and banked sharply to port to get away from the concentrated fire coming from the four-engined bomber. R. J. Roller, in the belly turret, kept pouring rounds into the victim.

The Betty turned to starboard, only to get the machine gun fire from R. Franko's tail turret. It then banked sharply, nosed over, and plunged into the sea. This was Searls' crew's second destruction of a Betty and their last. For all but one of the crew fate would deal them a bad hand in a few short weeks.[7]

For the Buccaneers of VB-104 March 1944 marked the last month of combat operations, yet it would be a deadly time, as the squadron lost two planes and their crews. Meanwhile, 104 and 106 continued harassing the enemy with attacks on Choiseul Bay. Choiseul was a staging point for barge traffic ferrying troops and supplies to Kolombangara and Bougainville. Since September, the American Navy had tried to stem the tide of barge traffic, and with the help of Navy PB4Ys they managed to put a dent in the amount of traffic. On 4 March, both squadrons staged strikes on the Choiseul Bay area, with 102 sending two bombers and 106 sending six. The result was barge traffic continued to diminish.

Failed to Return

Three days later, Searls and his crew took off in *Wata-Honey* and failed to return after conducting a routine search of Kapingamarangi. His co-pilot was Harp Joslyn, who had wanted to show off his scar and Purple Heart from being wounded—he never got the chance. Also aboard was a navigator from VB-106 who had taken the place of the regular crewman.

Fortunately for Searls' regular tail gunner Robert Franko, he was on R&R in New Zealand and missed the flight. What became of them? Were they the victims of an enemy fighter or a ship's anti-aircraft fire, or did something mechanical occur which happened so fast that a distress call could not be made? As often occurred in the Pacific, when a plane failed to return it left very few clues. Two days later, Lt. Feind was flying a search for the missing bomber and found a main wheel and other debris floating in the ocean. That was all that remained of eleven men and their plane.[8]

While searching for Searls VB-104 lost another plane and crew when Lt. Anderson's Crew 7 in PB4Y-1 *The Schooner* were apparently shot down while attacking an enemy cargo ship at Kapingamarangi. Fragmentary evidence extracted from radio logs of other search planes revealed the missing plane had sent a message that he was going to attack a small ship near the island. Later in the afternoon two search planes from VB-106 attacked and sank a small ship unloading inside the lagoon at Kapingamarangi. Both planes received heavy fire from 20 mm cannons and small arms fire from the ship and on shore.[9]

Maybe Anderson had received the same reception, but with catastrophic results. As with Searls, Anderson and his crew vanished, leaving very little information as to what

Mail call for members of VB-104 and 106 on Munda. ***Courtesy of the National Archives***

exactly happened to them. It was a hard time for the men; the Buccaneers were only days away from going home and they had lost twenty-two men.

During spring 1944, the Liberator squadrons were given a new weapon to use against Japanese submarines: the Mark-24 "Fido." On 16 March, Lt. Seaman attacked a surfaced sub with two of them. One ran around in circles on the surface before sinking, while the other porpoised several times, circled for forty-five seconds, and then turned toward the area where the sub had submerged. There was no explosion indicating the weapon had sniffed out its quarry, and with nothing else to do Seaman left.

There is no evidence that any aircraft operating in the Pacific successfully deployed the Mark-24. One pilot upon releasing his Mark-24 and watching it running around in circles remarked, "Fido is chasing its tail." Navy anti-submarine squadrons operating in the Atlantic had better luck with the weapon when it was successfully deployed in the destruction of I-51. The following year, three squadrons were provided with an air-to-ground guided missile which would fare little better than the "Fido."

For VB-104 engagements with Betty bombers resumed, with Lt. Donald's crew intercepting one on 22 March 400 miles southeast of Truk and 100 miles east of Nukuoro Atoll. The Betty, apparently on a reconnaissance search for American naval forces, was sighted at 11 o'clock, 4,000 feet, and four miles ahead of the PB4Y-1. Donald started a diving turn toward the Betty, and when directly behind and a range of 1,000 yards the crew opened fire. Bill Knudsen in the bow, R. L. Hammond in the belly, and Roho Rolland on the starboard waist gun concentrated machine gun fire on the Betty's engines and pilot compartment.

The Japanese gunners in the waist section and top blister returned fire, but were quickly silenced by the Liberator's belly gunner. The enemy plane then dove for the water with its starboard engine smoking. Donald closed in for the kill as W. L. Sams fired his twin guns into the plane. The Liberator was less than 300 yards from the Betty and every gun on Donald's plane that could be brought to bare fired at the dying bomber.

The Betty crashed in the water and exploded in a giant ball of orange flame. Scattered across the water were the bomber's tail wheel, main tire, and part of a wing with the distinctive red meatball. The lives of the Japanese crew had been snuffed out in forty-five seconds, the total time of engagement from beginning to end.[10]

The following day, Lt. F. L. Feind's Crew 6 aboard PB4Y-1 *Saints and Sinners* (Bureau Number 32070) intercepted another Betty while on patrol some sixty miles off of Kapingamarangi while cruising at 3,000 feet. Plane captain and port waist gunner Charlie Vex reported an unidentified aircraft at 1,000 feet heading directly toward them.

As the Liberator closed in the Betty's tail cannon and top blister guns opened fire. At maximum effective range W. R. Forrester in the bow and E. W. Goldbaum in the belly turret began firing at the Betty, now flying barely off the water. The larger bomber dove at the Betty like a hawk going after a sparrow, using altitude advantage to close the range, and with the Liberator's gunners acting as talons rounds began ripping into the Betty's engines, fuselage, and wings. The Betty hit the water and exploded.[11]

Those final bursts of .50-caliber rounds put into the Betty turned out to be the last shots fired by VB-104 on this tour of duty. Routine searches continued without enemy contact through 26 March 1944, and crews flying in battle-weary planes began returning to the US via Canton and Kaneohe. The Buccaneers headed home after a tremendous tour of duty that earned them the first of two Presidential Unit Citations. They had lost forty-two men killed in action during the tour. Many of the men who survived would offer their services again, and some their lives, as members of VPB-104 under the command of Whitney Wright, the man credited with being the first Navy Liberator pilot to attack at masthead height.

Little Green Apples*, a PB4Y-1P of VD-1, departs Guadalcanal for a photographic reconnaissance mission circa January 1944. *Courtesy of Robert Livingstone and Pete Johnston

The crew of *Little Green Apples* with the unit emblem painted above the name. The canvas cover between the two men in the back row is hiding radar antennae. *Courtesy of Robert Livingstone and Pete Johnston*

8

James Compton's Bulldog Squadron
March–April 1944

The last days of March saw the departure of Sears and VB-104 back to the United States for reformation. Five days before the Buccaneers' tour ended on 25 March, Cdr. J. R. Compton arrived on Munda from Kaneohe with the first three Liberators of VB-115 and reported for duty with Fleet Air Wing One under the Army's Fifth Air Force. This was the Bulldog Squadron, and they did not have to wait long before they underwent their first baptism of fire; in the process they found that the Japanese still had a lot of fight left in them.

The arrival of the new squadron coincided with orders to move VB-106 to Nadzab Airfield, New Guinea. Their new accommodations were a stark contrast to those they had grown accustomed to at Munda and Carney. Mud, humidity, and poor food were soon factors in causing one hundred cases of dysentery among squadron personnel. More frightening to some were the 15,000 foot mountains on both sides of the landing strip which were often enveloped in thick clouds. The crews prayed like hell that they would not hit one while taking off.

Three days after their arrival 115's Lt. (jg) Hamilton M. Dawes Jr. was on a routine search near Satawan. Looking down at the island from 5,000 feet and a mile off, Hamilton saw some ten to twelve aircraft parked in and near revetments; even more disturbing, three fighters at the end of the runway were scrambling to intercept the snooping Liberator. Dawes turned his bomber south and headed for cloud cover. The Liberator patrol plane commander did not like the twelve to one odds and sought a hiding place.

Before he could find a safe haven an Oscar, Tojo, and Zeke overtook the patrol bomber in four miles and began a series of runs that continued for twenty-five minutes. All attacks came from 2,000 feet above, with the fighters diving and coming in individually in rapid succession. Dawes' top turret gunner tracked and fired at each one as they dived down. The pilot of the Oscar took excellent advantage, using the blind areas around the bomber's vertical stabilizers with such effect that the waist gunners could not fire effectively.

All attacks came from the rear; consequently, the fighters were able to avoid the field of fire of the bow and belly turrets, which could only fire when the PB4Y-1 made radical turns. One burst from a fighter shattered the tail turret's glass, causing one of the guns to stop functioning.

The Tojo came in for a run but was hit repeatedly by top turret gunner, Louis A. Chiles, when it closed within 200 feet. Chiles kept firing though he had suffered a slight flesh wound in the arm. Pieces of the engine cowling flew off and it burst into smoke. The plane went into a dive, but was seen to level off near the surface. Seeing their comrade's plane smoking the others broke off the attack.

Dawes knew his plane had been badly damaged and was low on gas; he decided to head for a newly established airfield on Green Island for refueling. Dawes made it to Green and refueled. After fifty minutes the Liberator was airborne and headed for Munda. After leaving the ground he found out the

Squadron Patch for VB-115, the "Bulldog" squadron. ***Courtesy of Albert Mark***

VB-115's *So Sorry* (possibly bureau number 32169) with the words "LINDY'S PLACE" painted below the pilot's window and "THE RED NETWORK" written below the radio operator's window. *Courtesy of Larry Slavin*

landing gear could not be retracted and the plane flew 600 miles with its landing gear in a partially down position.

Reaching Munda, Dawes and crew landed safely, gassed up, and took off again, flying another 300 miles to base to deliver the photographs taken of Satawan. An exhausted crew climbed out of the Liberator, inspected the aircraft, and found it perforated with holes caused by the fighters' machine guns and cannon. Such was the tenacity of Navy Liberator crews and their willingness to go beyond the call of duty and complete the mission, even with a damaged plane and wounded men.

While 106 and 115 plugged away at bypassed islands and interrupting enemy supply lines, Rex Hardy, a pilot for VD-1 squadron, recalled a mission at the end of March. Two photographic Liberators staged from Nadzab, New Guinea, were sent out to photograph Palau with Army B-24s flying protective cover. The Liberators were the only planes capable of reaching the target. Knowing the flight would be at extreme range, the planes had to refuel on the newly acquired airstrip at Momote, in the Admiralties.

The mission took place at night, and photoflash bombs were used to illuminate the island. They succeeded without any problems and the bomber returned after a twenty-hour flight. The Army and Navy got the photographs for planning future bombing missions and the invasion of Palau and Hardy was awarded the Distinguished Flying Cross.[1]

The Bulldogs on Green Island

By April, the Solomons, Admiralties, and the Bismarcks were firmly under allied control, with the exception of Rabaul and its 100,000 defenders; the Japanese fortress was left to wither on the vine. Focus for the seventh fleet shifted to New Guinea, with the Hollandia Operation on the twenty-first. During this time VB-115 shifted base to Green Island. Based with them was a detachment of the Army's 17th Weather Squadron, who would often fly missions with the Bulldogs to conduct weather observations. On 11 April, Staff Sgt. Thomas F. Rhodes became the first member of the weather squadron to fly such missions. Although they flew with the PB4Y-1 squadron they received no flight pay.[2]

While on Green, 115 proceeded to deliver strikes in the Caroline Islands with almost daily missions to Puluwat, destroying small shipping, barracks, buildings, and supplies, and killing personnel from minimum altitude. For the next several months Puluwat became a favorite target of Army and Navy Liberators, receiving continuous attacks from squadrons based in the Central Pacific. The largest and most heavily fortified island in the atoll was Alet. Lt. S. B. Pitt hit Puluwat for the first time, finding a new runway under construction, destroying barges, and killing enemy personnel with a strafing attack at minimum altitude.

For VB-106, staging out of Nadzab, the squadron made a large number of enemy contacts, with eighty-two Japanese aircraft and 114 ships sighted. Additionally, six Liberators hit Wakde on 5 April. This was one of the few multi-plane missions flown by the squadron.

Mistaken Identity

War is possibly man's most confusing vocation. Unexpected events happen with regularity, and near tragedies happen with as much frequency. Commanders on down to the lowest rank must know what is going on at all times in a combat situation; without that knowledge anything and everything can happen.

In the Pacific, surface units engaging in land bombardments needed to know the location of allied ground troops or risked raining shells on their own men. The same was true of aircraft supporting land offensives. Therefore, logic would dictate that search planes know the position of allied naval surface units and submarines or risk sinking their own ships. However, it seems this area of communication failed, and almost resulted in the loss of an American submarine by a Liberator from VB-106.

Green Island. *Courtesy of the National Archives*

Operations building of VB-115 taken in September 1944. ***Courtesy of Albert Mark***

On 11 April, Lt. E. T. Morrison sighted a fully surfaced sub eight miles away from his position at 7,000 feet. He dove in for the attack and found the bomb bay would not open; instead, his gunners fired 500 rounds at the submarine.

As Morrison swung around for another run the crew managed to open the bomb bay and dropped three 500-pound bombs just as the sub submerged. The bombs went wide and missed the boat by over 100 feet. It was a good thing he came around for another bombing run, since dropping 500-pound bombs on a surfaced submarine probably would have blown it right out of the water, killing everyone aboard the American submarine USS *Cero*. Navy command did not like one of its own submarines being on the receiving end of a PB4Y-1 Liberator attack and told Cdr. Hayward as much.

Cdr. Hayward wrote a scathing rebuttal to the actions of his men when his squadron was reprimanded for the attack. In it he writes, "Besides the USS *Cero* there had been six similar incidents in the area in less than a year."

He pointed out that Morrison was not at fault because the submarine was 340 miles away from the closest friendly sub position furnished to his command at the time, and that it did not attempt to identify itself as friendly. He pointed out that antisubmarine warfare (ASW) required immediate attack by an airplane to insure success, and all pilots in the command had been well indoctrinated along those lines.

"This command was censured for taking too long to attack a sub off Nauru and for taking too long to identify the sub as enemy. This was caused by general information furnished to the command that the USS *Paddle* [the submarine in question] was northwest of Nauru for rescue purposes. Such vague information confuses air units. It is evident from the above incident that this command has been wrong no matter what course has been taken, and we are rapidly approaching a situation where all PPCs do nothing but hope they won't see any submarines. The present situation is not conducive to efficient ASW operations."

Hayward ended his memo by recommending that IFF (identify friend or foe gear) be installed on all allied submarines and be used on the surface day and night when operating in areas where friendly aircraft were operating, and that commands such as his be furnished with detailed locations of allied submarines. Higher command listened to Hayward and the number of aerial attacks by Allied aircraft on American submarines declined.[3]

There was some good news for Hayward. On 12 April, orders were issued sending them to Momote Airfield, Los

Richard Jeffreys (bottom left) and the rest of his crew after their arrival at North Island Naval Air Station on 16 February 1944. The crew served with VD-1. Note Emerson nose turret. ***Courtesy of Richard Jeffreys Jr.***

Negros Island. The short-lived stay in the deplorable conditions at Nadzab was over, and the move placed the squadron at the most advanced base in the Southwest Pacific. From here they would become highly successful in destroying Japanese shipping and aircraft.

For Compton's Bulldogs, the remainder of April was a time of continued assaults on Puluwat. The island's defenses were hard to neutralize, as Lt. H. E. Robinson of VB-115 found out when he attacked a radio station on Alet. He pickled off a 500-pound bomb from 150 feet as three machine guns fired back from the radio tower. The bombs detonated thirty feet from the station, causing it to rock back and forth. The Liberator took hits inside the open bomb bay that shattered the hydraulic lines. Damage to his plane did not stop Robinson from making additional runs on the radio station. As he left the three machine gun positions that had damaged the PB4Y had been reduced to one.

The Bulldogs continued with strikes against Puluwat, with Lt. A. P. Anderson hitting shipping in the lagoon from an altitude of only thirty feet on 22 April. Anderson came in so low that ocean spray hit the belly turret as the Liberator approached the atoll. Intense 40 mm defensive fire was received from the ships, but Anderson's gunners managed to set fire to a couple small coastal vessels without any damage to the plane. The same could not be said of Lt. W. R. Doerr and his crew (Bureau number 3222), who set out for the same target on the same day and never returned. On board was Staff Sgt. Russell Hill, an aerologist from the 17th Weather Squadron.

Crew 11 of VB-115 was shot down and killed while attacking Puluwat on 22 April 1944. Back Row (L-R): AMM3 John Wise Megginson, 2nd mechanic; CAP (Chief Aviation Pilot) Bernard Leroy Johnson, co-pilot; Lt. William Richard Doerr, pilot; Ens. Harold Elsworth Barrett, navigator; and AMM2 John James Marrapodi, plane captain and starboard waist gunner. Front Row (L-R): AOM2 Reno Anthony Chiste, 1st ordnanceman and belly turret gunner; ARM2 Robert Frank Holman, 1st radioman and top turret gunner; S1c Steve Campbell Burkhart Jr., port waist gunner; AOMB3 Thomas Franklin Reed, 2nd ordnanceman, bombsight mechanic, and tail turret gunner; and ARM3 Rocco Charles Capobianco, 2nd radioman and bow turret gunner. ***Crew 11 photo from William R. Doerr estate, courtesy of Charles J. Doerr III. Crew identification courtesy of Martha Collins and Alan J. Moore***

Doerr's crew was shot down over Puluwat and their remains were initially buried on the island. The remains were transferred to Hawaii after the war for identification and were eventually returned to the US for burial.

The following day Cdr. Compton decided to go with Lt. P. J. Bruneau and his crew to search for Doerr. On the way a Betty was spotted and Bruneau jettisoned bombs, applied full throttle, and climbed to intercept the bomber, which was 4,000 feet higher than the Liberator. Staying slightly under and behind the quarry, Compton ordered the gunners to hold their fire until they were at minimum range and to concentrate on the Betty's starboard engine, cockpit, and the tail turret. From some 400 yards the Liberator's top, bow, and belly turrets opened fire. The Betty's 20 mm tail gun responded with three bursts. The Japanese pilot weaved and dove, trying to keep away from Bruneau's gunners. Bruneau closed in, and at one point the two planes were separated by only fifty yards.

The PB4Y's gunners found their range and began riddling the Betty. The starboard engine burst into flames and fell off completely, with other pieces of the wing, fuselage, and tail flying off and dropping to the water. The Betty went into a steep glide, leveled off momentarily, then fell off in a steep, tight, diving spiral, exploding as it struck the water. The pursuit and attack lasted twenty-eight minutes over a distance of sixty miles before finally coming to an end only eighty-eight miles from Truk.

Killed along with Crew 11 was Sgt. Russell Hill, an aerologist with the Army Air Force 17th Weather Squadron who was aboard Doerr's aircraft to observe weather patterns. ***From Russell E. Hill estate, courtesy of Hill Family***

9

Farther into Enemy Territory May–June 1944

A Mitsubishi G4M "Betty" under attack by Lt. Porter's PB4Y-1 *Porter's Posse* of VB-106 off Biak Island, New Guinea, circa April–May 1944. *Emil Buehler Library, NMNA*

During May, Hayward had his squadron split between Momote, Mokorang, and Wakde, with strikes reaching the coast of New Guinea and beyond. Venturing deeper into enemy-held territory brought about increased contact with the Japanese. In doing so, VB-106 lost one of its greatest pilots.

The month started with the loss of Lt. Seaman and most of his crew. The young officer was now a father-to-be, and in tribute to his unborn child—hoping it would be a boy—named his Liberator *Mark*, after a son he would never see.

A PB4Y-1 of VB-115 chasing down a Japanese transport. *Courtesy of Albert Mark*

Kawanishi M8K2 "Emily" Flying Boat under attack by VB-115's Lieutenant Stoughton Atwood. *Courtesy of the National Archives*

Thin trail of smoke flows out of the Emily. ***Courtesy of Albert Mark***

His last mission was a strike against shipping off New Guinea. As with many servicemen who fight in a relentless conflict, they become detached to the human aspect of war. Seaman had become one of them. He had grown to hate the Japanese, and once remarked he would never be taken alive and always carried hand grenades with him.

After sinking a ship off Schouten and another off Biak, the Liberator was intercepted by four Tojos. The fighters came in dropping aerial bombs. One pass destroyed the bow turret with the gunner inside and knocked out the number four engine. Another hit the left wing's gas tank and it began to burn. The fighters then came in and knocked out the other three engines. As the flaming bomber made a gradual descent toward the water Seaman sent out a final message to base.

"I am going to alight upon the sea."

Miraculously he managed to ditch the aircraft; however, the top turret came down, preventing Seaman and his co-pilot, Lt. (jg) Alvin H. Saviko, from escaping, and they drowned. Three others who managed to exit the plane put on life jackets, but apparently sustained serious injuries and could not keep their heads out of the water and drowned. A fourth died from injuries a few days later after being rescued by a PBY Catalina of VP-33. On the announcement of Seaman's death, Cdr. Hayward commented that the lost patrol plane commander was the greatest aviator of the Pacific War. A twist of fate caused one of the regular crewmen, Jesse Samuals, to miss the flight due to a case of malaria. It broke the heart of the nineteen-year-old, because the men he considered family were now dead.

Targeting Japanese Reconnaissance Aircraft

May 1944 saw increasing efforts to neutralize remaining Japanese operational aircraft and shipping trying to flee to the safe havens Satawan and Truk. Compton's squadron was becoming more aggressive in these missions, with Lt. L. A. Johnson leading the Bulldog squadron with a strike on enemy shipping trying to get to Truk on the fifth.

It had been a long patrol for Lt. Johnson and his crew, with nothing to see but an occasional island. Nearing the end of his search sector, he climbed to 10,000 feet in hopes of spotting some of the enemy shipping reported to be fleeing to Truk. The sharp eyes of bow gunner G. R. Dewitt spotted a ship's wake ahead and reported it to the pilot. Ahead of the wake were five small ships steaming at ten to fifteen knots, riding low in the water with their decks full of crates and fuel barrels. They were in a tight defensive formation, with three in the front and two in the rear.

The Liberator pilot decided to fly a circle around the convoy to make sure there were no enemy fighters flying cover. As Johnson approached every ship in the convoy opened up with everything they had, from 7.7 mm machine guns to 40 mm cannons. The gunners were excellent and the Liberator began taking hits. A hydraulic line to the belly turret was hit and fluid began streaming across the Plexiglas; soon the gunner could no longer see to fire and the turret went out of commission.

Johnson continued with his run while his remaining guns raked gun positions aboard the ships, causing enough casualties among the ships' compliment that defensive fire began to slacken. A 500-pound bomb dropped by air bomber Goss exploded directly underneath one of the ships, lifting it up out of the water before falling back into the ocean and sinking.

Johnson's gunners continued to strafe, causing one of the smaller ships to catch fire. In the process, the top turret gunner had a finger cut off while he tried to clear his guns, but even through intense pain and bleeding he continued to fire his weapon. After ten runs two ships were sinking and the other was damaged.

Strange things can often occur in war, and what happened on a flight flown by Bulldog pilot Lt. L. M. Monroe and crew on the eighteenth was no exception. During a patrol the pilot spotted nine float planes at a small atoll named Lamotrok. At the end of a bombing and strafing attack which set six of the planes afire the port waist gunner lost his balance when Monroe banked the plane. The gunner fired his .50-caliber machine gun right into the number one engine. The damage was severe

The end of the chase results in the destruction of the Emily. ***Courtesy of Albert Mark***

Gunners of a VB-115 Liberator cause this Betty's engines to flame. ***Courtesy of Albert Mark***

enough that the Liberator had to land at an alternate airfield. The man was not awarded a medal for almost shooting down his own PB4Y-1 Liberator, and there is no evidence to suggest the Japanese would have done so, either.

For weeks 106 and 115 were surprised at the lack of aggression from Japanese pilots they had encountered. Many times patrol bombers were shadowed but never attacked by the agile fighters. Lt. Paul J. Bruneau of VB-115 found one Japanese pilot who still had some fight left in him when he encountered several enemy fighters while attacking a convoy of shipping on the nineteenth.

During the pre-flight briefing Bruneau and crew were told of enemy shipping approaching Satawan from Truk. Intelligence proved correct; as the PB4Y-1 approached Satawan from 6,000 feet they saw four cargo ships in the lagoon below. Coming in from the north, the ships began sending up 40 mm and machine gun fire as Bruneau closed in.

Crossing over one of the ships, he pickled off one 500-pound bomb that exploded thirty feet away. Bruneau banked the plane for another attack, only to see three Zekes and a Hamp approaching from the west at 3,000 feet. The Zekes peeled off and began runs while the Hamp stayed above, occasionally dropping phosphorus bombs. As the fighters approached Bruneau dived the Liberator down to fifty feet, throwing off the enemy's timing. One of the fighters came in and was immediately hit by the combined firepower of the bow and top turrets. The Zeke pulled away, smoking, then rolled on its back, with the pilot making a successful bailout before his plane crashed into the water.

Seeing one of their own go down in flames, the other three planes abandoned their pursuit and headed back to Satawan. Bruneau was not finished. He wanted the shipping, and decided to go back after making sure he was no longer being pursued.

An hour later he came back and saw the ships anchored in Satawan Lagoon. The enemy was still alert and began sending up anti-aircraft fire as Bruneau came in for a bombing run. As his gunners laid down suppressing fire the pilot pickled another 500-pound bomb that rocked one of the ships.

The enemy gunners now had the Liberator's range, as shore guns began hitting the bomber. The waist gunner was hit in the torso by a 40 mm round, but the flak suit he was wearing saved him from serious wounds.

Bruneau kept coming down and pickled off four depth bombs that straddled another ship. Another 40 mm round hit below the bow turret, sending shrapnel into the gunner's compartment. A flak suit he was sitting on saved his life. Seeing his plane was getting some punishment and with all bombs away Bruneau left Satawan, leaving two cargo ships severely damaged.

On the eighteenth, the island of Wakde, just a few miles off the coast of New Guinea, was invaded. Wakde would be a key airfield in the Southwest Pacific offensive toward the Philippines, and between May and July, an advanced echelon from VB-115 operated from there. The airstrip was built of hard, compact coral that made it operationally superior to the marston matting field at Carney. Climbing out of their aircraft, the men of 115 saw the remains of the recent battle—blasted palm trees and destroyed Japanese aircraft.[1]

Back on Green Island, the squadron lost another Liberator and her crew. As VB-104 was well aware, taking off with a fully loaded Liberator was quite dangerous. On 20 May, VB-115 found that out when Lt. Stephen B. Pitt and his entire crew were lost when their PB4Y-1 (number 32159) crashed at sea only four minutes after taking off from Green Island.

Towering black smoke rises from where the Betty went down. ***Courtesy of Albert Mark***

Nose art on a VD-1 Liberator. *Courtesy of the National Archives*

During the last week of May, most of VB-115 shifted base to Mokerang Airdrome, Los Negros Island, and joined 106 for duty with Commander Aircraft, Seventh Fleet. The search areas included one 1,000-mile and four 800-mile sectors. The following day an advanced echelon proceeded to Wakde Island for searches of the northern coast of New Guinea and the Philippine Islands. This detachment was based and operated with the 310th Bomb Wing, 5th Air Force.

Photograph Squadron One Reconnaissance to Guam

VD-1 continued their job, and was ordered on the twenty-seventh for a special mission to Guam. Again, as during the mission to Palau in March, Guam far exceeded the range from Guadalcanal, so the planes would have to stage from Eniwetok, in the Marshall Islands. The mission was to provide the latest intelligence of the island's fortifications for the impending invasion scheduled for late July. Japanese opposition was expected to be heavy, therefore, the usual tactic of one plane flying back and forth over the island to get full photographic coverage—a tactic that could cost the lives of the plane and crew—was abandoned in favor of using eight planes. VD-1 Liberators would be spread a mile apart, with each plane having an assigned sector to fly over once. The formation would be divided into four sections of three aircraft, with Army B-24s flying cover and engaging in a token bombing strike.

Arrival of a replacement crew for VD-1 taken in April 1944. *Courtesy of the National Archives*

The bombers took off at daybreak and formed up, climbing to 25,000 feet. As the formation closed in on Guam, the Army bombers closed up with the lead section of VD-1. Crossing the shoreline heavy anti-aircraft fire began, and Japanese fighters were scrambling to meet the bombers. Bombs were released, mapping began, and as the formation turned south Japanese fighters started closing.

The Japanese pilots were aggressive and tore into the formation, firing cannon and machine guns and dropping phosphorus bombs. Just about all the planes of VD-1 were hit, but not seriously. Not so for one of the Army B-24s, which took a hit from a phosphorus bomb and went down.[2]

Japanese Betty reconnaissance aircraft continued to be intercepted by patrolling PB4Y-1s. On 28 May, Lt. Memner of VB-115 overtook and shot down one of the twin-engine bombers thirty miles north of Manokwari. In an engagement which took hunter and hunted down to the water, the Liberator's bow and top gunners poured rounds into the Betty's cockpit, wing root, and fuselage before the quarry flamed and fell.

The Hellion's Head Back

On 27 May, VB-106 suffered one more lost before returning to the US when Lt. Morrison's plane lost power and crashed on take-off at Mokorang. The pilot, previously reprimanded for the attack on the USS *Cero*, was killed, along with the navigator and radioman; the rest escaped from the burning bomber, with some receiving extensive injuries, such as Charles Furey, the last man pulled from the burning wreckage, who suffered fractures and third degree burns. He would remain hospitalized for seventeen months.[3]

Late in May, pressure against Japanese bases in Western New Guinea began immediately after Hollandia fields became operational, with Biak receiving daily raids and numerous sorties sent out to harass the Japanese in the Wewak area. The new American bases were now a threat to Japan's inner defense zone, and that brought numerous enemy bases in range of land-based bombers.

The next major allied landing occurred at Biak on the twenty-seventh. Biak is in the Schouten Islands off the New Guinea coast. Capture of the island placed allied air power within 800 miles of the Philippines. The taking of Biak was followed a few days later by landings at Owi Island. By the middle of June, Owi's airfield was ready for Army and Navy Liberators.

After eight months in combat, it was time for Hayward's Hellions of VB-106 to be relieved. Taking their place during the first week of June was VB-101 at Los Negros, now under the command of Justin Miller. The first Navy Liberator squadron was back for a second tour of duty. VB-106 would be back the following year flying the PB4Y-2 Privateer and with the new nickname "The Wolverators." Some of the men would be transferred to other squadrons; for some the transfer to VPB-119 would result in their deaths. For Hayward, he would go on to work on the Manhattan Project, building the first atomic bombs, and rise to vice admiral before retiring.

Miller's squadron was another that experienced loss of men before their arrival in the Pacific. While training at Camp Kearney on 8 January, a Liberator flown by Lt. Philip Nelson crashed and burned after an engine failure, killing everybody on board.

The Japanese air forces still had some punch left in them, as they staged a bombing strike on Wakde on the night of 5 June. The result was that three Bulldog Liberators were destroyed and another two were damaged.

10

Mopping-Up in the Southwest Pacific June–September 1944

Much of American military activity had shifted to another area of the Pacific. Saipan, in the Mariana Islands, was invaded as a stepping stone to launch B-29 bombing strikes on the Japanese mainland. Playing a role in the invasion were Navy squadrons VB-108 and 109. The Japanese Navy, which had been relatively quiet for the past couple months, was about to launch a major counterattack in the Marianas.

The war was rapidly shifting to the Central Pacific, leaving the squadrons with harassing raids and reconnaissance missions. Such patrols, although long and tedious, provided an invaluable service to American surface forces operating in the region.

On 19 June, a Liberator from VB-101 searching the Philippine Sea sighted Japanese Adm. Ozawa's convoy, consisting of the carriers *Shokaku* and *Zuikaku*, two heavy cruisers, and five destroyers. Of all the aircraft sent from Los Negros and Manus, this Liberator was the only land-based search plane to spot the convoy. The battle of the Philippine Sea—the Marianas Turkey Shoot—was about to begin. During the two-day battle (19–20 June), the Japanese lost over 600 aircraft and three aircraft carriers.[1]

July began with the temporary transfer of VD-1 to Wakde. The squadron lived in tents and ate from mess kits while not flying photo flights to Palau and Morotai. Three weeks later they were back on Guadalcanal. Not long afterward, orders were issued sending the first Navy Liberator photographic squadron back to the United States. The squadron had been lucky as Navy Liberator squadrons went: they lost two planes, with one a crash landing and the other a ditching. The ditching occurred when pilot Lt. George Fairbanks was forced to make a water landing off the Japanese-held island of Yap, resulting in the death of his navigator, Ens. Douglas Brown. Fairbanks would later become a patrol plane commander with VPB-109, flying the PB4Y-2 Privateer from Okinawa.

The squadron had one more important mission to conduct before they could go home.

On the fifth, 115's Ens. P. R. Barker was at the end of a 640-mile search from Wakde at 8,000 feet when a small cargo ship and her escort appeared a mile off Cape Lelai, Halmahera Island. It had already been a busy day, with his crew bombing gun positions and buildings at Merir Island. The escort started throwing up intense 20 mm anti-aircraft fire, but Barker continued on his run. While his gunner strafed the ships Barker glided down to 500 feet and dropped three 100-pound bombs. A fire had already started on the bridge from the bow gunner's twin fifties as one of the bombs hit the ship.

The Liberator crew saw and felt a large explosion from the direct hit and the ship began to burn fiercely. A second run was then made; three more 100-pound bombs were dropped

VB-101 delivers an attack in September 1944. ***Courtesy of the National Archives***

but fell short, with two being duds. For forty minutes the Liberator's crew watched as the fire increased and the crew began abandoning ship by getting into lifeboats or jumping overboard. Another supply boat for the Japanese would never deliver its goods.

By July, the New Guinea Campaign was ending. Late in the month and on into August, Gen. MacArthur staged two major landings at Noemfoor Island and Sansapor. Both were desired as future sites for airfields on the drive to the Philippines. For VB-101 and 115, the capture of Biak, Owi, and Wakde allowed their Liberators to venture farther into the Celebes Sea, hence the Philippines. The last two weeks of July saw VB-115 making attacks on small shipping in the Celebes Sea, with searches extended toward the Mindanao area and many of the Bulldog's PB4Ys receiving considerable light machine gun fire on several occasions. During one such encounter Lt. R. L. White's Liberator had forty-eight holes punched into it, and during another flight involving a different crew on the twenty-third a bow gunner was wounded.[2]

On the twenty-second, Lt. Wiljo Lingren of VB-115 encountered a Betty off the eastern Philippines. While cruising along at 8,000 feet, the crew saw the enemy aircraft coming out of a cloud top at the same altitude a mile and a half ahead of them. Lingren applied full throttle and managed to get within 100 yards, with the Betty directly ahead and slightly below. The combined firepower from Lingren's belly, bow, and top turrets found the cockpit and starboard engine. The Betty's top gunner managed to fire off a few rounds but did not hit the Liberator.

The first rounds apparently killed the pilot and set the starboard engine smoking. The Japanese plane fell off into a deep spiral and crashed into the ocean. The destruction of the Betty marked the thirteenth multi-engined plane shot down in a seven-week period.

PB4Y Operations Reach the Philippines

August 1944 found Navy Liberators venturing into Philippine waters and increased sightings of enemy merchant shipping. On 4 August, Bulldog pilot Ens. P. R. Baker sighted a convoy consisting of a 5,000-ton freighter, two cargo ships weighing less than 500 tons, and three escorting gunboats. The pilot sent in a contact report to the 308th Bomb Wing, who was in operational command, but the Army never sent out a striking force. It was up to Baker to hit the enemy.

From 400 feet he salvoed his entire bomb load on the largest ship. All of them missed to the rear of the vessel. It was now up to the Liberator's gunners to inflict some damage. The gunboats started sending intense anti-aircraft fire from 40 mm guns, with one burst hitting the horizontal stabilizer and another the number four engine cowling. Baker's gunners managed to get the smaller cargo vessels burning before lack of fuel forced him to abandon his attack and head home.

For VB-101, venturing into Philippine waters and attacking an abundance of enemy shipping resulted in their first combat casualty. Lt. Forbes attacked an eighty-foot coastal vessel off Mindanao. During two successful bombing and strafing runs that left the ship burning a 7.7 mm round entered the Liberator through the bombardier's window and hit William T. Van Meter (AOM1C) in the throat, killing him.

On the twenty-third, Lt. Lindgren had a close call with enemy fighters while on a search through the Palau Islands. Two Oscars intercepted the Liberator, and in the ensuing aerial duel the bomber took a 20 mm hit to the number one engine. All instrument wiring was severed and the oil cooler was blown off. A fire broke out on the wing and burned for two minutes before going out. Finding cloud cover, Lindgren threw off his attackers and started for home. The engine could not be feathered during the trip back and all gear, including bombs, ammunition, and waist guns, were thrown out of the aircraft. They made it back to Owi with eighty gallons of fuel left. A week later the same Liberator crew had a similar experience while searching the Celebes. During the flight three Oscars made an unsuccessful attack with phosphorous bombs. After ten minutes of this the fighters left the Liberator alone.

During the last week of the month Bulldog Liberators struck enemy shipping in the Celebes and Mindanao, sinking and damaging an estimated eighteen enemy ships. Lt.Cdr. Harwill E. Robinson earned the honor of coastal killer when he found twelve of the small vessels off the eastern coast of Mindanao on the twenty-ninth. In several bombing and strafing runs the Liberator crew damaged five of the vessels.

On 25 August, VD-1 ended their tour of duty with a climatic mission to Palau. Their photographic mission was coordinated with a bombing strike by the 307th and 5th Bomb Groups of XIII Bomber Command. Under the leadership of

Destruction of small vessels by VB-101. ***Courtesy of the National Archives***

Cdr. Richard O. Greene, six VD-1 Liberators joined up and reached Babelthuap, Palau, just after 11:00 a.m. East of the island the formation was intercepted by a group of six Zeke fighters, and soon the number grew to fifteen. For the next hour the Liberators slugged away at the attackers, with the bombers scoring hits on three enemy aircraft. However, the Liberators received serious damage in return.

During thirteen separate runs on the bombers the fighters inflicted serious damage on five Liberators, wounding several men. On one plane a photographer had his right elbow shattered by a 7.7 mm round, another received a wound to the groin, and the tail gunner suffered a head wound when his turret was shattered. All VD-1 aircraft managed to make it back to base; not so fortunate were three Army Liberators that were lost. A week later VD-1 received orders sending them back to the United States.

Do Not Attack

Frequent contact with the enemy was replaced by a ban against attacks throughout the following month. During September, as preparations were being made to invade the Philippines, the Navy Liberator squadrons were ordered by Commander Aircraft 7th fleet not to attack enemy shipping, installations, or aircraft unless they were a direct threat to United States forces. VB-101 and 115 engaged in few attacks on enemy forces; instead, they continued to cover their assigned search sectors from Owi.

Before the restriction was imposed crews from 115 managed to damage a few coastal vessels in and near the Celebes. On the first, Lt. (jg) Harold Boche bombed an oil-laden barge to pieces; the following day the Japanese showed Lt. (jg) Warren Johnson and his crew that they still had serviceable aircraft left when he was intercepted forty miles west of Palau. Eight fighters closed in on the Liberator, but Johnson was able to escape by hiding in heavy clouds. The last score for the Bulldogs in September came on the seventh, when Ens. John Gregory attacked a small sub chaser off Yap. The seventy-five-foot long boat managed to hit the Liberator in the number three engine once with a 12.7 mm round as Gregory came in to bomb and strafe. After three runs the Liberator left the vessel sinking with a dozen of her crew swimming in the oily water.

On the horizon was the Philippines, and Navy Liberator, and later Privateer squadrons would take part in Gen. MacArthur's return. Operations continued in the Southwest Pacific throughout the remainder of the war, with naval squadrons taking part in every major allied offensive. The assault on the Philippines would also coincide with the designation of Navy bomber squadrons being changed to Navy patrol and bombing.

In less than a year, VB-104 and 106 had perfected the art of masthead height attacks patterned after B-25 squadrons of the 5th Air Force. In the coming months squadrons such as VB-108 and 109 would take it a step further by conducting prolonged minimum altitude approaches to the target.

During the approach, the four-engined Liberators would fly at twenty to fifty feet off the water to escape enemy radar detection, pulling up to 200 feet over the target. Bombing was done with precision at 200 feet and at 200 miles per hour by the pilot pressing his bomb release mechanism, called a "pickle." Only on high altitude attacks, which were a rarity, did the bombardier—an enlisted crewmember—initiate bomb runs. Instead, the pilot dropped by "seaman's eye." While the pilot made the bomb run all ten machine gun positions trained on targets of opportunity.

Part II: Operations in the Central Pacific

While the allies slogged their way through the tropical islands of the South Pacific towards the ultimate goal of returning to the Philippines, Naval planners turned their eyes towards the island chains of the Central Pacific. The generally flat terrain and abundance of coral on the islands were well suited for the construction of airstrips, and the lagoons afforded natural harbors for shipping. The region had two strategic values for naval planners. First, establishing bases in the area would provide a stepping stone for future advances in the Philippines or Formosa. Second, the islands would later serve as bases for American naval and air power for strikes against mainland Japan.

In the autumn of 1943, Air Force Central Pacific was established under the command of Admiral John Hoover, which at first consisted only of the Ellice, Fiji, and Samoan Islands. It was set up as a mobile unit that could move westward through the Central Pacific area as American forces gained control of Japanese strongholds in that region. Ultimately it would include the Gilberts, Marshalls, Marianas, Palau Islands, and Iwo Jima.

The function of Commander Air Force Central Pacific was generally twofold. Hoover maintained all the land based aircraft in the Central Pacific, and controlled all the occupying forces which garrisoned the islands in that area. On 1 May 1944, the command title was changed to Forward Area, and on 1 June 1945 it was changed to Marianas Area. The task force number, originally 57, became 94 on November 20, 1944.

11

Hayward, Stroh, and Renfro October–November 1943

March 1943 in San Diego, California, found enlisted naval aviation pilot Allen C. Morgan and his friend and fellow NAP Dick Panther hoping to receive orders for a England-bound PB4Y-1 squadron, where an abundance of pretty women, good food, and pubs could be found. They both figured they would bomb the Germans and get shot at, but the perks of such duty outweighed the risks. When they received orders for duty with VD-3, according to Morgan: "We were going to a VD squadron. Nobody even knew what in the hell it stood for. Cdr. Renfro on the orders requested that two of the smoothest pilots become photo recon pilots."

That is how he and Panther found themselves in Stroh's office, who informed them of the squadron's mission and asked Morgan what he thought. Morgan recalled, "He asked me what I thought. I told him right out. I didn't care, he was just a lieutenant commander. I didn't give a damn who he was, I was going to tell him what I thought."

"He said, 'well what do you think?'

"I said, 'what I think is that I want to kill goddamn Japs! I want to bomb and shoot them goddamn people; I don't want to take their picture!'"

Allen Morgan (left) and Dick Panther were given a mud bath by officers of VD-3 after being commissioned as ensigns on 7 August 1943. Both would later serve as patrol plane commanders on a second tour of duty with VPB-102. ***Courtesy of Joseph Morgan***

The squadron emblem of VB-108 from the front cover of the squadron's cruise book. ***Courtesy of James Andrews***

Stroh responded that he did not want to have pilots who did not want to be in the squadron, so he would cut new orders for them. Morgan and Panther were ecstatic, visualizing orders sending them to England. The following day they waited outside Stroh's office, and minutes turned into a few hours before they were finally summoned into the commander's office. Stroh told Morgan, "I like men with a mind of their own. Hell, I'm going to make you my co-pilot."

Morgan didn't want the job, because according to him, "Now, nobody wants to be the skipper's co-pilot because they like going on suicide missions and Stroh went on several of them."[1]

Morgan's statement does describe the typical commanding officer of a PB4Y-1 squadron, who would fly the most missions and conduct the most dangerous attacks. Cdr. Stroh recommended Morgan and Panther to receive direct naval reserve commissions as ensigns, which were granted.

Morgan and Panther's first official job as commissioned officers was the grim task of recovering the wreckage of a squadron PB4Y-1 and the remains of its crew after it crashed into a mountainside near NAS Barber's Point, Hawaii. The plane (bureau number 32005), piloted by executive officer Lt.Cdr. Alfred Wilstam, took off on a training flight and made a half circle before going into a small cumulus cloud. According to Morgan:

"Almost immediately they came out of the cloud upside down. He dove down toward the ground upside down with this B-24 with a full crew and he tried to do a half roll to get it back upright. He got it almost back upright and the left aileron tore off the wing and went right into the mountainside. The skipper called us both in and gave us two dump trucks, one for Panther and a crew and me and a crew, and told us to pick up everything we could find that had anything to do with that airplane and not to leave one scrap of a burnt parachute a buckle or anything, or any part of a body.

"We took sheets to bring the bodies back home in. The largest piece we found of anybody was a foot. We found pieces of burnt flesh and stuff. The biggest thing we could find of the aircraft was the landing gear oleos. We brought every piece of that airplane. I did find Kovaleski's shoes, my navigation officer (Lt. Charles Kovaleski): his shoes were fused into the rudder pedals. It took several dump truck trips to bring everything in and we piled it on our hangar floor. That was our first official job as commissioned officers."[2]

While the Carney Field squadrons were engaged in operations during October 1943, the third pacific squadron was preparing to join them via a short stop in the Central Pacific.

Cdr. Robert J. Stroh's VD-3 had arrived earlier in the month at Canton, and along with VB-106 would make some photographic reconnaissance and bombing missions against Makin, Tarawa, and other minor atolls in the Gilberts. Earlier in the month VB-106 began operations from Midway, with squadron aircraft flying 300-mile CAP in advance of Task Force 14, which was about to deliver strikes against a place named Wake Island.

Rule for Bombing Wake Island

Wake was captured by the Japanese in December 1941, and ever since had been a thorn in American military planning. Aircraft from the atoll could monitor fleet movements heading for the Gilberts and had to be eliminated. The job for Task Force 14 and Midway-based VB-106 was to deliver a death blow to Wake's air power. Between 5 and 6 October, 106 flew missions with the job of preventing any Japanese air or surface units spotting American ships before the strike.

Two days later Hayward's squadron was ordered to conduct a bombing raid after the completion of the carrier-based strike. Their operational order was to, "Attack sufficiently in advance to permit photographing of results of own bombing and of previous bombing and bombardment attacks. Attack Wilkes and Peale Islands. Decide choice of targets on the spot as conditions permit and results of previous strikes become apparent. If conditions permit, and any of the following installations remain, select targets in accordance with the following order of

Kwajalein under attack by VD-3 and VB-108 in December 1943. ***Courtesy of the National Archives***

PB4Y-1 Liberators of Cdr. Renfro's VB-108 parked on the flight line at an unidentified airfield circa late 1943–early 1944. The plane in the background is bureau number 32107. ***Author's Collection***

Probably the same crew from the previous image removing the rubber de-icing boots from the horizontal stabilizer in an effort to reduce weight and increase fuel efficiency. ***Author's Collection***

priority: aircraft and installations; fuel and ammunition dumps; anti-aircraft guns and batteries; coastal defense guns; and water storage tanks and distillation plants. Conduct strafing attacks after bombing attacks and taking photographs if ground opposition permits. The dredging wharf, East Peale Island, and all dredging equipment are not to be attacked."

The "hands off" order for the dredging equipment is quite interesting, in that the equipment was civilian owned before the Japanese captured Wake. Possibly the United States Navy did not want to pay reparations for destroyed material after the war?

At Midway, each PB4Y-1 was loaded with three 325-pound depth bombs with instantaneous fuses and two clusters of six 30-pound fragmentation bombs. Six planes, led by Cdr. Hayward in *Chick's Chick*, took off and joined up at 8,000 feet in a loose formation of two three-plane sections. Hayward's Hellions attacked the atoll individually from altitudes ranging from 4,000 to 9,000 feet.

The Liberators came roaring in over the island, taking the garrison by surprise. The first section attacked Wilkes and the southwestern section of Wake Island, concentrating on fuel tanks, revetment areas, and barracks at Peacock Point. The second section attacked Peale Island and the northern section of Wake. They struck planes on field, a barracks area, the shop area, and plane dispersal areas along the northwestern section of Wake. As ordered, aircraft dispersal areas, heavy gun batteries, barracks, gasoline storage tanks, and runways were bombed. Several of the bombers came in lower as their belly

Members of an unidentified VB-108 crew relax while another appears to be checking an engine at an unknown airfield. ***Author's Collection***

Men of VB-108 playing softball on Nanumea, Ellice Islands, with PB4Y-1 bureau number 32109 ***Little Joe*** **in the background.** ***Courtesy of the National Archives***

and tail turrets strafed during and after the bombing runs, hitting planes, revetments, and barracks.

The Japanese, still stunned from the pasting they had taken by carrier-based planes, could only put up weak and inaccurate anti-aircraft fire from fourteen three-inch guns in several areas on Peale, Wilkes, and Wake Islands. Ten Betty bombers and six Zekes on the ground either damaged or destroyed were the evidence of Task Force 14's passage. Additionally, bomb craters in each runway, the barracks area, and the shop area were evidence of the damage inflicted by the earlier strike.

Unknown to either VB-106 or the American task force that preceded them, there were ninety-six American POWs on the island, the last of 1,600 American servicemen and civilian contractors captured when the atoll fell in December 1941. After the bombardment the men were rounded up, tied, blindfolded, and machine gunned, their bodies thrown into a long mass grave by the shore.

A week after their attack on Wake the squadron moved to Canton Island. The stage had been set for Operation Galvanic, and VB-106 and VD-3 would be heavily involved. Missions were now centered on the Gilbert Islands to reduce enemy air capability and to get the latest reconnaissance of the area. The first such mission was to Makin, in the Gilberts.

Reconnaissance of Tarawa and Makin

The Gilbert Islands consist of fifteen atolls that run north to south and cover a total land area of 166 square miles. A British possession, the Japanese occupied the islands at the outbreak of hostilities and began fortifying the larger atolls, especially Tarawa and Makin.[3]

After staging through Baker Island, five Liberators from the squadron escorted three planes of VD-3 on a reconnaissance and bombing mission against the atoll at 20,000 feet. The two commanding officers—Cdr. Stroh of VD-3 and Cdr. Hayward of VB-106—would lead the Liberators toward the target that would forever be ingrained in the minds of Marines in just a few weeks.

The eleven planes flew in a loose formation toward Baker; Stroh developed engine trouble and had to return to Canton. At Baker the planes were gassed up with 3,300 gallons of fuel. Porter took over as section leader, and takeoff was made in three sections. Lt. Mitchell could not rendezvous, and after two hours trying to find the group returned to Baker.

The formation arrived at a point twenty miles southwest of the atoll and split up into sections for the run over the target. Anti-aircraft fire was inaccurate, with puffs exploding behind and below the formation. In all, sixteen 100 and three 300 pound bombs were dropped, with most hitting the water and beach near some boats moored west of the seaplane base. Hits were scored on a large gun position and a parked truck, while four hit a village near the seaplane ramp on Butaritari Island. If anything, the air strikes on the Gilberts alerted the Japanese of American intentions in the region and moved them into building improved fortifications.

On the twentieth, VB-106 again escorted VD-3 into the Gilberts, this time for a photographic and token bombing mission against Tarawa. Leading the mission was Lt. Porter of VD-3 and Lt. Seaman of VB-106. The planes took off in the late evening, flew in a loose formation, and arrived at Funafuti four hours later for refueling. On the way one of the 106's bombers flown by Lt. Patella disappeared; neither the crew nor the plane was seen again. Upon landing the crew found facilities on the island were seriously inadequate, with no ground crews to tow the planes into revetments and no accommodations for the crew to sleep. Also meals were unavailable at that time of night.

The remaining aircraft at Funafuti gassed up to 3,400 gallons and loaded an additional twenty-five 100-pound bombs. On the way to the target Lt. Seaman developed engine trouble soon after take off and had to feather his number four engine and turn back. Jettisoning his bombs, Seaman flew around for two hours to burn off gas; he did not want to land a fully gassed bomber on an unfamiliar airstrip. After landing it was discovered that a paper plate blown into the engine had stopped up the oil cooler.

The gunners of Cdr. R. J. Stroh's bomber strafe a 2,400-ton vessel at 100 feet off of Majuro Atoll on 10 December 1943. ***National Archives***

As the formation proceeded onward toward Tarawa they encountered bad weather for the first few hundred miles. Less than four hours later they neared Tarawa and climbed to 20,000 feet in a tight formation. Twenty miles out the sections split up for their attacks.

The first and third sections encountered heavy anti-aircraft fire from numerous gun positions on Bititu Island, commencing while they were still out of range and continuing as they passed over the island and well beyond. The fire was very accurate, with several of the planes being rocked from time to time by the concussion of flak exploding around them. The formation released their bombs as the photographers of VD-3 took pictures of the atoll.

VB-108 Tokyo Rose's Four-Engine Fighters

Although Hayward's Hellions (VB-106) was the first Navy Liberator squadron to operate in the Central Pacific from Midway Island, they were not the first permanent squadron. Hayward's Hellions departed on the twenty-third, and the following day nine planes of VB-108, commanded by E. C. Renfro, reported for duty with Task Force 57.3 Search and Reconnaissance Group, thus becoming the first permanent Liberator squadron to begin operations in the Central Pacific. Cdr. Renfro's squadron is fabled to have earned their nickname from the famous propagandist during the unit's first tour November 1943–July 1944.

Renfro's squadron had two missions: they were to provide armed escort for planes of Photographic Squadron Three, and second, patrol throughout the Caroline and Gilbert Islands and report any Japanese naval movements which may interfere with Operation Galvanic. Two days later bad weather prevented them from conducting their first joint mission to Wotje. The following month was busy operationally for VB-108 and VD-3, as the invasion of the Gilberts began. During this period both squadrons would lose men to the enemy and to nature. On November 11, the squadron moved to Nukufetau.

With assigned search sectors of 800 miles, several missions over the Gilberts and Marshalls were conducted that provided CINCPAC with valuable intelligence on Japanese installations, in addition to protecting the fleet from the prying eyes of enemy air reconnaissance. During the weeks culminating in the invasion Adm. Hoover ordered nighttime sorties against Makin and Tarawa in the Gilberts. The bombings caused relatively minor damage, which was a disappointment to Navy brass, but they did provide invaluable photographic coverage of future landing areas.

Adrift at Sea

Both squadrons, hitting targets of opportunity during the course of their searches, inflicted damage on shipping and shore installations at Ebon, Majuro, Nauru, Arno, Kwajalein, Ujae, and Eniwetok. During one of these strikes on the seventeenth Lt. Paul Hardy, taking along a war correspondent, was forced to ditch his plane near Nukufetau on 18 November 1943. After days drifting in the Pacific Ocean they were finally rescued. Hardy recounts what happened:

"The time of take off from Nukufetau was 1113 hours for a routine search and reconnaissance patrol. The patrol was negative. Returning, the flight reached Nanomea at 2330 hours, 17 November 1943 (local time). Navigation was in all respects OK. We were flying at 7,000 feet and observed searchlights at Nanomea. We could see the field at this time, and it was agreed to return to Nukufetau without landing at Nanomea to avoid an extra night landing and take-off.

"Our trip from Nanomea to Nukufetau should have taken about an hour and a quarter. After approximately one hour we saw flashes in the distance in the vicinity of Nukufetau, which we thought were bomb bursts. This was corroborated by the war correspondent, who had experienced such things.

"To avoid this supposed condition we chose to fly an east and west course until the situation was all right, flying five minutes in each direction. During this procedure we commenced to let down. Between 0030 and 0130 hours we decided to go into Nukufetau and flew a course that we believed to be toward it, but did not pick up the island.

"During this time we made constant use of our radio but picked up no radio aids whatsoever, nor could we contact Funafuti or Nukufetau by voice or CW on any assigned frequency. We then tried to get a vector by calling Fighter Director, but did not succeed in establishing communication. The transmitter was putting out, but my radioman felt certain the circuit was being jammed. We then commenced a radar search, making a 360 degree circle, and picked up a blip believed to indicate land about thirty miles distant. We followed the blip about seven miles and it disappeared. Another 360 degree circle was commenced, but we were unable to pick up the blip again.

"No anxiety was felt yet; we sent message after message, both voice and CW, and thinking our message might be getting through while we could not receive an answer, we included a report that our search was negative.

"By 0200, we realized that we were hopelessly lost. We had no lights, no radio aids. With approximately a one-hour supply of gas we chose to make a water landing with power. Bombs were jettisoned and we threw out our waist guns and all loose gear. During this time we were circling, hoping to pick up land, and our emergency IFF was turned on. About one-half hour before landing we dropped four or five flares, in the vicinity of which we eventually landed. The crew was then told to prepare for a water landing. Every man in the crew was cool and everyone did his job. Everyone was ordered to fill his canteen.

"Prior to landing the crew was ordered aft, in the vicinity of the belly turret, bracing themselves against the command deck by their feet and to stay relaxed. The navigator, Ens. Robert D. Plice, asked to remain on the flight deck but was ordered aft. We let down to 1,000 feet and headed east into the moon. When we reached 500 feet I went on instruments. I did not look out the cockpit, instead using my radio altimeter.

During the descent I had my co-pilot read out the altitude as we both put on our shoulder straps. The tail hit first, and according to the crew ten or fifteen feet of the tail section was sheared off.

"The tail hit with a terrific impact, as we hit the water at ninety miles per hour. The impact knocked me unconscious momentarily, and I had the feeling of going down and taking in water. I felt I was drowning and tried to take in water to hasten the procedure. When this did not take effect the desire to live returned and I unfastened my safety.

"I went out the window on my side of the cockpit and popped to the surface. I must have been the last to leave the plane, as Ens. Welshonce was on the wing and Strouse and Widell were making frantic efforts to rescue him and me. I believe had it not been for their efforts, without thought of their own safety, my co-pilot and I would not have survived.

"My co-pilot's arm was broken and a deep gash under his eye covered his face with blood. My own face was mashed and bloody, and I nearly drowned. Strouse, Widell, and I climbed on top of the plane and tried to release the starboard life raft. It was jammed and we were unable to release it. The port raft released but failed to inflate fully and would hold only one man. Even then the raft was mostly under water. I asked how many were killed and they said that they thought everyone was out. The war correspondent who was with us had not, in fact, gotten out. I believe he did not go aft with the crew when instructed to do so and that he remained on the catwalk in the bomb bay and was probably crushed. The seven-man raft inflated fully, all aft climbed aboard, and they had it secured by a rope to some part of the plane. The plane started to change attitude and the cord holding the raft broke. We attempted to move away from the plane, feeling it was about to sink, and tried to join with the raft.

"The rafts were not connected and we were unable to join, as the partially inflated raft was so heavy and soggy we could not move it through the water. I did not see the plane go down. Each raft had a flashlight that worked for fifteen to twenty minutes. Voice communication was impossible due to sea and wind. We called for help, as Widell was the only one in full possession of his faculties.

"We placed Ens. Welshonce in the raft, located the pump, and started to inflate it. We were too weak, and there is quite a technique to working the pump. Three of us remained holding on to the raft for probably an hour. We then succeeded in pumping the raft up and got into it. At first everybody vomited.

"We made Welshonce as comfortable as possible and everybody slept a bit. In the morning we took stock. My Mae West was torn during the landing and leaked either through a tear or an open valve. The other Mae Wests worked perfectly. We had no water, no rations, no navigational instruments, no emergency equipment, and no smoke bombs.

"If there had been one we could have been picked up the second day. The first day we sighted three or four planes: two SBDs and a PBY. The SBDs passed fairly close, but not close enough to see us. We had no way to signal them except with a mirror.

"The second day we sighted eight planes, all a good ways off and all on the same general course. We thought we were on the route from Nanomea to Funafuti. The third day we saw no planes, a rainstorm came, and that night we got ample water and sucked up the surplus by mouth, putting it in the Mae West. We heard several planes in the night. The fourth day, late in the afternoon, we saw one plane that must have been fifty miles away toward the sunset.

"We heard planes again that night, and again it rained. On the fifth day we saw more planes, which from their altitude appeared to be searching, but not in range of any signaling device we had. The sixth day we saw no planes until noon, then saw several apparently searching for survivors. At about 1500 we identified five B-24s and one PBY that were turning and covering the area.

Cdr. E. C. Renfro's PB4Y-1 *Sugar* (bureau number 32098) on patrol over the Central Pacific during 1944. *Author's Collection*

"We put out our dye, feeling confident we were about to be saved. Soon one of the B-24s came on a course that would pass about five miles. We stood up and waved the sailcloth. When it came abreast of us it deviated and came directly toward us. We knew we had been saved. In five minutes all the B-24s were circling and dropping smoke flares and life preservers with canteens attached. The PBY appeared to start home and one of the B-24s was seen to head back. The 5-A landed and we all got aboard."[4]

Hardy and his crew were rescued after a harrowing six days adrift at sea. How many other airmen in the same predicament did not survive? While Hardy's crew recovered from their injuries and exposure, VB-108 continued with operations.

In the course of operations in November, the two squadrons were intercepted and managed to shoot down several enemy aircraft in their assigned search sectors. On one such mission, six Zekes between Makin and Mille jumped one of VB-108's Liberators flown by Lt. Stickell.

While searching his sector and after leaving the area of Makin, Lt. Stickell sighted a plane in the distance. About fifteen or twenty minutes after the sighting the Liberator had closed within three miles. Stickell climbed to 1,800 feet while the other plane continued at an altitude of 150 feet.

When the PB4Y was a half mile away the rising sun marking on the other plane was seen and Stickell nosed over the bomber to attack. By this time the plane had been identified as a Betty. As soon as Stickell put his nose over the Betty fired his tail 20 mm cannon. He fired two or three rounds, paused, then fired again.

The Liberator's airspeed now indicated 210 mph as the chase continued for eleven minutes, with the planes dropping down to about 200 feet. The tail gun of the Betty did not have much flexibility, and by staying alongside the enemy plane Lt. Stickell avoided being hit. Fire was also observed from the top blister and waist guns of the twin-engined bomber. As the Betty was overtaken Stickell's bow and top turret gunners hit it. The Japanese pilot dropped his bomb load as Lt. Stickell closed in. The Betty lost speed and the PB4Y-1 passed by as the tail gunner got in a final burst. The aircraft burst into flames and went into the water.

On the twenty-sixth, the squadron moved to the donut-shaped tropical isle Apamama, in the Gilberts. The move would extend search sectors out to the Marshall Islands, the next operation in the Central Pacific Campaign.

12

Apamama Operations December 1943

Apamama lies 75 miles southwest of Tarawa. The island is approximately fifteen miles in diameter, shaped like a letter "C," and covered with lush coconut trees. Unlike most of her island sisters, Apamama was spared from complete destruction during Operation Galvanic. Marines who landed on the island found that the twenty-four Japanese troops garrisoned there had committed suicide.

The airfield on the island was O' Hare Field, named after "Butch" O' Hare, USS *Enterprise* fighter pilot and recipient of the Congressional Medal of Honor who was killed during the Gilberts operation. The 95th Seabees built the 8,000-foot coral runway, and by 1 February, 5,000 men and 112 planes would be based at the field. In addition to native villages, which were out of bounds to service personnel, there were five separate American military establishments on the island. The Army Defensive Fighter Group's P-40s were based north of the strip, while a second army camp housed the 47th and 48th Medium Bombardment Groups' B-25 Mitchells.[1]

The crew of *Hound Dog* served with VD-3 in the Central Pacific. Third from left "Me" is Lt. Allen C. Morgan, who attended flight school and was designated an enlisted naval aviation pilot (NAP). He then earned a directed commission and served with VD-3, followed by VPB-102. ***Courtesy of Joseph Morgan***

A crewman sits out of the top hatch as his PB4Y-1 turns on to the coral runway of O'Hare Field on Apamama, Gilbert Islands, January 1944. VB-108, 109, and VD-3 operated from this island January–February 1944. ***Courtesy of the National Archives***

O'Hare Field on Apamama. ***Courtesy of the National Archives***

Kwajalein and Eniwetok

Now that the Gilberts had been taken, the next move would be the invasion of the Marshalls. Adm. Chester W. Nimitz, Commander Pacific Fleet, informed Hoover of the impending Marshalls invasion, code-named Operations Flintlock and Catchpole, that was to begin in February. The operation would consist of two phases: the first, "Flintlock," would begin on 31 January with the invasion of Kwajalein, followed by "Catchpole," the invasion of Eniwetok, on the seventeenth.

The Marshalls were a former German possession given to the Japanese by the Treaty of Versailles after WWI. The archipelago is one of four groups that make up Micronesia: the Gilberts, Carolines, and the Marianas. The Marshalls consist of thirty-three coral atolls containing some 1,100 islands that extend 800 miles from the southeast to the northwest. In the 1920s, the Japanese began fortifying the larger islands, and by the beginning of the Pacific War Kwajalein had become one of the most important enemy bases in the island group. The atoll is comprised of three major islands and some ninety other smaller islets, all of which surround one of the world's largest lagoons. The three largest islands—Kwajalein, Roi, and Namur—had been turned into major Japanese military installations.

Kwajalein resembles a pistol, with Roi and Namur on the northern end representing the cocking assembly, while Kwajalein is the grip of the weapon. Roi and Namur are small islets connected by a man-made causeway. Both had been turned into an airfield, with Roi having three runways and facilities for basing seventy-two torpedo bombers and 100 fighters consisting mainly of G4M2 Bettys and A6M5 Zekes. The Japanese Air Groups preparing to meet the American forces were 252, 281, 752, 753, and 952. These squadrons would be annihilated in the coming weeks. Before this happened these pilots would go up against Army and Navy Liberators bombing their Marshall Island bases. The outcome would mark the Liberator as one of the Navy's most successful fighters—a job it was not designed for.

On the southern end of the lagoon off Kwajalein Island was a naval base that held a supply depot and the advance naval headquarters of the Japanese Navy. Two squadrons of scout seaplanes were stationed on nearby Ebeye Island. Defending the atoll were over 8,000 troops. Only a handful would survive the battle to come.

Eniwetok is the westernmost atoll of the Marshalls and lies some 300 miles from Kwajalein. It is a large round atoll, resembling a donut, is comprised of forty islets, and has the second largest lagoon in the archipelago. The Japanese had made military use of the three larger islands Engebi, Parry, and Eniwetok. Engebi, to the north, had a 4,000 foot runway with anti-aircraft defenses, while Parry and Eniwetok were the sites of search radar stations, coastal defense guns, and barracks.

Unlike Kwajalein, which took years of effort to fortify, the Japanese did not make use of Eniwetok until 1942, when construction of the Engebi airstrip began. Unlike its sister atoll Kwajalein, the Japanese had made no attempt to defend Eniwetok until the Gilberts fell and then used it as a staging point for the Marianas and Carolines. There were 3,400 troops ready to defend the atoll.[2]

Seek, Destroy, Take Photographs

The job for Hoover's land-based planes preceding the invasion was to reduce Japanese air power in the Marshalls, particularly at the Japanese garrisons on Wotje, Maloelap, and Mili. American military strategists did not have the intention of landing forces on these three islands, but they held strong enough military forces to become a nuisance to the invasion force if they were not neutralized.

Mili is the nearest atoll to the Gilberts, and the Japanese had built two runways, barracks, and bomb and torpedo storage facilities. Taroa Island, in Maleolap Atoll, had two runways over 3,000 feet long and numerous installations.

Wotje, which many land-based squadrons would become quite familiar with, had two runways, a seaplane base, more than fifty buildings, and plenty of anti-aircraft gun emplacements. Jaluit, in the southern Marshalls, had a seaplane base with two squadrons of four-engined flying boats and one squadron of fighter seaplanes. Additionally, these islands had ample radio facilities and some had search radar. It was the job of land-based squadrons to neutralize enemy garrisons stationed on the islands. From 8 December to the end of January, Hoover's land-based planes assumed all air preparations for the Marshalls Campaign.

Rear Adm. Hoover defined the primary mission of VB-108—and later VB-109—as, "Searching and patrolling assigned sectors and obtaining and transmitting information of the enemy, particularly ship movements." Secondarily, search planes were to "use any opportunity to attack enemy submarines or small vessels." Daily reconnaissance of enemy-held bases, often at low levels for photographic coverage, was soon added,

Living conditions on Apamama.

Lt. Ackerman's Crew Six of VB-108 standing by their PB4Y-1 *PISTOL PACKIN MAMA*. Their last names (back row, L to R) are: Martin; Mares; Ens. Lowman, navigator; Lt. Ackerman, PPC; Lt. (jg) Folsom, co-pilot; Thomson; and Culbertson. Front row (L to R): Schiefelbein; Etscorn; and Kenesky. *Courtesy of James Andrews*

and special missions and strikes often exceeded routine patrols in number of planes employed and hours flown.

Adopting Low-Level Strikes

Taking their queue from VB-104 and 106, with their use of low level attacks, Renfro realized the unrivaled possibilities of this type of offensive tactic and so began training his crews. Early results would prove so successful that permission was obtained in February from Adm. Spruance to attack all enemy land installations and ships in the Lesser Marshalls deemed worth the risk involved based on the judgment of the individual patrol plane commander. Planes were permitted to go beyond and outside search sectors to strike enemy targets when such attacks did not minimize the effectiveness of the assigned patrol.

Two routine searches per day were conducted from Apamama initially about 800 miles in length, covering the Marshall Islands area from Mille and Maloelap to Kwajalein and Jaluit. With the invasion of the Marshalls search sectors were extended to 1,000 miles to Eniwetok, requiring twelve to fifteen hour flights. Four were flown daily, each one scheduled to hit the end of their cross legs at or near sunset, necessitating night flying and night landings in all instances. After Eniwetok was secure these patrols were flown principally during daylight hours. After setting up their tents in the jungle of Apamama Renfro's men began patrol operations. During the late afternoon of 1 December, Lt. Stickell went out to investigate the Marshall Island group. He found out first hand that the Japanese could still send up air power.

Approaching Mille Island from 100 feet, it did not take long for the Liberator to attract six Zeke fighters. Seeing he was in trouble, Stickell turned south as the enemy planes intercepted. The first fighter dove and made a frontal attack, but bow turret gunner Marvin L. Blakely (AOM2c) got in seventy-five to one hundred rounds on it, while top turret gunner Edmund J. Schmitt (ACOM) got in another fifty to seventy-five rounds. A piece of the Zeke's wing fell off and it went back to base wobbling. Stickell kept throwing off any attempt at a coordinated attack by the fighters by changing course and altitude. At one point the Liberator flew only thirty feet above the waves.

Another fighter came in, and the tail turret, manned by Daniel P. Licht (AMM3c), and the top turret hit the enemy plane, drawing smoke. The fighter was not finished with the PB4Y-1, as he came back around for another attack. Pulling up at 500–750 feet, the Zeke exposed its belly. Stickell's tail and top turrets converged on him and the fighter took hits; smoking from his port wing, the Zeke spun out of control and hit the water.

Another attack came from the rear, out of the sun. Blakeley fired one hundred rounds and knocked off the oil scoop under the fuselage. Black smoke billowed, soon followed by flames, and the plane passed below the bomber and was not seen again. The pursuers had enough and left the American bomber

Lt. J. H. Stickell of VB-108. *Courtesy of the National Archives*

alone, flying home and licking their wounds from the devastating attack conducted by a lone Liberator and her crew. Adm. Hoover took note of Stickell's actions and he sent a personal letter congratulating the Liberator crew that fought off six enemy fighters.

Three days later the squadron received a radio message concerning the existence of enemy shipping at Mille. Cdr. Renfro sent Lt. Frank W. Ackerman to get them. Approaching the atoll at fifty feet and using cloud cover and rain to conceal his approach, the Liberator neared the northern tip of the island. Nine Zekes were seen taking off from an airstrip, but heading away from the Liberator. Ackerman continued on course and attacked, with his gunners strafing gun positions before starting a bombing run on a ship. From forty feet he dropped two 325-pound depth bombs. One of the Liberator's crew, Robert F. Kenesky (AMM2c), saw the bombs hit close to the vessel's bow, sending up debris into the air. He continued at an altitude of fifteen to twenty feet with his gunners strafing both sides of the runways, destroying radar, control towers at the airfield, and five small boats.

The Zekes came back, probably after getting a report that their airfield was under attack, and surrounded the Liberator. Ackerman's gunners were excellent shots, as the first fighter came and was hit by starboard waist gunner Fred Mares (AMM1c) and top turret gunner William J. Martin (AOM2c). The fighter's engine broke out in flames and it spiraled down and hit the water.

As the fighters attacked the Navy pilot turned his bomber and set a course for base, diving and turning to break up the attacks. Another Zeke came in and seemed to stall as he pulled up, exposing his belly, and was hit in unison by the tail, port waist, and top turret gunners. The plane was smoking as it headed toward the water. Seeing two of his comrades hit, a third fighter came in to brave the intense machine gun fire pouring from the Liberator. His attack did not last long, as the top and starboard waist positions hit him. After leaving the island behind two Zekes followed and shadowed the PB4Y-1 but turned back. They had had enough with the Navy bomber after losing two—possibly three—fighters during the engagement outside Mille.

Snapping Pictures and Avoiding Flak

The Japanese occupied the phosphate-rich island of Nauru on 25 August 1942 and built an airstrip. The allies decided to bypass the island since it had no strategic value; however, reconnaissance and bombing missions were flown to keep the airstrip from becoming operational. Lt. Dick Satterfield, Ens. Morgan, and crew aboard *Hound Dog* participated in a VD-3 squadron effort on 11 December 1943 to obtain a complete photographic display of the island; the crew barely survived the mission. Allen Morgan recounted: "That was the island that shot the hell out of us! We had to fly through a screen of anti-aircraft fire. Flak sounds like throwing rocks on a tin roof.

"The group finished the run but complete photograph coverage was not obtained, so Cdr. Stroh ordered one plane to go back.

"It seems we missed a strip [a portion of the island to be photographed] somehow over Nauru and the skipper sent Dick Satterfield and I to take another run by ourselves. We went over at 20,000 feet. We had just started on our run and those sons of bitches starting shooting, and boy, I mean the first pop and they were on us. We were getting yelled at from all over the airplane: tail gunner, waist gunner, the belly gunner—all of them. The belly was hollering that he was hit and that scared us—most everybody else seemed alright. The tail gunner said he was sitting there and suddenly a big rush of air hit him and he looked over and his left hand gun was gone. One .50 was shot right off the damn turret!

"The belly gunner couldn't get himself up 'cause his hydraulic line was shot into. We had a crank on it like a bicycle chain and sprocket and you could crank that thing up manually, so I grabbed the damn walk around bottle [portable oxygen], snapped it on, and ran back through the bomb bay. Me and the guys in the waist hatches cranked him up and he was white as a sheet. This was our semi-pro baseball player Neely, Art Neely. He kept telling us he was hit. We got him up to the flight deck. He was trying to die on us from shock.

"I kept asking him, 'Neely, where you hit, where you hurt?' He said, 'all over.' So we got his damn flight suit off of him. His foot was shredded, his big toe was gone. His toes weren't even bleeding; we were high enough altitude and cold enough that it was just flayed flesh. I took the sulpha and dusted all over his foot and started bandaging his foot up. What had happened is flak had hit inside his ammo box and blew up the ammo. That was the only man I ever got hit."

Satterfield dove the Liberator down to where it was only twenty feet off the water and headed back to the base at Funafuti, where according to Morgan, "When we got back that goddamn airplane had over 400 holes in it!"[1]

Deadly Jaluit

On 12 December, Cdr. Renfro sent out two of his planes flown by Lts. Stickell and Daley to bomb Jaluit. For Stickell, this mission would turn out to be his last. Renfro's patrol plane commanders had learned to approach Japanese-held islands from a minimum altitude of fifty feet to avoid enemy radar. This mission was no different.

The two Liberators reached the target in the late afternoon and swept down on the island, whose garrison was ready for the attacking Navy bombers. Gun positions and personnel were strafed as the troops below tried to man their guns. Five Rufes were found—three on a seaplane ramp and two in water—and were destroyed by strafing. Next Stickell swooped in and dropped five bombs on installations at Emij town. One landed next to a two-story building and the others landed near radio towers and a building area.

The Japanese had succeeded in manning their anti-aircraft positions and began sending up a thick blanket of machine gun and cannon fire. Coming in behind Stickell, Daley dropped five bombs on Emij and one on a radio station south of the town. Fires were now raging among the hangars. However, the enemy gunners had both Liberators in their sites and Daley's number four engine was hit.

In front of Daley defensive fire was pounding the other Liberator. A 12.7 mm round went up through the floorboard in the cockpit and hit Stickell in his foot. Seeing the pilot was wounded, co-pilot Lt. Alfred J. Laupheimer took control of the aircraft and headed back to base. Stickell was taken out of the pilot's seat and given first aid as plane captain John Jabara (ACMM) climbed into the vacated seat and helped the co-pilot with the controls.

Lt. Stickell lost a considerable amount of blood from a wound some two inches long. Gravely wounded, his crewmen took care of their pilot throughout the six-hour trip home. After landing, the ambulance arrived and took Stickell to the hospital; he never left. Pneumonia set in and he died a week later. A man who had survived as a pilot over Europe and who wanted to continue serving could not survive the severe blood loss from his wound and complications. A great, heroic man was gone, but not forgotten by the squadron. An airfield in the Marshall Islands would be named after him.

Targeting Jaluit by VB-108 cost the life of Lt. Stickell and may have led to the loss of a crew that disappeared on 13 December 1943. Lt.Cdr. John J. McCormack took off from Nuku Fetau, Ellice Islands, in PB4Y-1 32099 for a routine patrol and disappeared. Japanese records state a B-24 was shot down that day seven miles south of Jaluit, near Kili Atoll. Three survivors—identified as members of the US Army Air Force—consisting of one officer and two enlisted men drifting in a life raft were picked up by the Japanese ship *Ran-Maru* and taken to Jabor, and from there to Emidj, where it appears they were interrogated. American intelligence officers found Japanese military documents after Kwajalein was occupied in February 1944. Those documents held the names of three crewmen that were part of McCormack's crew: Ens. Darrel D. Whitmore, ACRM Lonnie Powell, and AMM1c John A. Zillis. A section of a document, "Treatment of American POWs," reveals that an unknown Japanese warrant officer was contemptuous of the three Americans and enjoyed watching the interrogation, but became frustrated when the captured officer would not break, even when subjected to punches and kicks. Finally he became satisfied when the prisoner was punched in the jaw hard enough for the prisoner to let out a scream.

On 17 December, the three men were placed aboard the *Ran-Maru* and taken to Kwajalein. The ultimate fate of those men remains a mystery, but it is probable that they, along with other captured Americans, were either executed or killed during American bombardments.[2]

The air war against Japanese shore installations and shipping in the Caroline and Marshall Islands began intensifying late in December, with continued attacks on the Marshalls and regular anti-shipping sweeps. On one such mission Lt. M. J. Ebright found a 1,200-ton cargo ship west of Jaluit. The ship began sending up anti-aircraft fire from gun positions on the bow and stern to no avail as Ebright's gunners began concentrating their fire on the ship's defenses. The Liberator reduced altitude to one hundred feet and Ebright pickled off two 325-pound depth bombs as the aircraft crossed over the ship's bow, barely missing the mast. Both bombs landed twenty-five feet off the port side and exploded, sending debris flying into the air. The ship settled over on her starboard side, rolled up, and sank by the stern. The ship was larger than Ebright reported; it was the 1,900-ton *Nankai Maru* Number 2, which was on a mission to re-supply the island.[3]

Christmas Day 1943 did not stop the continued conduct of the war, with VB-108 sending Lt. Hop to conduct a one-plane attack on enemy shipping at Kwajalein. Taking off from Apamama at 10:00 p.m., the PB4Y-1 reached the Japanese base in the pre-dawn hours. Passing the atoll at fifty feet, Hop spotted ten vessels three miles off shore. Seeing that three of them appeared to be destroyer escorts the Liberator pilot decided to look for easier game.

Thirty miles south a smaller convoy consisting of two cargo ships and their armed escorts was sighted. The ships spotted the intruder and began firing at the plane as Hop came in for an attack. The ships turned to evade the three 500-pound bombs that Hop pickled off, two of which straddled the lead cargo vessel, with one a direct hit. Coming back around for another run, the Liberator took hits from machine gun and cannon fire that severed the hydraulic lines and put holes in the port wing and the tail. Shrapnel from one round hit Hop, causing minor wounds to his knee and hand.

The wounds and damage inflicted on him and his bomber did not stop the pilot from making additional strafing and bombing attacks. By the end of his strike one of the merchant ships was listing and burning, and it is doubtful it continued to stay afloat. Ten hours after leaving O'Hare Field Lt. Hop and his crew were back at their base.

13

The Marshall Islands Campaign January 1944

On the last day of 1943, Renfro's squadron was joined by Cdr. Norman Miller's VB-109, soon to be called the Reluctant Raiders. The heat and humidity of Apamama greeted the men of 109 fresh from Hawaii. It would be their home for the next two months.

Before the Marshalls could be assaulted aerial photographs had to be taken of the fortified islands to determine their defenses. This job fell to VD-3; providing armed protection for Stroh's planes fell to Renfro and Miller's squadrons. On the twenty-ninth, two planes from VD-3 and four from VB-108 went on a photographic reconnaissance mission of Kwajalein Atoll with a secondary mission of bombing it.

The Liberators from 108 carried three 500-pound bombs with delayed fuses. They took off and flew in a V formation of two sections at 8,000 feet and a speed of 150–160 miles per hour. About one hour from the target the formation started to climb and reached 20,000 feet.

Section one started on their photographic run at the southernmost point of Kwajalein Atoll, continued up the eastern side of the atoll to near its most northerly point, and then reversed course, staying to the lagoon side and paralleling their original course. Section two started at the same point and progressed northwesterly along the western side of the atoll to a point almost south of where section one had turned, then reversed course by retracing its original course.

As the first section began covering the eastern part of the atoll some anti-aircraft fire was observed from Kwajalein, and puffs were reported coming up through the clouds near the middle of their run. At the turn the formation started getting some anti-aircraft fire from Roi. The flak was inaccurate and did not cause any trouble. Heavy shipping, mostly in the Kwajalein anchorage, was observed with estimates of up to forty-five ships.

When they were about one-third up the northerly leg Lt. Hop's tail gunner reported fighters at their level. They were not attacked until after they had completed the northerly run and were coming back over the lagoon. After turning south Lt. Hop saw at least half a dozen fighters coming from the south about 1,000 feet above them. Lt. Ebright's co-pilot reported he counted ten fighters and thought they were Zekes. Lt. Hop reported there were at least three or four Tonys among them.

The fighters stationed themselves above the Liberators and began dropping phosphorus bombs that made light-colored streamers as they exploded. The formation could not take any evasive action during the photographic run and had to watch as the bombs exploded above them, hoping none would hit. Afterward, the fighters came in for well-coordinated, diving attacks through the formation, coming down almost vertical and shooting for the main gas cells in the wings.

They were capable and aggressive in their attack, and followed the section about twenty or thirty miles beyond Kwajalein. One fighter came underneath Lt. Hop's plane, and the waist gunner, Robert S. Larson (AMM3c), got in a burst into one of the Zeke's cockpits and on top of the plane. It burst into flames and fell off on a wing. However, one round hit, causing three .50-cailber bullets to explode in Hop's starboard gun linkage, injuring waist gunners Larson and Alvin C. Hall

Shipping under attack by VB-108 and 109. ***Courtesy of Thomas Delahoussaye***

(AMM2c). Top gunner Harold R. Pfieffer (ARM2c) was also injured when a bullet smashed his goggles. Then a 20 mm burst damaged Hop's port wing and flap.

While Hop battled it out the fighters made high side runs against Lt. Ebright's plane. One Zeke, making such a run from about three o'clock, was hit by the top gunner and the port waist position manned by Donald W. Gleason (AMM1c). The bullets went into the top of the plane in the vicinity of the cockpit. It went over on its back, and instead of pulling out of its run about 3,000 feet below as the rest were doing, it was seen by the belly turret to continue to fall, smoking. Lt. Ebright made a successful landing with his port tire flat on reaching base.

While the first section was slugging it out the other ran into trouble. Some anti-aircraft fire was drawn from Kwajalein, bursting about a half mile behind. Lt. Kile, while climbing to altitude, had all four of his engines overheat. He was unable to get power out of them and only reached 19,000 feet. When his Liberator reached the target he had fallen a mile behind the others. He therefore went about three-quarters of the way on the north leg and then turned south and met his section leader coming back at the southeast end of the atoll. He managed to drop his bomb load, with at least one of his bombs falling on Kwajalein, starting a fire near the pier. On the way out one fighter came into attack but was quickly driven off.

Another VB-108 Liberator flown by Lt. Niebruegge, flying on the port wing of Lt. Allen of VD-3, became the focus of a series of concentrated attacks. According to Allen, the number two and three engines of Neibruegge's plane caught fire and the bomber fell away out of control, hitting the water a few miles off the island. No parachutes were seen, and if there were survivors nothing could have been done to rescue them.

After the raid on Kwajalein Renfro received orders to begin a mining campaign against the Japanese. On New Year's Day 1944, VB-108 began the operation of neutralizing enemy strongholds prior to the conquest of the Marshall Islands. During the predawn hours Cdr. Renfro led four Liberators to Maloelap on a mining operation and planted sixteen Mark-13 mines in Enijun Channel. The same type of mission was followed two days later at Taroa Harbor.

Mission Scratched

The Japanese were still capable of sending out harassing attacks on the new American bases in the Gilberts, and according to one man from VB-109, they could do some damage. Andy Halaz, a member of Miller's squadron, remembers his arrival on the island and an enemy air attack that occurred shortly thereafter that destroyed his aircraft *Our Baby*:

"After landing on Apamama all the planes were lined up on the strip. One man from each plane had to stand watch, though, not because of any Japanese, but to keep our own ground crews and CASU [Carrier Aircraft Service Unit] outfits from stealing parts. I took the first watch and the rest of my crew, along with the other crews, was trucked to camp.

"Next morning one of the guys relieved me, and I was driven the four and a half miles to camp in a little Marine jeep—my first jeep ride. I left my flight jacket and a few other things in the plane and took my sea bag and the rest of my gear to camp. The other guys had already pitched the tent and done everything else.

"We didn't have to fly the following day, January 3, but we did have an early morning flight scheduled for January 4. Shortly after 9 p.m. on January 3, the whole crew was swimming out on the reef and having a great time when sirens went off. The Marines hadn't told us what to do in case of an air raid, and being brand new on the island, we didn't know what the sirens meant. We thought it might be a drill until a bomb landed not too far from where we were swimming and the Marine guns on the beach started firing. Then we knew it was a raid and raced back to the beach, grabbed our helmets, and dove into our tents and foxholes. After the all clear sounded, we went to bed sleeping on cots in the tent. About midnight the chief came in and shook me awake.

"'What's going on?' I asked.

"'Come on outside. Don't wake the crew,' he said. When we got outside he continued. 'You know we were bombed last night.'

"'Yeah.'

"'You remember seeing that big red glare out there on the other end of the island?'

"'Yeah. I thought maybe the Japs hit a munitions dump or something.'

"'No, they didn't.'

"'Well, what was the fire?'

"'Well,' he answered. 'I want to tell you, you don't have a flight tomorrow morning.'

"'What do you mean?'

"'That was your airplane that was burning.' I couldn't believe it.

"'Come on, chief. You got to be kidding.' 'No,' he replied. 'Your airplane's gone, Andy, and that's it.'

Smoke rises from a direct hit from a Central Pacific Liberator.

"I must have made a lot of noise, because the rest of the crew woke up and came outside, asking what was going on. I told them and everybody got dressed. We tried to get transportation to the airstrip, and finally, around daylight, the whole crew, along with the pilot, co-pilot, and navigator, jumped in to a couple jeeps and went down to the airstrip.

"Our plane lay smoldering. Except for the two scorched tail fins still standing, it was flat. There was nothing left of it. I was told three bombs had hit the plane on the tail, amidships, and just in front of the nose, igniting the fuel, oxygen, and 4,100 rounds of .50-caliber ammunition on board. The fire had been so hot that the propellers had melted like candles, and with bullets flying in all directions, the firefighters hadn't been able to get close enough to put out the fire and save the plane. It's amazing none of them was hurt.

"Matters could have been much worse. The bomb truck with four trailers had just left the ordnance shack with our load (four 500-pounders for the forward bay and 100-pound demolition bombs for the rear bomb bays) when the sirens had sounded. The ordnance crew immediately turned back to the bomb shelter, but given another half hour they would have finished their work. Had the Japanese attacked then, the detonation of our own bombs would have destroyed much of that half of the island and many more planes. As it was, the two on either side of ours were grounded for bullet hole repairs.

"I asked where the two men were who had been with the plane. One had been on watch. The other had asked to go down to the plane that night because he needed to clean his guns before the flight. I learned that shrapnel from a bomb had hit one of them [E. O. Ray] in the back and collapsed his lung. He was transferred to Honolulu and later back to the States. The second man [Idleman] was badly burned. His clothes had caught on fire and he was in sick bay. He was also sent back to Honolulu and treated. About two months later he rejoined the squadron and was assigned to Crew 7.

"From then on Crew 9 was spare crew and flew just about every airplane in the squadron, including the skipper's.

"The only thing I lost with *Our Baby* was my flight jacket. With the heat in the Pacific, though, and the heat in the bow turret (my combat assignment), I didn't need one. We only used flight jackets during high-altitude flights, and most of ours weren't."[1]

Deadly Kwajalein

Two PB4Y-1P photographic aircraft commanded by Cdr. Stroh and Lt. Allen departed Apamama at 2330 on 4 January for a 1,300-mile round trip mission to obtain low oblique photographs of Kwajalein's southwestern section preparatory to the American amphibious landing scheduled for February. The Liberators arrived at the atoll initially undetected as dawn approached and started a photographic run from 200 feet at 200 mph when Stroh observed a dozen enemy fighters lifting off from Roi Island. The Zeke pilots appeared to be experienced, as the planes paired up and took positions 1,500 to 2,000 feet above and on both sides of Stroh and Allen. The pilots ordered the ball turrets retracted and then dove their aircraft down until both were twenty-five feet off the water, thus restricting the fighters to make high-end attacks. Allen's plane became the focus of the fighters' attention as the aerial battle reached its climax some fifteen miles south of Kwajalein, when without warning and no signs of visible damage to his plane, Allen's Liberator suddenly pulled up into a tight loop and then dove into the water, exploding on impact. Since his plane (Bureau Number 32019), according to witnesses, showed no visual damage, Lt. Allen may have been wounded and pulled back the yoke in response; however, the reason will never be known and eleven men perished off deadly Kwajalein. After the loss of Allen's plane the squadrons now understood the threat from Kwajalein-based fighters.

The loss of Allen's crew did not inhibit the determination to photograph Kwajalein. Lts. Thomas Seabrook and William Bridgeman joined with two planes of VB-108 and two photographic planes of VD-3 on a high-altitude mission over Kwajalein. From analysis of photographs taken on 29 December, the Japanese appeared to be building an airstrip on the atoll. Therefore, photographic coverage was needed of the enemy airstrip under construction to determine the progress that had been made since the last coverage. The Reluctant Raiders knew the area to be hot with enemy fighters, as witnessed by the loss of a VB-108 aircraft near the atoll.

After taking off from Apamama the planes rendezvoused and flew in a tight V formation for mutual support. Arriving

Crew Six of VB-109, led by William Bridgeman, was one of the most combat efficient crews, sinking approximately 14,000 tons of enemy shipping and destroying six enemy aircraft on the ground. Back row (L to R): Peter T. Fay; C. W. Tischoff (transferred to Crew 11); Lt. William Bridgeman; Ens. Herbert H. Rittmiller; and Edwin P. Watts. Bottom row (L to R): Warren G. Griffin: Howard E. Bensing; Robert A. Tovey; George E. Murphy; and Robert W. Carey. *Author's Collection*

over Kwajalein, the aircraft received anti-aircraft fire from the southeast side of the island that damaged the starboard wing and fuselage of the last VD-3 plane in the formation.

Below, in the lagoon, 120 Japanese ships laid at anchor, consisting of large freighters, two destroyers, and smaller merchant vessels. Just as the formation crossed over the southern part of the island on their bombing run Lt. Bridgeman's number one and three engines lost power and the plane fell out of formation, nearly colliding with a plane from VD-3 as it fell.

After losing nearly 1,000 feet in altitude Bridgeman managed to get the engines restarted, but it was too late to release his bombs. Lt. Seabrook released his bombs over the target and they missed the island entirely, falling harmlessly into the water. Bombs released by VB-108 managed to hit the island but damage assessment was impossible to determine, and damage, if any, was minimal. The primary mission of obtaining photographs of the atoll was achieved without damage to the aircraft and the formation returned to Apamama.

Upon careful examination of the photographs VD-3 obtained a strike in force was ordered and target assignments were made. Ten planes from VB-108, 109, and VD-3 would hit the shipping seen in Kwajalein Harbor. All planes except VD-3, Lt. Ebright of VB-108, and Oden Sheppard of VB-109 were to cross the island from the south and select and attack the largest shipping targets. Upon reaching Kwajalein, Ebright and Sheppard were to drop back and provide cover for the formation. Upon reaching the island Ebright would swing right over the island and drop two 500-pound bombs on a headquarters building east of a runway and three more bombs on heavy gun positions at the eastern tip of the island. Sheppard was to cross over to the west with a boat basin as his primary target for two bombs and three others for a heavy gun position on the western tip. His alternate mission was to neutralize the runway and prevent enemy planes from taking off. All planes would then swing left and retire over the atoll above Enubuj and head home. On 11 January, the order was given, the crews were briefed, and the planes were loaded for the strike.

VB-109 Crew One, led by squadron CO Cdr. Norman "Bus" Miller, who became the most decorated US naval aviator of WWII. Standing (L to R): Adron G. Whitson, ACRM, radio chief; unknown; Cdr. Norman M. Miller, pilot PPC and squadron commander; Ens. Ira Smith Jr., navigator; and Paul K. Ramsay, ACMM, plane captain. Kneeling (L to R): Lawrence B. Johnson, AOM2C, belly gunner; Jack A. Simmen, AMM3C, bow gunner; Bernard R. "Whiskey" Jaskiewicz, AOM2C, port waist gunner; Edwin L. Dorris, ARM2C, top turret gunner; and Robert Gariel, AMM2C, tail gunner. Note: not shown is Thomas Delahoussaye, added to the crew in March 1944. ***Author's Collection***

After taking off, VB-108 and VB-109 planes flew in a line formed on the leader, Cdr. Renfro, while the two VD-3 planes formed on Renfro's left wing. The planes flew from Apamama to Makin and then to Kwajalein, passing midway between Mille and Jaluit at an altitude ranging from 500 to 600 feet. Forty miles from the target the formation dropped down to fifty feet to avoid radar detection, with Lt. Ebright and VB-109's Lt. Oden Sheppard dropping back four miles behind the formation. The bombers, in line, roared over the island near high noon with all guns blazing as they struck anchored shipping.

Complete surprise was achieved, as Japanese personnel began running in every direction on the island while very little anti-aircraft fire was received. Striking the anchored shipping, Cdr. Renfro dropped 500-pound bombs on two one hundred-foot long merchant vessels and two more at a larger freighter. The first two bombs missed the smaller vessels, but the third one was a direct hit on the stern of the freighter. Crossing over Enubuj, he dropped his fifth bomb on a radio installation, blowing it to pieces.

Renfro's attack awakened the defenses on the ships and the island, and anti-aircraft fire began peppering the sky around the attacking planes. At the same time Lt. Wengierski dropped a string of four bombs among the shipping. The first bomb hit a boat dock and the second landed among small wooden coastal vessels. His third bomb was a direct hit amidships on a freighter, while his fourth bomb hit the stern of another ship anchored nearby.

Attacking a 6,000-ton freighter, Cdr. Miller dropped a string of five bombs toward the ship. The first two bombs fell short and ran like torpedoes, detonating against the ship's hull. The third and fourth bombs were direct hits on the ship's deck and the vessel began burning. The fifth bomb sailed over the intended target and hit another cargo vessel nearby. Finishing his bombing run, Miller's plane took several hits in the aft section from anti-aircraft fire.

Another 109 Liberator flown by Lt. Jackson Grayson spotted another medium-size freighter off the northern part of the island, made a run on it, and released a string of 500-pound bombs. The first two bombs fell short, while the third torpedoed through the water and exploded against the ship's hull. The fourth bomb hit the stern of the ship and the fifth sailed over and hit the water. The ship was left burning and listing to starboard when Grayson's tail gunner saw the ship explode and sink.

Over the island Lt. Ebright dropped two bombs in the headquarters area and two more on a gun position. His fifth bomb ricocheted off the gun installation and exploded in the water. As Ebright was hitting the headquarters area Lt. Sheppard's plane crossed from the right of the formation and observed the airstrip with eight "Zekes"—four parked on the runway and four on the taxiway—two of which were preparing for take-off. He immediately attacked from 300 feet and dropped two bombs that landed near the four fighters on the runway while his gunners strafed those on the taxiway. Swinging over, he dropped his third bomb on a gun position seen firing southwest of the airstrip.

As each plane completed their strike they left the island and headed back to base. Of the eight attacking planes, all but Lt. Daley's, whose bombs failed to release, had successfully completed their strike. In Kwajalein Harbor, the *Ikuta Maru*, a 3,000-ton cargo ship, was sunk, and at least six more merchantmen were severely damaged.[2]

Strikes Continue

On 13 January, VB-109 had their first combat loss when Lt. Coleman and his crew took off on a routine patrol and never returned. The plane he flew had been parked next to one of the aircraft damaged in the air raid. Whether their plane was damaged that night without being noticed will never be known. No trace of them could be found, and the men and planes from VB-109 continued to look for the next three days without any luck; they simply vanished in the great expanse of the Pacific Ocean. Lost with Lt. Coleman were Lt. Amos Shriener, who had flown with the Royal Air Force, and Harry Donovan and Don Dujak, who had risked their lives saving squadron planes during the air raid.

Mid to late January marked increasing anti-shipping sweeps by the two Navy Liberator squadrons. Five planes of the squadron piloted by Cdr. Miller, Lts. Sheppard, Wheaton, and Mellard, and Lt. (jg) Herron, along with five planes of VB-108, escorted six photographic planes of VD-3 over Kusaie, in the Eastern Carolines, on the seventeenth. The primary mission of the VD-3 planes leading the sections was to obtain vertical photographic coverage of Kusaie Island, particularly of an airfield under construction. The escorting planes were to give added protection to the photographic planes in case of interception by enemy fighters, and all planes were to bomb Lele Harbor on the eastern side of the island. If there was shipping in the harbor it would be the primary target; if not, the harbor installations on the south shore of Lele Harbor became the target.

The planes joined after leaving base and climbed to 18,000 feet. Visibility was unlimited when five miles from the target the formation broke up so that each section could make their bombing runs. Shortly before reaching the target Lts. Piper's and Webster's planes suffered mechanical failures and were forced to turn back.

To effect maximum surprise all runs over the target started at Lele Harbor. As well as being the primary bombing target, Lele Harbor was considered the most strongly defended. After crossing the harbor the second section broke off from the formation and made its photographic run over the most northeasterly part of the island. The first section then took the next sector westward, followed by the third section, fourth section, and the sixth section. The fifth section took the most southeasterly sector, including the airfields. No defensive anti-aircraft fire or interceptors were received as the planes made their runs.

The first photographic plane, piloted by Cdr. Stroh, had difficulty with its bomb release mechanism and was unable to release any bombs on the target area. Lt. Mullron, following Stroh, dropped his bombs on a warehouse on the south side of Lele Island with unobserved results. The third plane, piloted by Lt. Martin, dropped all of his bombs across the harbor entrance and on the reef. Lt. Idleman dropped one 500-pound bomb and two 100-pound bombs on a radio station with unobserved results. Lieutenant Daley dropped a 500-pound bomb and five 100-pound bombs on a building near a seaplane base area on the southern side of Lele Harbor, again with unobserved results. Lt. Kiem dropped his bombs near a large wooden pier on the south side of Lele Harbor.

A crew of VB-109 that failed to return on 13 January 1944.

Bombing runs made by the other planes achieved similar results. One plane dropped eight 100-pound bombs on the northwest end of the harbor and all but one fell in the water. Two pilots had trouble opening their bomb bay doors and the bombs fell into the water. Another pilot dropped thirteen 100-pound bombs for a direct hit on a native village on the western edge of Lele Harbor.

The accuracy of bombing runs made by VB-109 planes was more successful. Lt. Sheppard dropped fifteen 100-pound bombs in a built-up area on the southern shore of Lele Harbor. Miller dropped fifteen 100-pound bombs in a building area on the south shore of Lele Harbor, and Lt. Herron dropped fifteen 100-pound bombs on the eastern side of the island between the harbor and the airfield. Bombs dropped by Lts. Mellard and Wheaton fell harmlessly in the harbor.

The medium altitude strike over Kusaie was over and the planes headed home after conducting a somewhat disappointing bombing mission. From a strategic standpoint the strike on Kusaie was a dismal failure, with the enemy suffering only minor damage. The strike was one of the few missions conducted from medium and high altitudes, and such raids, except for a handful of similar strikes conducted in the months to come, would be conducted at minimum altitude.

Lt. Hop decided to snoop around Kwajalein on the seventeenth, and in the process was barely lucky to get back to base alive. During the late afternoon, the pilot spotted a small cargo vessel fifteen miles off the southern end of the atoll. Coming up from behind the target at fifty feet, Hop pickled off four 500-pound bombs while his gunners strafed the vessel. The first two bombs skipped over the ship from stern to bow and exploded. The first exploded close to the side and the fourth exploded under the ship's stern. While preparing for another strafing attack the tail gunner reported four Zekes 1,000 feet above coming in to intercept. Seeing he was outgunned, Hop abandoned the attack and headed south toward a rain squall.

The fighters closed in and the aerial duel began. Using the strategy of turning in on the attackers with his gunners firing Hop was able to upset the enemy's timing. Robert Lawson, in the port waist position, fired a burst into one fighter's engine; the Zeke headed away, losing altitude, with heavy black smoke coming from the engine compartment. After Hop made it to an area of heavy overcast, and after watching one of their own go down, the remaining three Japanese fighters broke off the attack.

Attacks on shipping continued four days later when Lt. (jg) G. H. Webster of 108 attacked a 700-ton cargo ship off Maloelap, resulting in another loss for the Japanese merchant marine. On 24 January, VB-109 received a radio message from an American submarine saying that a crippled enemy ship was being towed into Kwajalein and was being escorted by four gunboats. Cdr. Miller decided to send Lts. Hicks and Bridgeman after it.

Both aircraft flew alongside each other after climbing to 4,000 feet before gradually dropping down nearer the water until they were skimming over the tops of the waves. Less than an hour later the *Ogashima Maru*, a 1,400-ton freighter, was spotted thirty miles southeast of Kwajalein being towed by a tugboat and three escorts. The ships spotted the aircraft and knew they were not friendly, and began firing a barrage of heavy anti-aircraft fire. The towing and escorting tugs cast off their lines and all five ships commenced circling while continuing to put up intense anti-aircraft fire. The gunfire between the ships and the two aircraft became intense, and the air was filled with black puffs of smoke from exploding anti-aircraft shells. Because of the defensive fire Hicks' plane took minor hits to the port wing.

While Hicks began his bombing run, Bridgeman's plane came low alongside one of the gunboats, with it not more than 100 feet beneath the plane. The gun crew from the stern of the ship started running down to the port side to man their 40 mm bow gun. The four Japanese had a look of total terror on their faces as they stared at the American plane flying alongside them. Robert Carey, the starboard waist gunner, opened fire, and one by one the four bodies of the gun crew fell into the ocean. After the death of the gun crew the boat ceased firing and the gunners began shooting at the boat's waterline, leaving it burning as Bridgeman circled around to protect Hicks during his bombing run.

Lt. Hicks, about a mile ahead of Bridgeman, took on another gunboat and began working over it quite well before making his bombing run on the starboard bow of the freighter. Hicks released three 500-pound bombs that went over and exploded fifty feet beyond the ship. He circled around and made his next run from the aft section of the ship at seventy-five feet before pulling up and over as he crossed the ship, releasing the remaining two 500-pound bombs. Both bombs

Kusaie under attack by VB-108 and 109. ***Courtesy of the National Archives***

skipped across the water and hit the starboard side of the ship. Now it was Bridgeman's turn to make a run on it.

Bridgeman came in from the stern to bow and dropped a string of five bombs ten to fifteen feet from the port side of the freighter. The explosions lifted the ship out of the water, exposing the starboard hull almost to the keel as she began listing to port. As the planes left the *Ogashima Maru* keeled over and sank. A day later Lt. Wengierski was searching an area near the small Marshall island Ailinglapalap when he spotted two Japanese warships anchored in the lagoon.[3]

Wanting a closer look, the pilot turned toward the ships, but his investigation was short-lived, as five Zekes approached single file toward the Liberator. The bomber pilot turned, dove his aircraft down to twenty-five feet, and for the next twenty minutes the Japanese fighters and the patrol bomber played a game of cat and mouse over the Pacific.

The fighters began making head-on runs on the PB4Y-1, with one machine gun burst shooting away the Liberator's radar antenna. As soon as one completed its run it broke away, exposing its underside to the Liberator's gunners. Bursts from R. L. Minton in the bow, W. E. Mills in the top, and W. J. Stout at the starboard guns went into the fighter's engine; the fighter flipped over on its back and fell into the ocean.

At the same instant one Zeke was being shot down the bomber's port waist gunner opened up on another Zeke, hitting it in the engine. This fighter went down, bounced on the water a couple times, and then crashed. The Japanese planes were not finished, as another attack was begun. A few moments later bursts from the bow, top, and port gunners sent a third enemy plane to a watery grave. Three fighters the Japanese could ill afford to lose had been shot down to the loss of one radar antenna.

The same day, while on anti-submarine duty near Eniwetok, 109's Crew 13, commanded by Lt. Grayson, spotted the 4,000-ton Japanese ship *Special Submarine Chaser Number One* being towed by three gunboats. Carrying only two Mark-47 depth bombs, Lt. Grayson made a run on the ship as his gunners took on the three gunboats.

The four ships put up heavy, accurate anti-aircraft fire and the plane took several hits from 7.7 mm machine gun rounds to the starboard wing and the aft portion of the fuselage. One round entered the fuselage and one of his gunners, Bobby W. Fickling, received a minor splinter wound.

Through the intense defensive fire the pilot continued on his bombing run and released the depth bombs, both falling twenty-five feet short of the target. The ship became enveloped in a thick cloud of black smoke and began listing heavily to port when Lt. Grayson ended the attack. *Special Submarine Chaser Number One* never made it to Eniwetok, and for some of those aboard Grayson's plane they too would become casualties of war.[4]

On two successive days beginning on 26 January, Renfro's Liberators sighted and attacked shipping throughout the Marshall Islands. For Lt. Muldrow, a reconnaissance of Eniwetok on the twenty-sixth was a routine flight until he was forty miles east of the atoll, where he found a tanker escorted by two patrol boats. Sixty seconds later two depth bombs exploded underneath the ship's stern, lifting the ship out of the water and exposing the propeller. Muldrow banked his plane sharply and his gunners started strafing the escorts. The patrol vessels did not sit by as they were being attacked; they began sending up heavy machine gun fire that hit the number three engine, knocking it out. With one engine smoking Muldrow headed away, leaving the freighter smoking and sinking.

The Reluctant Raiders' Lt. Joseph Jadin also had an interesting time a day later when his crew spotted three freighters cruising at ten knots eighty miles south of Eniwetok. Coming in for a strafing attack which left two of the three ships in flames, the plane was considerably damaged by anti-aircraft fire, and his tail gunner, Joseph McKernan, received serious wounds to the back and head from fragments of a 12.7 mm round. The bullet entered through the lower starboard side of the aft fuselage and then continued aft and up, entering the upper part of the tail turret before it wounded the gunner. After leaving the ships co-pilot Ens. Tischoff climbed back to the rear of the plane and administered first aid to the wounded gunner. Because of the aid rendered to the man he survived.

The Apamama squadrons were not done with enemy shipping for the month, as two different crews of Cdr. Renfro's squadron hit shipping at Uterik and Eniwetok. Lt. R. B. Daley attacked a small merchant ship at Uterik, leaving it burning. Going over the atoll, Daley's gunners strafed a radio station and killed two of its operators before returning to base. In the early afternoon Lt. R. N. Rice conducted a one-plane war against installations on Eniwetok.

Going in at fifty feet over the eastern tip of the atoll, the Navy Liberator took the enemy completely by surprise as the bomber came roaring over the island. Japanese personnel climbing down a ladder of an observation tower, as well as thirty-five men standing on a dock, became victims of the bomber's .50-caliber fire. Three Rufes moored nearby were heavily strafed in passing as Daley went after a 1,400-ton merchant ship. Both depth bombs he dropped failed to detonate because the water was too shallow. The PB4Y-1 headed back out over the ocean, leaving well over three dozen men dead or wounded on Eniwetok.

For VB-109, January meant the loss of an entire crew to enemy action and two other bombers being destroyed: one during a night landing and the other through enemy bombing. For Renfro and his men, it was the first month they went without losing a man or machine.

Through December and January land-based planes had failed to gain air superiority over the Marshalls and the Japanese still had 150 operational planes during the last week of the month, but by February 1, American carrier planes had destroyed most of these planes.

14

Operation Galvanic February 1944

The first day of the month the invasion of the Marshall Islands began with Marine landings on Kwajalein. The doomed Japanese garrison of some 8,000 men must have been quite impressed to see twelve carriers and eight battleships before them. They probably eagerly awaited to see the invincible Imperial Japanese Navy appear over the horizon and deal the Americans a crushing defeat, a sight they would never see; instead, a few days later only a handful of the garrison would be alive.

For Renfro and Miller, February was a very heavy operational month for their squadrons. During the operation they flew some 200,000 miles of search and patrol, covering millions of square miles of water and assuring the Pacific Fleet in its Marshalls campaign that no major enemy shipping was within striking distance. The softening up of the Lesser Marshalls intensified with strikes on Jaluit, Rongelap, Wotje, and Mille, while shipping and installations at Kusaie were destroyed and heavy damage was inflicted at Wake. Almost every day lone Liberators went out to strafe and bomb bypassed islands in the Marshalls. The purpose: to stop any effort on the part of the Japanese to launch a counterattack on the Kwajalein forces. These one-plane missions were risky, with many planes encountering anti-aircraft fire, and for one Navy Liberator crew such an encounter proved deadly.

Deadly Wotje

On the thirteenth, 109's Lt. (jg) Herron and crew, including a photographer from VD-3, borrowed Lt.Cdr. Bundy's plane and headed for Wotje for a routine search. They never returned. Searches for them were conducted for five days by all available planes without success. The day after Herron disappeared, Radio Tokyo claimed the destruction of a B-24 over Wotje on the day in question, and even read the names of the crew. However, the names she read were Lt.Cdr. Bundy's that were written on the floor of the cockpit by a member of his crew. Herron's plane must have been hit close to shore and crashed on the beach, or in shallow water. The ultimate fate of Herron and his crew will never be truly known, as their bodies were never recovered. If some of the crew had survived they would have been killed shortly after their capture.

Central Pacific Liberator crews knew the Japanese gunners on Wotje were some of the best. A PB4Y-1 flying at 200 feet or less and at 200 miles per hour was an easy target for a gunner, and if a plane were hit at that altitude the crew would not have enough time to bail out. The effectiveness of enemy gunners on Wotje became quite apparent, and would almost cost VB-109 another plane and its crew two days later.

On the fifteenth, Lt. Grayson's Crew 13 was sent out to Wotje on a close photographic reconnaissance mission accompanied by a photographer from VD-3. Grayson approached the eastern portion of the atoll from the south and crossed into the lagoon just south of the island. The approach was made at 100 feet, then increased to 500 feet, enabling the photographer to get his pictures. Above the lagoon six of Adm. Spruance's Grumman TBF dive-bombers were glide bombing the island.

VB-109 crew lost on 13 February 1944.

Wake Island under attack by VB-108 and 109. ***Courtesy of Thomas Delahoussaye***

Grayson skirted the western edge of Wotje 1,500 feet above the beach and his gunners started strafing the island, blowing up a large gasoline storage tank on the island's southwestern tip. Just as he was preparing for a steady photographic run and he was just about opposite the southern end of a runway enemy anti-aircraft fire opened up.

The fire was so intense and accurate it seemed like the whole island was firing at him. Fire from a 12.7 mm machine gun shot out the plane's hydraulic system and the number three engine, starting a fire. Grayson feathered the prop and the wind extinguished the flames. Navigator Ens. Harry Bigham received a minor wound from a spent 12.7 mm bullet, and fragments from a 20 mm round inflicted minor wounds on two other crew members: Hugo L. Kluge and Bobby W. Fickling.

Seeing that his plane was getting badly shot up and having three wounded crewmembers Grayson flew directly to Roi. After lowering flaps and landing gear manually Grayson made a successful landing on the partially completed strip. Upon inspection seventy-five bullet holes were counted on his plane. The mission over Wotje was Grayson's third close call. Within two months he was out of the squadron and some of his men were transferred to other crews.

Grayson's mission was the climax of a costly five-day operational period over Wotje in which a PB4Y-1 of VB-109 and a B-25 of the 398th Bomber Command were lost, while two PB4Y-1s were badly shot up, one from VB-108. The taking of low oblique photographs of enemy installations protected by strong concentrations of light and medium anti-aircraft batteries with a PB4Y-1 was extremely hazardous. There was no opportunity for adequate evasive action if the photographer was given a reasonably steady platform to work from, and the enemy gunners could ask for no fatter target than a Liberator bomber coming in at 200 miles per hour and 200 feet.[1]

Kusaie Struck Again

On 17 February, Eniwetok was invaded and would soon become another base for Liberator squadrons. Until then 108 and 109 continued their strikes. A day after the invasion began Cdr. Miller and Lt. Seabrook joined Lts. John Muldrow and H. G. Crowgey of VB-108 to strike shore installations and shipping at Lele Harbor, Kusaie, at masthead height in the first of several such strikes.

During the attack Lt. Seabrook seriously damaged a 400-ton cargo vessel, but abrupt hills close ashore protected a larger ship from the low-level attack. Lt. Seabrook and the two VB-108 planes dropped eighteen 500-pound bombs on a 200-ton patrol vessel at Fukiru Point, scoring five hits, but they failed to sink her. Miller had problems during three runs when his bomb release mechanism malfunctioned and the bombs had to be dropped by emergency release. The bombs went over a barracks south of the harbor and landed among a grove of trees.

A week later the squadrons returned to Kusaie at dawn, this time at masthead height. A successful low level attack was difficult to make against shipping moored off the main island in a cove off the southern part of the harbor. Hills rise abruptly and the cove is sheltered, making low level runs virtually impossible. The whole harbor area is sandwiched between the mainland hills and Lele Island, which made masthead level approaches of any kind limited and very hazardous.

The four Liberators took off at 2 a.m. to strike Kusaie at dawn and proceeded to the target independently. The original plan called for Miller to lead his section into the harbor over a pass between mountains from the western side of the island. However, when landfall was made low hanging clouds enveloped the mountain pass, so plans were altered and all planes approached at low level from the north.

American fleet at anchor in Kwajalein Lagoon. ***Courtesy of the National Archives***

Lt. Kile and Crew 15 standing next to *Gypsy Caravan*. Back row (L to R): Bocade; Ens. Rendig; Lt. Kile; Ens. Howe; and Hunter. Bottom (L to R): Widell; Brent; Duff; Mason; Grant; and Waligura. ***Courtsey of James Andrews***

Miller entered Lele Harbor from the north between Kusaie and Lele, made a sharp turn to port, and proceeded through the harbor on an easterly heading. Light to medium anti-aircraft fire was received from several locations on Lele Island as the planes flew over the harbor. Miller spotted a 1,500-ton tanker at anchor off Fukiru Point and made a run on it as his gunners strafed the ship. The pilot dropped a string of 500-pound bombs that straddled the ship. The ship listed heavily to port before sinking a few minutes later. During the bombing run the plane took four hits to the starboard wing from 7.7 mm machine guns, causing fuel to begin streaming across the wing.

As Miller left, Lt. Muldrow spotted a 100-ton escort vessel docked west of Yepan Point. Muldrow's plane closed for an attack and dropped five bombs that missed the ship. He made a sharp turn to starboard and then, in a turn to port, flew over hills to the west of the harbor and made another attack on the escort. Coming in at a forty-five-degree glide from 200 feet, Muldrow released a bomb but missed again. After finishing his run on the escort Muldrow's gunners strafed a gun position on Yepan Point at close range and silenced it. Not content on scoring misses on the escort, he went clockwise around Lele Island, entering the harbor from the east, and made two runs, but both times the bombs would not release. He finally gave up and finished by making a strafing run on installations on the eastern coast.

Lt. Kile, flying behind Miller, attacked from the east and dropped one bomb on the escort that missed. Returning for another run, he decided to target the freighter still afloat and dropped five bombs, scoring one direct hit amidships. A fire broke out, followed by a violent explosion, and the ship sank a few minutes later.

Lt. Sheppard finished the raid by dropping three bombs on installations on the eastern coast adjacent to a cultivated field before meeting up with the three other planes. Sheppard's plane took a hit from a 40 mm shell, knocking out the number three engine and causing a fuel leak. The Liberators departed Kusaie leaving two ships sinking, one of them being the 2,600-ton *Shunsan Maru*, and two other merchantmen severely damaged.

Sheppard turned for home on three engines and with no way of determining how much fuel remained. Cdr. Miller pulled up and flew alongside for several hours, surveying the damage before he had to return to Apamama for refueling. As Sheppard looked at the three Liberators disappearing ahead, the pilot requested his navigator plot the best heading to Apamama, 750 miles away. There were no landmarks and no stars, just the compass and a best estimate of wind drift for the navigator to get the plane back to base.

Some five hours later the shoreline of Apamama appeared in the distance. Any slight error in navigation would have forced Sheppard to ditch in the water, because as they were coming in on final approach the plane ran out of fuel. The landing gear hit the beach hard, just beyond the water, and the plane bounced along the runway before stopping short of the approach lights. The mission to Kusaie had taken some elven hours to complete.

With the increased tempo of the Marshalls Campaign toward the latter part of February, plans were laid to move VB-109 to Kwajalein. To test the new airfield Cdr. Miller piloted the first four-engined plane to land on the newly completed airstrips at Majuro and Kwajalein on the twenty-fifth and twenty-sixth.

Wake Island Struck Again

Pursuant to an operational order, VB-108, 109, and VD-3 were directed to conduct a daylight, low level bombing and strafing attack on Wake Atoll in conjunction with photographic coverage. The evening of the twenty-eighth, after completing a night take-off and rendezvous over O'Hare Field, Apamama,

PB4Y-1s lined up on Kwajalein. ***Courtesy of the National Archives***

the formation flew to Kwajalein Island to pick up two VD-3 planes. All eight planes then proceeded to Wake.

A low-level approach from the east had been selected to take advantage of prevailing winds. Miller's section was to fly over Wake and Wilkes Island, flanked by a photo plane on the port wing taking pictures of the south portion of Wake Atoll. Muldrow's section was assigned a similar task along the northern part of Wake Island and Peale Island, with a single photo plane on the starboard wing to cover that portion of the atoll.

The formation, excluding Lt. Webster, who was never able to join up after investigating what turned out to be a friendly submarine, reached a point eighty miles east of Wake before making its turn and then proceeded toward the target in a loose line abreast.

Altitude was maintained at fifty feet before finally dropping down to twenty-five feet as they neared the atoll. When the atoll was finally sighted some ten miles out the formation flew the last few miles on a southeasterly heading. As the planes closed in a few rounds of light and medium anti-aircraft fire were encountered. When they were 2,500 feet out the plane's gunners started strafing and continued until they had passed over the atoll. The cumulative effect of this fire, coupled with what appeared to be complete surprise, resulted in relatively meager return fire throughout the attack. Many of the guns were still covered with canvas as their crews scurried to man them.

As the attacking planes pulled up to 200 feet to make their drops, Miller, to avoid cutting out his wing man, crossed Wake Island on a southeasterly heading. Along the southern edge of an airstrip were four fighters, one two-engined bomber, and one torpedo bomber. As he crossed over the runway he dropped a string of four 500-pound bombs along the northwestern side of the airstrip.

Lt. Piper and Crew 9 of VB-108 next to *Goosin' You*. Back row (L to R): Di Pasquale; Gatlin; Lt. Piper; Lt. (jg) Kurz; Ens. Scott; Blanc; and Hebert. Bottom row (L to R): Burkhardt; Pattison; Morton; Parise; Racke; and Christensen. *Courtesy of James Andrews*

Destroyed installations on Rongelap Atoll, Marshall Islands. *Courtesy of the National Archives*

Lt. Hicks, to Miller's port, swung behind him and proceeded along the southwestern part of Wake, dropping his bombs on installations. No shipping was found, except two small craft in the lagoon and a large dredge near the seaplane base. Jobe, parallel to the course flown by Hicks, released sixteen 100-pound bombs among the parked planes south of the runway, on pillboxes and fuel tanks on the western end of Wake Island, and on installations at the eastern and western portions of Wilkes Island. Six of the bombs landed on a barracks, resulting in a large explosion.

Muldrow and Piper came over Wake Island from the southeast, with Piper flying in close formation on Muldrow's starboard wing. They turned right and flew a course taking them over a heavily built up area on the northwestern tip of Wake and over Peale Island. While Muldrow dropped 500-pound bombs among the installations on the tip of Wake and one near the large dredge in the seaplane base, Piper dropped a string of twenty 100-pound bombs along the northern part of Wake and along Peale Island.

While the pilots were initiating their bombing runs the gunners strafed pillboxes, buildings, planes, and personnel with devastating effect. As the planes left fires were burning throughout the atoll.

Retirement was made to the southwest, and all attack planes landed at Roi to refuel before heading back to Apamama after a trip lasting twenty hours. This was not VB-109's last visit Wake, and throughout the remaining months of their tour squadron planes visited the former American possession to remind the Japanese garrison on the atoll that they had not been forgotten.

15

Hitting the Caroline Islands March–May 1944

Four PB4Y-1s of VB-108 and 109 struck Ponape Island in the Caroline Group, where an airfield and a garrison of approximately 8,000 members of the Japanese Imperial Army and Navy were based. The targets for the 3 March strike consisted of a destroyer, freighter, and two escort vessels reported in the island's harbor. In the early afternoon, the planes joined up for a night rendezvous and proceeded to Ponape at an altitude of 8,000 feet. After reducing altitude to 500 feet one hundred miles from target the formation flew the last fifty miles at fifty feet. Lt. Ackerman from VB-108 lost the formation during the night and never reached the target. As the flight passed Ponape some 20 miles to the east the course was changed, bringing the formation due north of the harbor area. Lt. Hicks turned to port and proceeded on a southerly course into the target. Lts. Daley and Jobe followed him in column spread 2,500 feet apart.

When Hicks saw that the reported shipping was not present he made a 180-degree turn in the harbor area and passed over the eastern coast of Langar Island. Intense but inaccurate anti-aircraft fire greeted the formation as they arrived. Coming in, Hicks' gunners strafed a multi-engined seaplane on the water. Passing the burning seaplane, Hicks proceeded to a large built up area on Langar Island. Strafing and four 500-pound bombs caused considerable damage to a pier on the southern tip of the island, a seaplane ramp, a hangar, and a warehouse building on the southern end of the island. Lt. Daley, following behind Hicks into the harbor, spotted a 100-foot long coastal vessel under way and dropped four bombs. One near miss caused the ship to catch fire and to circle to port out of control. Lt. Daley followed Hicks out of the harbor on a northerly heading, strafing the western slope of Langar Island heavily as he retired.

Jobe, following Daley, selected Langar Island as his target and dropped four bombs in a string across the center of the southern portion of the island. Jobe's gunners finally sank the coastal vessel damaged by Lt. Daley in the harbor. After joining up northeast of Ponape the planes landed at Apamama after refueling at Kwajalein.

For Miller and the Reluctant Raiders, orders were issued which sent them packing for Kwajalein. To keep them company Renfro sent an advance echelon consisting of four crews and their Liberators. Throughout March, VB-109 continuously launched one-plane strikes on minor Japanese installations on Oroluk, Kusaie, Pingelap, Rongerik, Pakin, and Ant Islands. For VB-108, Satawan was added to their list. As the South Pacific squadrons new quite well this island could be dangerous, as the crew of Liberator *Nippo Nippin Kitten* found out on 12 March 1944. Their mission was an armed reconnaissance of Satawan Island.

Lt. Daley lifted the Liberator off Apamama at 0700 with the intention of hitting Satawan around noon. As they neared the island, the electronic countermeasures operator reported they had been picked up by enemy radar. The plane was also equipped with a special countermeasures radar detecting receiver manned by its own operator. Daley reduced altitude, and in a short time crossed the northeast corner of the island.

Lt. Oden Sheppard of VB-109 closing in on a radio station on Oroluk Atoll, Marshall Islands. ***Courtesy of Oden Sheppard***

Destruction of the radio station. ***Courtesy of Oden Sheppard***

Below, a large gun battery was targeted with a 500-pound bomb and put out of action. The pilot made a left turn to come back around. Doing so, he suddenly found himself lined up on a runway of a Japanese airfield that had been hidden by a tree line. A couple fighters were preparing to take off as Daley dropped two 500-pound bombs among them, destroying one and extensively damaging the other.

The Liberator reversed course again and came back toward the airfield. This time enemy batteries and heavy machine guns were ready and opened fire. The first bursts hit the bow turret, killing gunner John R. Blattner (AOM2c). The same bursts knocked out both port engines. One shell struck the propeller spinner on the port inboard engine, causing damage to the gear case which prevented it from being feathered. It then caught fire, but plane captain John Candy (AMM1c) cut the fuel to the engine and the fire went out.

The co-pilot, seeing smoke coming into the cockpit, thought there was a fire on the pilot's side and was fishing around for a hand extinguisher. As they approached the northeastern end of the runway the remaining bombs were jettisoned. Tail gunner Joseph Mintz (AOM2c) reported hits on the runway, effectively preventing any use by the Japanese planes. However, the Liberator was now in a very steep left bank, both port engines were out, and the prop on the inboard engine could not be feathered. Both pilots were now on the controls, fighting to bring the plane back to level flight. In seconds the aircraft was out over the ocean and out of range of anti-aircraft fire.

After regaining control of the plane the pilot ordered anything removable jettisoned to lighten the plane. The crew threw out the guns, ammunition, radios, countermeasures gear, all armor plate that could be removed, and the belly turret was unbolted and prepared to be dropped if it became necessary.

It was apparent with the loss of fuel that making it back to base was not possible. Navigator Ens. Robert D. Plice plotted a course for Eniwetok that would take them across a reef that lay on an almost direct line between Truk and Ponape. This reef would be their only physical checkpoint between their present location and Eniwetok. The crew debated whether to ditch, set down on the reef if they came to it, or to try to make Eniwetok.

The first two options meant probable capture by the Japanese, and most likely execution if captured. It was decided if they came to the reef that they would try for Eniwetok. Even if they could not land, they could at least ditch in the vicinity of the invasion fleet and be picked up. There was also the possibility that the Marines had taken Engebi, the island in the atoll on which the Japanese had built a fighter strip.

Plice's navigating was perfect, and they approached the reef on course and time as he predicted. Though this reef was within fighter range of Truk and Ponape, no Japanese fighters were encountered.

As they approached Eniwetok plane captain John Candy told the pilots that the hydraulic reservoir had a hole in it and they were without brakes. He was told to patch it and fill it with whatever was available—if nothing else, use urine. In searching around it was discovered that the crew had overlooked some cans of pineapple juice when jettisoning all they could to cut down weight. Once the hole in the reservoir was patched the best it could be filled with was the pineapple juice, giving the pilots one shot on the brakes.

The plane captain was told to fasten a chute to each waist gun mount and pop them the second the plane touched the runway. He would have done so, except for one thing: every chute had been tossed overboard when reducing the weight of the plane.

The plane came in with two dead engines on an unfamiliar strip, and the instant the wheels touched the runway both pilots were on the brakes, hoping the tires would hold. If they didn't, the Liberator would plow into a sea wall at the end of the runway.

Lt. Daley and Crew 11 of VB-108 standing next to *Nippo Nippin Kitten* (bureau number 32116). Back row (L to R): Schoch; Ens. Mulligan; Lt. Daley; Ens. Wells; and Eshman. Bottom row (L to R): Quilici; Gilchrist; Driscoll; Cady; Mintz; and O'Connell. ***Courtesy of James Andrews***

Instantly, as the plane touched down, Daley knew he was going too fast to avoid hitting the wall. He hit the left brake and threw the plane in a sliding turn to reverse course and prayed the landing gear would take the stress and the brakes would continue to function. Jumping and sliding along the coral strip, the plane finally came around and coasted to a stop.

Daley and his crew climbed out of the aircraft, two of them carrying the body of the dead bow gunner. They were greeted by Marines as they climbed out. One of them was Maj. Faust, commander of a Marine F4U squadron that had landed there the same day. The major took the Navy crew and helped them prepare for the coming night by providing them a foxhole for protection and M-1 carbines. He also saw that a coffin was provided for Blattner. The next day the crew dug a grave and buried Blattner with full military honors, with a Marine Chaplain performing the service and a Marine firing squad the salute.

After the burial Daley went and reported the details of their findings at Satawan, leaving Ens. Wetherill in charge. During the day Adm. Hoover, Commander Central Pacific, arrived with his aide and came over to inspect the plane and her crew. Wetherill went up and saluted. Seeing no insignia on him and looking at the shabby, dirty men behind the ensign, Hoover asked who in the hell were they. Wetherill told him and was immediately chewed out for being out of uniform and not being presentable. It did not matter that the crew had barely escaped from being shot down, had not taken a bath in two days, and had just buried one of their own. Later in the day the admiral allowed Daley's crew to fly back to Kwajalein in his R4D (the Navy version of a DC-3 cargo plane). Hoover could not stand the smell of them and kicked his co-pilot out of his seat and road up front.[1]

At their new home on Kwajalein, the men of VB-109 were greeted to the sites and smells of the recent battle and the toiling of engineers building a new air base. Noises from heavy construction equipment and the sound of dynamite exploding was a constant annoyance and strain on the men, as was the smell of Japanese corpses rotting in the hot tropical sun. There were no smiling natives to take the men fishing as there had been on Apamama, nor were there any other type of activities to keep the men's morale up. The strains of being on an advance base began to show.

Staging through Eniwetok on the fourth, Cdr. Miller was ordered to attack a reported enemy carrier and two destroyers in Nonwin Lagoon, in the Hall Islands. Upon arriving at the reported position he found no shipping and radioed back to base that he was proceeding to Truk.

Before the Marshalls Campaign began Truk was considered by some military strategists to be the Japanese Pearl Harbor, or Gibraltar. The atoll is in the Caroline Islands and consists of twelve major islands rising to 1,500 feet above sea level.

The islands can be approached by any of four passes through the coral reef encircling the atoll. It possesses one of the best anchorages anywhere in the Pacific, and the Japanese acknowledged the importance of it by building one of the world's best military fortifications.

The Japanese had built strong fortifications on Moen, Dublon, Fefan, Uman, Eten, Param, Ulalu, Udat, and Tol. Coastal artillery and anti-aircraft guns heavily defended all military fortifications on these islands. Moen had a 3,300-foot bomber strip, a fighter strip, radar, a torpedo storage area, and a torpedo boat base. Dublon was the primary town in the atoll and contained docks, a seaplane base, a submarine base, naval headquarters, oil and torpedo storage, ammunition magazines, and an aviation repair station. Fefan was the main supply center, with a pier, warehouses, ammunition dumps, and search radar.

Other islands being utilized were Uman, which had search radar and a torpedo boat base. Eten had a 3,300-foot airstrip and revetments for fighter aircraft. Param had a 3,900-foot airstrip. Ulalu had a radio direction finder. Tol had radar and a torpedo boat base. Usually the lagoon at any one time held countless merchant ships and naval ships of all sizes and classes.[2]

The Japanese expected that once the Americans took the Marshalls it seemed likely that Truk, with its military fortifications and anchorage, would be the next target. They planned on keeping it at all costs. However, the usefulness of Truk as a major staging point for the Imperial Japanese Navy came to a disastrous end 17–18 February 1944.

Two American Carrier Forces under the command of Vice Adm. R. A. Spruance and Rear Adm. M. A. Mitscher converged on Truk, won a decisive victory over the Japanese, and effectively neutralized the offensive capability of Truk. During two days of air strikes carrier-based planes sunk an estimated 137,000 tons of shipping in the lagoon. In addition, twenty-four merchant vessels, two light cruisers, two sub-tenders, and 250–275 planes were either destroyed or damaged. The air strikes did not destroy the atoll's defensive capability, and

A PB4Y-1 heads out on patrol in the Central Pacific. ***Courtesy of the National Archives***

Preparing to load bombs. ***Courtesy of the National Archives***

it still had formidable anti-aircraft positions and some one hundred serviceable fighters.[3]

Cdr. Miller Hits Truk

Closing in on Truk under an overcast sky, Miller crossed the northern part of Truk Atoll just east of North Pass and proceeded directly to the main anchorage west of Moen at minimum altitude. He saw what appeared to be a small destroyer anchored a half mile south of the island and he mentally noted it as a possible target should nothing more promising develop. Continuing southward to a point north of Fefan and circling to port, he flew northward along the western side of Moen. The faint, diffused light of the moon through the overcast disclosed land at a distance of five miles, but he was unable to see the destroyer until she suddenly loomed three-quarters of a mile ahead on his port bow, lying approximately a mile off the center of Moen.

Still not content to accept this ship as the final target, he returned and investigated the area between Moen, Dublon, and Fefan. No shipping was found, and then anti-aircraft fire and searchlights started up from several locations. Miller abandoned the search and proceeded to attack the destroyer. After making one run to orient himself he made his bombing run, crossing the port quarter to the starboard bow of the ship. As he closed for the kill the destroyer opened up with gunfire. Roaring through the face of this fire Miller pickled off four 1,000-pound bombs. The bombs exploded, straddling both sides of the warship. There was no opportunity to further appraise the results of the attack, as the plane was immediately caught in the glare of two searchlights from the airfield area on Moen.

For the next thirty seconds he maneuvered as best he could without diving into the water, trying to break out of their billowing circle and evade the blistering anti-aircraft fire from Moen Island. This was finally accomplished by a radical turn to starboard followed by a turn to port. Flying northwest, Miller departed the atoll and thus completed the first attack on Truk by a lone plane. The destroyer was claimed sunk by the squadron, but no records substantiate this claim.

Unknown to Cdr. Miller, the raid was more devastating to the enemy than he realized. At the time of the attack Truk had five submarines at anchor in the lagoon. All were ordered to submerge and one of them, *I-169*, made an emergency descent to the bottom of the lagoon, but a ventilation tube did not close and flood damage in the control room prevented the boat from surfacing. A crew of seventy-seven was trapped inside and two days of rescue efforts failed to raise the boat. Many of the crew safe behind closed compartments survived the flooding but perished when the sub's air supply ran out.[4]

Anti-Shipping Strikes

April on Eniwetok was a month of long patrols, with steady pounding of minor enemy bases punctuated by several brilliant long plane sorties. On the ninth, Cdr. Miller bombed and strafed installations at the new Ponape airfield, killing enemy personnel and destroying equipment. After bombing the airstrip Miller left Ponape, only to return an hour later to surprise the enemy repairing the damage. Two small freighters were also destroyed during the raid. Lt. Janeshek destroyed a sawmill, lumberyard, and small boatway at Ponape on the elventh. The same day Lts. Rogers and Kile of VB-108 were ordered to make a dawn attack on enemy shipping at Ulul.

On 12 April, Lt.Cdr. Muldrow, executive officer of VB-108, spotted a fully surfaced submarine from 2,000 feet and dove his plane in for an attack; by the time the lumbering PB4Y-1 arrived the submarine had submerged, but the periscope was still visible as a pair of 500-pound bombs left the bomber's belly. The first hit close to port and the second forward of the

A wrecked Japanese ship on Minto Reef. ***Courtesy of the National Archives***

Japanese installation on Ponape, in the Caroline Islands, as viewed from a VB-109 Liberator at 300 feet on 19 April 1944. The island became a favorite target of Central Pacific-based Navy bombing squadrons. ***Courtesy Joe Jobe Family Collection***

conning tower. The explosions hurled up a fountain of dirty brown water. Twenty seconds after the water settled air bubbles appeared. He circled for ten minutes, when suddenly there was a flash under water, followed by an explosion, and oily water appeared. Muldrow left and continued with his search, only to return one-and-a-half hours later.

He found a large oil slick measuring 200 yards wide and stretching almost a half mile long; within the slick was yellowish debris. *I-174*, on her ninth war patrol and under the command of Lt.Cdr. Suzuki Katsuhito, was lost with 107 souls aboard. The amount of oil and debris could only indicate the submarine was severely damaged or destroyed. Aircraft from the squadron would continue to meet with enemy submarines several times during the month without obtaining a confirmed kill.

The neutralization of Truk continued throughout the month, with special mining missions, code-named Project King Two, conducted by the Liberator squadrons and VP-13, a Navy patrol squadron flying PB2Y flying boats. On the eighteenth, Lt. Jobe successfully sowed mines in Northeast Pass, Truk Atoll, and on the nineteenth, Cdr. Miller and Lt. Hicks, Lt. Cdr. Bundy, and Lts. Seabrook and Clifton Davis sowed mines in South Pass, Truk Atoll. The same day Lt. Janeshek bombed coastal gun emplacements on the coast of Ponape, returning on the twenty-second to destroy more. On the nineteenth, Lt. Mellard gave chase to a Betty bomber but was unable to make a kill. The following day Lt. (jg) Kasperson bombed a ship beached on Minto Reef, and on the twenty-first Lt. Seabrook attacked an enemy submarine north of Truk.

During the late afternoon of the twenty-second Miller, on a regular search through the Caroline Islands area north of Truk, reached Namonuito Atoll after having gone the full length of his sector. He dropped an incendiary bomb on a V-shaped building in the radio and weather station area on Ulul Island. On Igup Island (Norwin Atoll), a large storage building and a fifty-foot long boat drawn inland received a second incendiary bomb. Miller's next stop was at Ruo Island (Murilo Atoll), some sixty miles from Truk, where five small wooden coastal vessels were anchored in the lagoon.

Light and medium anti-aircraft fire at first was received from several of the ships as well as from the shore, but there was no damage to the plane. Bombing runs were made and 100-pound bombs were released without a direct hit, but a number of near misses contributed to the final destruction. For the next fifteen minutes Miller made twelve strafing and two bombing runs. Explosions rocked the two ships, one emitting a large yellowish cloud of smoke. As the ship's crew tried in vain to put out the fires they were caught in the fire from Miller's gunners and were killed. The two ships, together with a third one, were either burned to the water line or gutted beyond repair. The remaining two were seriously crippled, with large holes, oil streaming and spreading on the water, and parts of the ships torn off and afloat. Members of Miller's crew hung two more 100-pound bombs to the bomb racks and a visit was paid to Murilo Island.

Two coastal vessels larger than the first five were tied up alongside a small patrol vessel in the lagoon with Japanese flags waving in the breeze. Miller made a run on the ships but the two bombs missed. The vessels got underway and started circling as strafing runs were made. They suddenly gave up this defensive strategy and the patrol vessel and one coastal ran for the reef, where they beached themselves. Ten strafing runs inflicted extensive damage that caused fires to spring up as oil covered the water. Approximately thirty of the ship's crew leaped into the water, but few survived the devastating

A newly constructed runway area of Japanese-held Ponape was found and bombed by Cdr. "Bus" Miller on 9 April. Thereafter, American land and sea-based squadrons sought to keep it from being used. ***Courtesy Joe Jobe Family Collection***

.50-caliber fire from Miller's gunners. The other coastal vessel never reached the reef and she shuddered under several violent explosions, stopped dead in the water, and became engulfed in a mass of flames.

The only damage to the plane and crew occurred during the strafing attack. The port waist gun mounting post broke away during firing, and before the gunner could quit firing he shot a three-inch hole in the fuselage below the port waist hatch. Gunner B. R. "Whiskey" Jaskiewicz fell back and struck an object behind him, causing a large contusion on his back. Having expended all his bombs and 3,500 rounds of ammunition, Miller returned to base after completing a flight of nearly fifteen hours. Examination of photographs taken the following day at Ruo found two ships sunk near the beach and two farther out in the lagoon. At Murilo, the patrol vessel had drifted downwind across the lagoon to the opposite side of the reef, beached and deserted.

On the twenty-eighth, Cdr. Miller went to Puluwat, and through intense anti-aircraft fire that damaged the plane destroyed buildings in a radio station area, as well as equipment along the runway. This attack marked the beginning of a personal six-week campaign by Cdr. Miller to reduce Puluwat defenses. While Miller was punishing Puluwat, Lt. R. B. Martin of VB-108 was flying his sector and saw a single-engined plane heading into the clouds. Engagements with enemy aircraft had been nonexistent since the Marshall Island Campaign, as carrier-based and land-based squadrons had all but eliminated Japanese aircraft in the Caroline and Marshall Islands.

The pursuit began and Martin caught up to the aircraft, now identified as a Kate. Getting into range, R. S. Strause (AOM2c) in the bow turret and H. H. Murray (AMM1c) in the top turret began firing. The rounds found their mark on the Kate's port wing root and gas tank. Fuel began streaming across the fuselage as R. A. Smith (AOM1c) in the belly turret and port waist gunner F. Ciavarra (AMM2c) opened up. Their rounds hit the starboard wing root and ignited the streaming fuel. In a fiery ball, the Japanese plane went out of control and hit the water. In less than five minutes the crew of the Japanese torpedo bomber had met their fate.

Truk Hit Again

On the twenty-ninth, sneaking into Truk at 200 feet at night, Cdr. Miller approached the atoll from the northeast and crossed the reef five miles south of Northeast Pass. Reaching a point eight miles northeast of Dublon, a large red flare arched into the sky and was visible for about five seconds, apparently an air raid signal from a hill on the north side of Efan. Miller maintained his southwesterly heading as he entered the lagoon and proceeded directly to the Eten anchorage. The moon was still in its early phases and almost directly overhead; a thin film of haze partially obscured its light, but the islands rising out of the lagoon were outlined at ten miles.

The outlines of Eten and Dublon took definite shape when Miller spotted two warships lying at anchor between the islands. Unable to turn in time he continued on his course, skirting around the south end of Eten before swinging wide as he made a 180-degree turn to bring him back between Eten and Dublon. As he was executing a radical flipper turn it became difficult to gauge his height above the water. His co-pilot, Lt. (jg) N. L. Burton, while watching the radio altimeter, saw the plane heading perilously close to the water and pulled up on the yoke in time to prevent the plane from crashing into the water. Miller regained control and in a moment the plane was righted and heading back on a northeasterly course.

The larger of the two warships again appeared dead ahead three-quarters of a mile away and was identified as a light cruiser. Miller closed the range, flew down the length of the ship from stern to bow, and dropped three 1,000-pound bombs. The three bombs hit the water ten to fifteen feet from the starboard side of the hull, near the fantail. Explosions lifted the stern out of the water and the ship was turned ninety degrees to starboard and began listing to port. Miller turned towards Eten and flew down the enemy runway at 200 feet as his gunners opened up and blasted installations along the airstrip.

The attack on the cruiser woke the enemy, anti-aircraft guns started firing up, and for the next two minutes the fire was the most intense and accurate that Miller and his crew had ever experienced. The plane was caught in crossfire from gun positions on Eten and Dublon. A steady hail of tracers streamed across the top of the plane from both directions, inexplicably not hitting the plane. Miller's gunners returned fire and the muzzle blast of the bow guns nearly blinded the pilot. The muzzle flashes from the plane's guns forced Miller to fly almost completely on instruments at low altitude through murderous crossfire.

Passing to the northwest between Dublon and Fefan, Miller's gunners strafed the western shore of Dublon while continuing to receive heavy accurate return fire. The seaplane base at Moen and a number of small naval auxiliaries anchored west of Moen were also strafed in passing. The Liberator then flew down the length of the Moen airfield, strafing heavily, but received no return fire. Miller then flew to the North Pass in search of further targets for the M-47 depth bomb he carried; finding none, he turned around, made his exit from the lagoon over the Northeast Pass, and returned to base.[5]

On the last day of the month, Lt. (jg) Kasperson attacked and severely damaged a 500-ton freighter and a 600-ton escort ship north of Truk during a thirty-minute engagement. Through intense and accurate anti-aircraft fire that damaged the leading edge of the wing between number one and two engines and the port horizontal stabilizer, Kasperson made four strafing runs and dropped Mark-47 depth bombs on the ships.

By the end of the month the old hunting grounds in the lesser Marshalls were in friendly hands. A small force of Marines landed on Ujae, only to find the six Japanese on the island had committed suicide. On Ailinglapalap, thirty-seven out of forty-six enemy troops were killed. Fourteen were killed on Uterik. At Ujelang, the Army's 11th Infantry Regiment landed and quickly dispatched eighteen of the emperor's troops. The only bypassed islands left were Wotje, Maleolap, Mili, and Jaluit. These last islands were too heavily fortified and not worth risking American lives, so they were left alone but not forgotten. These islands became target practice for fresh squadrons arriving in the area.

16

A Close Call over Puluwat
May 1944

During May, like the month before, Japanese surface and air power continued to decline in numbers, with shipping being reduced to small coastal vessels; none of the large merchant ships were to be found short of Saipan. It would not pick up again until late June. Until then, Renfro and Miller sent out patrols to seek out enemy forces. Between 4 and 12 May, the squadrons sent out planes to search Wake. They did not find much. Occasionally the Japanese on the island would send up weak anti-aircraft fire as a sign that they were still very much alive.

On 7 May, Lt. John D. Keeling, on a routine search through the northern Caroline Islands, had reached a point eighty-five miles north of Ulul at an altitude of 3,500 feet when his radioman in the port waist hatch sighted a plane silhouetted above the cloud layer at 5,000 feet. The other plane apparently sighted the PB4Y at the same time, reversed course, and started to climb.

Keeling turned to port, increased power, and in a slight climb rapidly gained on the other plane, shortly identified as a four-engined flying boat. The PB4Y-1 jettisoned its two Mark-47 depth bombs as the distance closed. The Mavis started to dive, turning to port toward the cloud bank. Now two miles behind, Keeling dove to keep between the Mavis and Truk. The Mavis reached the cloud before Keeling's gunners could open fire and both planes were continuously in and out of the clouds during the next twenty minutes in a hide-and-seek chase.

After the initial attempt of the Mavis to out-climb the PB4Y, the Japanese' evasive tactic became a continual turning and variation of altitude in an unsuccessful search for cloud cover sufficiently large enough to hide. No attempt was made by the enemy pilot to get down on the water where its gray-green camouflage might have complicated the race. The flying boat began a turn before entering the cloud, enabling Lt. Keeling to turn with him despite the concealment of the cloud. The Mavis came into the clear a little above and to the starboard side of the PB4Y and headed for a rain squall.

The bow turret of the PB4Y fired a few bursts at extreme range and opened up again as soon as the planes came into the clear. Keeling broke out at 1,500 feet with the Mavis close above on the starboard bow. The Mavis turned to port, presenting its starboard beam side to the Liberator, and tracers from the top and bow turrets of the PB4Y began hitting between the number three and four engines and at the starboard wing roots.

A long burst from the starboard waist gun entered the fuselage at the red disc and the tail gunner reached the trailing edge of the port wing, drawing smoke. As the Mavis banked, the tail gunner raked the top of the flying boat from the bow to the center of the wing. The enemy top rear, tail, and starboard side gunners opened up immediately, and one bullet hit the bow turret of Keeling's plane. Both planes went into a cloud again and Keeling broke out fifty feet below and 500 yards directly behind the Mavis. The bow turret knocked out the Japanese tail gun, and as Keeling pulled off to starboard about one hundred feet from the Japanese, both the bow and top turret shot through the wing to the number three engine.

The engine began to smoke, followed by a stream of fire, after apparently hitting the fuel tank. By now all the enemy guns had been silenced and the PB4Y port waist gunner, who

An airfield on Puluwat discovered by Cdr. Miller. ***Courtesy of the National Archives***

A crew from VD-4 circa mid-1944 standing by *HOGAN's GOAT*, with one individual identified as ARM2c Owens "Pete" Washington Bostick Jr. (bottom row far left). This unit relieved VD-3 for photographic reconnaissance operations in the Central Pacific. *Courtesy of John Bostick*

alternated at the starboard gun while the other gunner acted as cameraman, turned his fire to the red disc on the fuselage.

Fragments of the Mavis' wing peeled off, and a sheet of flame from the fuel tank between number three and four engines came back and seared off the starboard rudder and a portion of the starboard horizontal stabilizer and elevator. The plane lost speed and began to side-slip down and under, and the PB4Y pulled up and over him in a turn to port, reversing the bank with the top turret still firing at the number three engine nacelle. At 3,500 feet the Mavis entered a dive to starboard out of control toward the water and the Liberator's tail gunner raked the bow as it dropped off. The starboard wing of the Mavis folded back just before it struck the water and blew up. Keeling circled at an altitude of 1,000 feet, but only an oil slick remained to mark the position where the enemy plane had crashed.

Miller's Reluctant Raiders

After four months in the forward area enthusiasm for going out on strikes began to wane. Being woken up from sleep, rolling down toward the field in the dead of night to their plane, they were now too tired to be apprehensive. With their heads bobbing on their chests and arms hanging loosely they appeared to be most reluctant to go out again. They had become Miller's Reluctant Raiders, but they kept on going again and again.

Exposure to combat and the real possibility of death impact individuals during a tour of duty and years after the events have become part of history. Fear, strain, detachment, fatalism, dark humor, anxiety, and depression are some of the symptoms experienced by individuals throughout the history of warfare. Having a strange and dark sense of humor is one method of dealing with war. For example, the author's father, at the time an eighteen-year-old aerial gunner with VB-109, actually stripped the uniform of a dead Japanese sailor on Kwajalein, boiled it, and wore it, with boots painted bright red, on at least one combat mission. When asked why he simply remarked, "If we get shot down and captured the 'Japs' might think I'm one of them."[1]

Those suffering from what was called "battle fatigue" during WWII were often seen as demoralizing to the unit's combat readiness. The author's father remarked that such men diagnosed with this psychological trauma were quickly "evacuated" to Hawaii. Commanding officers did not want this "disease" to spread. One such individual that was evacuated wrote a letter to his former crew members: "Maybe I don't think you miss me anymore in the crew…It wouldn't be fair to you boys to have me along when I couldn't do my best and give everything I had."

On the back of a photograph enclosed with the letter he wrote, "My only regret is that I am not the man now that I was back then."[2]

On 9 May, Lt.Cdr. Charles H. Clark's "Shutter Bugs" of VD-4 officially relieved VD-3. Clark, a 1934 graduate of the Naval Academy, would head a squadron over the next seven months that would fly 239 individual sorties over enemy territory without the loss of a single plane. During their tour they would fly combat reconnaissance, aerial surveys, damage assessment, and photo mapping, producing 93,000 photographs a month.[3]

On the fourteenth Cdr. Miller continued his trips to Truk and Puluwat. Having completed the coverage of his sector he headed for Truk, approaching the atoll at low altitude from the northeast and crossing the reef near North Pass. Miller scanned briefly for shipping reported at anchor north of Moen but found the anchorage empty. He proceeded directly to the anchorage west of Dublon and north of Fefan. Eight to twelve freighters from 1,000 to 5,000 tons were at anchor in the lagoon.

A PB4Y-1 of VB-109 piloted by Lt. Elmer Kasperson crossing over a small 500-ton Japanese cargo ship on 30 April 1944. The skipper of Crew 13 has just released a M47 depth bomb, the only type of explosives carried aboard the aircraft while on anti-submarine patrol. *Courtesy of the National Archives.*

The atoll's defenses were now alerted, and intense and accurate heavy and medium anti-aircraft fire was encountered from the ships and from shore installations on Fefan and Moen. Selecting one 5,000-ton freighter as a target, the range was closed and Miller continued through the increasing tempo and uncomfortable accuracy of the anti-aircraft fire. The bombing run was made across the ship's beam and Miller released four 1,000-pound bombs. The bombs went over; the first explosion occurred thirty feet from the starboard side of the ship. Before an attempt could be made to determine the results of the attack the plane took two hits on the number two engine from anti-aircraft fire.

Proceeding east of Fefan on a south and southwesterly heading, Miller passed another eight to twelve merchantmen anchored off Uman but did not attack; Miller left Truk bound for Puluwat. Eight miles from Puluwat at 100 feet altitude a red flare shot up from the water in front of the plane. A quick glance showed three men in two yellow rubber life rafts southwest of Puluwat. One turn was made to sight them again and check the position before continuing to Puluwat.

Coming in over Puluwat field, a sporadic burst of heavy but accurate anti-aircraft fire was received from a gun position on the eastern point of Alet Island. Miller dropped five 100-pound bombs that hit directly in a housing and lighthouse area. Having expended his bomb load, Miller returned to the sighted life rafts to pinpoint the position. To avoid attracting the attention of the Japanese he did not remain in the area, but sent in a contact report and continued on patrol.

A Close Call

Cdr. Miller was now providing most of the enthusiasm for the squadron and went out on some of the most dangerous missions. On the sixteenth, Cdr. Miller gave his crew a rest and took Lt. Bill Bridgeman and his crew along for one of the most successful masthead height attacks against Truk.

It was five o'clock in the morning and not quite daylight yet, with a full moon clearly outlining the islands at eight miles. Miller proceeded directly to the anchorage north of Fefan and west of Dublon where he had seen ships at anchor two nights before. Searching the harbor, Miller soon found a 5,000-ton freighter dead ahead lying at anchor. Approaching from the stern of the ship, he dropped three 500-pound bombs. The bombs hit ten to fifteen feet from the starboard side of the hull; the ship was rocked by explosions and began listing heavily to starboard. The explosions were the first indication the enemy had of the plane's presence. Miller turned south and then to the east, skirting Dublon, then circled widely around Eten in an attempt to locate the ships he had seen two days before, but they had moved. Returning between Fefan and Dublon through increasingly intense anti-aircraft fire, Robert Carey, the port waist gunner, sighted a 10,000-ton tanker a half mile off Dublon. Miller acknowledged the gunner and a moment later flew across the ship, dropping three 500-pound bombs.

A Mavis flying boat under attack by Lt. Keeling of VB-109. ***Courtesy of the National Archives***

The first bomb fell short fifteen feet from the starboard side of the hull; the second one hit directly on the deck, forty feet from the stern; and the third fell long over the ship and hit the water. The explosions lit up the whole sky behind the plane as the ship became engulfed in flames. The exploding tanker finally stirred the enemy into action, as anti-aircraft fire from the ships and shore installations became accurate, and searchlights on Moen and Fefan closely followed the plane's course. Miller headed westerly across the lagoon and left Truk by Piaanu Pass with a course set for Puluwat.

Approaching Puluwat from the northeast just before dawn, Miller made a run down the airstrip at an altitude of twenty-five feet, surprising a party of Japanese on their way to work in a battered pickup truck. Bow gunner George Murphy started shooting at the truck and both seemed to be on a head-on collision, except the plane was just barely higher than the truck. Bullets slammed into the truck with such force that the two front fenders went flying in different directions and the truck caught fire. The bow gunner killed Japanese troops when they jumped off the truck and tried to find shelter from the attacking plane. Forty more troops along the edge of the runway were decimated as they tried to take cover behind some coconut trees. Twenty more men running out of a barracks also became victims of the Liberator's gunners.

Miller dropped one 500-pound bomb at the end of an airstrip for a direct hit on a revetment, destroying it. Miller then circled to starboard for a run on the radio station and lighthouse on the northwest corner of Alet Island. Several new gun positions were encountered, as bursts of heavy and medium anti-aircraft fire began appearing around the plane. Miller dropped two more 500-pound bombs for direct hits on the radio station on this run, but smoke and dust from the explosions obscured the results. The Liberator made a little climb, banked to the right, and came down the runway again from the same direction as the first pass. This time the enemy had their guns in operation and began firing.

Miller flew past the lighthouse again, but this time an enemy gunner in the top of it opened fire with a 7.7 mm machine gun. Returning fire, the tail turret knocked the enemy machine gunner right off the top of the structure and he fell to the ground 135 feet below.

Closing the range for a second attack on the radio station, a three-inch anti-aircraft shell exploded directly above the plane. The plane lurched and debris came flying past outside the waist section. Howard Bensing, the top turret gunner, was firing straight ahead over the cockpit when the shell exploded just above him. The blast forced the twin guns downward and the mechanical stops on the turret designed to keep the guns from firing into the cockpit broke off. The concussion from the blast dazed the gunner and he continued to fire off rounds into the cockpit before he finally released the trigger. The bullets demolished the greenhouse and both pilots sustained wounds to their heads, arms, and backs from shrapnel, flying glass, and metal. The navigator was hurled from a position between the pilots back against the bomb bay hatch, happily escaping the shrapnel.

Although he was wounded Miller continued the run, instinctively pressing the pickle, and four bombs struck directly on the weather and radio station, while two others landed over and on the beach. After leaving Puluwat the pilots were given first aid by plane captain Ed Watts. The pilots were incapacitated, so both the plane captain and Pete Fay, the radio operator, took turns at the controls. Closing in toward their base, Cdr. Miller recovered enough to fly the plane and land at Eniwetok seven hours after the mission.[4]

17

Eniwetok Operations June–July 1944

With the invasion of the Marianas June was a busy month for the squadrons, with special flights and additional searches expanding and augmenting an already heavy operational schedule. On the sixth and seventh, a continuous special search for Japanese naval shipping was flown west of Truk; nightly searches were conducted west of Truk and in the surrounding areas of Puluwat and Pulap from the twelfth to the twenty-first. Special six-plane fleet protection patrols to intercept possible enemy search planes from Truk, Marcus, Guam, and Saipan were flown from the tenth through the thirteenth, and similar four-plane patrols were flown on the seventeenth and eighteenth. Except for two four-hour periods, continuous special anti-submarine searches were conducted from the seventeenth through the twenty-second.

The base at Eniwetok was well established when the squadrons arrived. Stickell Field was an 8,200-foot airstrip named after VB-108's Cdr. John H. Stickell, who was mortally wounded on a strike at Jaluit on 12 December 1943. The Bomber Camp, built and operated by VD-3 (later relieved by VD-4), supported the photographic squadron and Bombing Squadrons 108 and 109.

With the invasion of the Marianas on 14 June code-named Operation Forager, most of the squadron's operations were restricted to flying twelve to fifteen hour patrols and providing air cover for the task force. The Marianas consist of fifteen islands that stretch 425 miles across the Pacific. The four largest—Saipan, Tinian, Rota, and Guam—were the targets for invasion. With Saipan taken, B-29 Superfortresses would have a base close enough to bomb the Japanese mainland. In front of the invasion force were 32,000 Japanese defenders, and for the first time American forces would confront Japanese civilians. Before Saipan was declared secured on 9 July, there would be 16,500 American casualties, including 3,400 killed.

After recovering from his wounds sustained on 16 May, Cdr. Miller conducted a masthead-height raid against Truk on 2 June. Approaching Truk just after dusk, a rising moon provided excellent visibility for a low-level attack against shipping targets. While still fifteen minutes away from Truk, a searchlight appeared low on the water fifteen miles ahead and made one quick sweep in the plane's direction.

Cdr. Miller held his low altitude and entered the lagoon over Northeast Island. As the plane swung wide two miles west of Moen on a southerly heading, a 7,000-ton freighter at anchor was sighted three miles ahead. Miller turned to port and headed toward it, dropping three 500-pound bombs toward the ship's starboard bow. The first bomb struck approximately one hundred feet short of the intended target and the second fell twenty feet short and torpedoed on to strike the ship just below the water line, while the third was a direct hit amidships on the bridge.

A VB-109 Liberator chasing down a Jake torpedo bomber. ***Courtesy of the National Archives***

A great internal explosion lifted the ship out of the water and blew the central bridge structure off and upward into the air. As the plane left the water an intense red glare of towering flames had broken out amidships. As Miller's plane departed the burning ship intense anti-aircraft fire followed the plane's course. Continuing through the atoll, his gunners strafed a parked plane at Eten airstrip while silencing two medium anti-aircraft positions, blew up an ammunition dump at Dublon, and set fires to buildings on Moen, Eten, and Dublon.

After completing the strafing run, Miller turned to starboard toward the seaplane base at Moen as medium and heavy anti-aircraft fire increased in intensity and accuracy throughout the remaining runs. Installations at a seaplane base on Dublon were heavily strafed at 300 feet. Continuing on a southeast heading, the bomber passed a dozen freighters anchored northwest of Dublon. Concentrated fire from the belly turret, starboard waist gunner, and bow turret started fires on five of the freighters. As the ships were being strafed, heavy and intense anti-aircraft to port disclosed the presence of a destroyer anchored between Moen and Dublon. The port waist gunner and tail turret gunner immediately answered the warship's fire, scoring direct hits and silencing some of the destroyer's guns before their fire was directed to new targets along the western shore of Dublon. When last observed, the fires on three of the five burning freighters seemed under control, but two others remained burning and were engulfed in flames.

VB-109's Crew 7 led by Lt.Cdr. George Hicks. Standing (L to R): Charles A. Murphy, ACMM, plane captain, air gunner; Lt. William A. Warren, co-pilot; Lt.Cdr. George L. Hicks, pilot; Ens. Asa L. Branstetter, navigator; and Joseph L. Oppenheimer, ACOM, USN, leading chief. Kneeling (L to R): Edward C. Mazewski, AMM1C, mechanic, air gunner, detached; Sidney Metcalf, chief ACOM, ordnanceman, air gunner; Donald V. Conry, ARM2C, radioman, air gunner; William A. McNeil, AMM2C, mechanic, air gunner; and Hale D. Fisher, AMM1C, plane captain, air gunner (killed in action 4 June 1944). ***Author's Collection***

Stopping the Supply Chain

On 3 June, with the long absence of enemy shipping in assigned search areas and by the constant presence of it in the lagoon at Truk, Lt.Cdr. Hicks became convinced that the enemy was supplying Truk largely at night south and west of current patrol limits.

Navigator Ens. Dicky Wieland sighted an enemy convoy of eleven ships consisting of a large freighter, two medium freighters, a destroyer, and seven escorts five miles off to port and on the same course as the plane. With the darkness and poor visibility sight contact was lost, so Hicks circled, hoping to locate the convoy silhouetted against the moon. Dropping from an altitude of 1,500 to 400 feet, Hicks circled and came directly over the convoy.

The enemy gave no sign they were aware of the plane's presence. Course was reversed and the plane circled to starboard wide around the convoy and dropped to 200 feet on a northerly direction before heading directly over the middle of the convoy. Hicks selected the large freighter as a target and the range was closed.

One of the escort vessels on the near flank of the convoy opened fire when the plane had closed to 1,000 yards, and tracer fire was received from all the ships when the plane was 500 yards from the freighter. Immediately the tail, belly, and waist gunners returned fire, having held their fire while the advantage of surprise existed. The tail gunner directed his fire at gun positions on one of the freighters, which ceased firing abruptly. The belly turret fired steadily at the freighter, silencing some of the more accurate anti-aircraft. The gunners then trained their fire on a destroyer to the port of the convoy. Then the waist gunners fired at the escorts with the top turret joining them, starting flash fires on two of the ships.

As the plane passed over the nearest escort on the bombing run, the bow turret joined the belly turret's fire on the target freighter, shifting to a second freighter at the bomb drop and then to a far escort, knocking out two anti-aircraft guns. The bombardier, after coaching the pilot on the bombing run by means of the low altitude sight, manned a .30-caliber machine gun through the bombardier's starboard window against an escort gunboat on the far side of the convoy.

Hicks made his bombing run across the ship's port beam. A 1,000-pound bomb was released and hit directly on the deck approximately sixty feet from the stern, and a 500-pound bomb went over, entering the water fifteen to twenty feet off the starboard side of the hull. A violent explosion aboard the freighter followed the bomb detonations. The freighter was left on fire, dead in the water, and listing heavily to starboard. Hicks' plane was caught in the deadly crossfire of the larger ships over the center of the convoy.

Plane captain and starboard waist gunner Hale Fisher was hit by a shell after it entered the fuselage beneath the cockpit and traveled the length of the plane, holing the bomb bay door actuating cylinder, the bomb-bay tank, and two bulkheads before striking the gunner in the abdomen. Hicks, with the aid of his co-pilot, began radical evasive maneuvers as soon as bombs were away, skidding sharply and dropping down almost to the water.

When out of range Hicks reversed course and climbed to an altitude of 7,000 feet. The navigator went aft when the waist gunner was wounded and remained with him for a large part of the return flight, giving first aid. With the loss of hydraulic pressure Hicks found it impossible to close the bomb bay doors. One of the doors was finally closed manually, but the other was impossible to close until return to base. Reaching Eniwetok, a safe landing was effected with manual lowering of flaps and wheels despite the loss of outboard brakes. Two days later the entire squadron lined up outside the church on Eniwetok as the flag-draped coffin bearing the remains of Hale Fisher passed by on the way to the cemetery.[1]

The following evening, the sun had just set as Lt. Wheaton of VB-109 set his plane on a course west of Puluwat, hoping to find enemy shipping targets along the Truk-Guam lane that Hicks had found the night before. When the plane was at an altitude of 1,500 feet, the starboard waist gunner sighted a convoy at a distance of six miles. Wheaton turned starboard and reduced his altitude to 800 feet with the intention of circling the convoy, silhouetting them against the remaining daylight in the western sky for his bombing run.

The gunfire from every ship began as soon as the turn was initiated, with heavy anti-aircraft fire from a three-inch gun on a destroyer being consistently accurate. The enemy fire was an intense protective barrage as the plane passed to the rear of the ships on a southerly course. As the plane circled, three escort patrol vessels a half mile apart were sighted four miles behind the main convoy. Wheaton selected the escorts as his targets and the plane passed at 500 feet between the first two ships.

The starboard waist gunner opened fire on the leading escort as Wheaton turned to port, circling the second patrol vessel, and was soon followed by the other gunners. The two patrol boats answered with accurate 20 mm tracer fire, but concentrated fire from the PB4Y stopped all defensive fire from both vessels and stopped the second ship dead in the water.

Wheaton turned to starboard and headed for the third escort as intense, accurate gunfire was being received from a freighter and destroyer in the main convoy. Climbing to 1,500 feet, Wheaton approached the escort on a northerly heading, and through intense and accurate fire made a glide bombing run, releasing four 500-pound bombs in train at 500 feet and recovering from the run at 200 feet. This was one of the very few attacks made by VB-109 pilots at an altitude above masthead.

The first three bombs fell short, with the third striking the water twenty feet from the port hull. The fourth bomb dropped directly on the deck amidships. The explosion picked the ship up, twisted it forty-five degrees to starboard, and as the starboard waist gunner described "laid it on its side," as flames amidships rose twice the height of the ship. Before the plane had completed its pullout and began to turn to port the ship had sunk. With the help of his co-pilot Wheaton pulled out of his dive and climbed to 6,000 feet as anti-aircraft fire followed the plane during its departure.

Kate vs. Liberator

During the late afternoon of the sixth, Lt. Janeshek, on routine search through the Northern Caroline Islands and having partially completed the outward leg of his search sector, altered course toward the area west of Truk where enemy shipping had been encountered by Hicks and Wheaton. Cruising at 1,400 feet, he reached a point in sight of Truk when the bow gunner, Joseph Yates, sighted a Kate torpedo bomber slightly

Climbaboard*, a VB-109 Liberator piloted by Bill Bridgeman. *Courtesy of Oden Sheppard

PB4Y-1 Liberator *Thunder Mug* (bureau number 32108), with chamber pot nose art, was the personal plane of Cdr. Norman "Bus" Miller, skipper of VB-109. ***Author's Collection***

off the starboard three miles away at 1,000 feet and headed straight for Truk. Janeshek increased power, headed toward the enemy plane, and closed on it rapidly. While still two miles away the enemy plane apparently sighted the PB4Y and nosed over. Janeshek nosed over as well and the PB4Y's bow turret opened fire at the Kate at 1,200 feet.

The first burst hit the Kate's engine and the fuselage by the starboard wing root. Flames appeared on the cowl flaps on the Kate's port side and began streaming up and over the cockpit. The second burst at 800 feet went under the Kate harmlessly, but the third burst at 500 feet hit the Kate's tail as the bow turret gunner held the Kate directly in his fire. Port waist gunner Jack Biggers picked the Kate up under the wing at 300 feet range and riddled the rear cockpit and then the engine as the Liberator banked slightly to port. The rear cockpit gunner of the Kate pushed his canopy back and was standing up, preparing to bail out, as the Kate came into the sight of the PB4Y port waist gun. Jack Biggers fired a short burst and observed the enemy gunner suddenly sit down again.

Janeshek started a 180-degree turn to starboard, and as soon as he had passed the Kate Joseph Rodgers, the tail turret gunner, opened fire at 600 feet, followed the smoking Kate almost to the water, and was joined in the final stage by Robin Allen, the starboard waist gunner. About 500 feet from the water the Kate jettisoned two depth bombs, fell off on the port wing, and then hit the water without bouncing and exploded.

As the PB4Y completed its turn to starboard the water subsided and the starboard wing of the Kate appeared before it slowly sank. The red disc of the rising sun was gradually swallowed up by the oily and wreckage-strewn waves. The entire action had taken less than five minutes. The Liberator circled the position—fifteen miles from the reef of Truk Atoll with Tol Island plainly visible—observing the wreckage before returning to complete the coverage of his assigned search sector.

Anti-shipping Strikes Continue

The Japanese were still trying to reinforce the Mariana Islands by sending small convoys, but most were spotted and attacked by land-based and carrier groups. Lt. R. B. Daley of VB-108 sighted one of them, consisting of ten ships, 150 miles southeast of Guam. These were large merchant ships, the type that had not been seen in months—two tankers and three cargo ships weighing in excess of 5,000 tons escorted by five armed escorts. Seeing that his one Liberator did not stand much of a chance against the convoy's potential fire power, Daley prudently left them alone and went hunting for other targets. A few minutes later a small coastal vessel was sighted fifteen miles away from the main convoy.

The Liberator went down to seventy-five feet and began the attack. A machine gun opened fire as the bomber approached, but Daley's gunners strafed the position, killing the gun crew. For the next thirty minutes Daley and his crew flew around the vessel, dropping bombs and strafing. Afterward, there was very little left afloat as the Liberator headed home. Another Liberator from 109 was the next to make contact.

VB-109's Lt. Mellard, on search for shipping through the northern Caroline Islands and in the lanes west of Truk, was at an altitude of 1,000 feet when his radioman made a radar contact at fourteen miles. Through poor visibility Lt. Mellard made a thirty-degree turn to starboard. Five miles away a convoy of ships silhouetted against the moon was sighted at a speed of twelve knots. Mellard circled briefly, diving to 300 feet, picked a large freighter as a target, and began a bombing approach. However, with deteriorating visibility the target was shortly lost and Mellard turned to starboard. A few minutes later a freighter was sighted just as the plane flew across the length of the ship.

The bow turret opened fire on the freighter at 1,500 feet and his tracers hit the ship. The top and belly turrets joined in, and their converging fire started a blaze forward of the superstructure that burned throughout the attack. As the bomber passed to starboard of the freighter the bow and tail turrets, along with the starboard waist gunner, shifted their fire to an escort on the starboard side of the formation. The belly turret and port waist gun directed their fire at a possible destroyer off to port and to the rear of the freighter.

Mellard turned to port in front of the freighter, banking sharply, and came down to 200 feet for a run on the destroyer. A bombing run was made from the starboard bow to port quarter across the warship, and two 500-pound bombs struck the water ten feet from the starboard side of the hull and near enough together to form a single bomb splash before they exploded. The ship's stern rose out of the water and was kicked around forty-five degrees to port. Thick black smoke poured from the stern but there were no visible flames. When last observed the ship was down by the stern with a heavy starboard list and was stopped dead in the water.

The bombing run carried the plane close to an escort vessel that fired a little 20 mm tracer fire in the plane's direction—the only anti-aircraft fire noted during the entire run. Pulling out after the run, Mellard flew up moon for about ten miles, debating further possibilities. Aware of the destruction possible to achieve with machine gun fire and persuaded by the lack of anti-aircraft fire, he decided to return and try to finish off the cripple.

Mellard returned on the port side of the convoy, turning to port when abreast of the burning freighter, and crossed the beam of the formation with all guns strafing. The crippled destroyer had dropped behind the formation and out of lethal range of the plane's concentrated gunfire, but now the enemy was thoroughly alert. The convoy, with the exception of the destroyer, began firing simultaneously and sending up a barrage of light and medium anti-aircraft fire. Remarkably, the plane was not hit. Deciding to end the attack, Mellard turned to port and set course for base.

A Japanese coastal vessel under intense machine gun fire from a VB-109 Liberator on 16 June 1944. Such vessels were used to supply Japanese-held islands throughout the Caroline and Marshall Islands. ***Courtesy of the National Archives***

Miller's Puluwat Finale

Cdr. Miller's personal war with the Japanese on Puluwat ended during the second week of June 1944, as few structures remained after constant harassing attacks by land and sea-based aircraft. On a search through the Northern Carolines, he left his search sector in the Hall Islands and proceeded to a point twenty miles west of Truk to investigate the enemy shipping lanes. Sighting no shipping targets, Miller approached Puluwat from the east and attacked the concentration of gun emplacements on Alet Island that had given him difficulty on previous raids.

A low-level approach ranging from fifty to 200 feet for thirty miles was made toward Puluwat and complete surprise was achieved. An initial run was made across the northern part of Puluwat Island and down the length of the eastern point of Alet Island, directly over the target gun positions. Miller released ten 100-pound bombs on the gun positions. The first two bombs fell short, exploding on the beach. The succeeding eight hit directly in a string across the concentrated gun positions, shattering the emplacements and wrecking the guns.

The tail turret of a VB-116 Liberator as it looks today. ***Courtesy of Ed Robinson ©1999. Ed Robinson/Hawaiian Watercolors***

The bow turret opened fire at 1,500 feet, followed by the top turret and both waist gunners. The gun positions were the primary strafing targets, with the top turret and starboard waist shifting fire to a group of six tents and shelters adjacent to the gun emplacements and along the beach. The fire of the tail and belly turrets on the same targets after the bomb drop added to the devastation.

Skirting the shore to the western end of the runway, Miller circled to port and flew wide around the island group for a bombing run on the remaining installations in the lighthouse area on the northwest side of Alet. Heading toward the lighthouse, heavy and medium anti-aircraft fire was received from positions along the southwestern shore until the plane passed to the east around Puluwat Island.

Bombing runs against targets in the lighthouse area were made from the north and south, with recovery in a circle to starboard. On the first run, three 500-pound bombs were dropped over the lighthouse area of northwest Alet. The second drop was a direct hit on a generator building adjacent to the lighthouse. The third run was made on the radio station, and the bomb detonations destroyed the station and blew the roof off the last remaining building in the area. Anti-aircraft fire by heavy three-inch guns on the southern shore of Alet became very intense on the third run.

While attacking the lighthouse area, the plane was damaged by small caliber rounds to the starboard side of the fuselage, vertical stabilizer, tail, belly, starboard wing, and the lower starboard waist hatch, barely missing the waist gunners. Only a badly damaged lighthouse remained standing. Miller returned to his search sector by way of Ulul before returning to base.

VB-109 Scores Again

Four days later Lt. Mellard, on fleet protection patrol in conjunction with Lt. Harvey H. Hop of VB-108, was flying along a north-south line some 400 miles east of Saipan when Hop reported a Betty at 9,000 feet.

Mellard immediately altered course to parallel that of the Betty and climbed to 11,000 feet to obtain an altitude advantage. The pilot, 1,500 feet above and eight miles ahead of the Liberator, soon sighted the enemy bomber. Mellard increased power and climbed to 14,500 feet in pursuit. Twelve minutes later he brought the PB4Y in position to attack and nosed over and closed the range. A crossover from the Betty's starboard side was planned, keeping the belly turret retracted until ready for the attack.

Bow turret gunner Thomas C. Lee opened fire at a range of 1,500 feet. The initial burst was extremely accurate, with incendiaries splashing over the starboard wing root and fuselage of the enemy plane. Robert L. Dumais in the top turret fired a short burst, scoring hits along the fuselage and in the cockpit area. There was no return fire from the Japanese plane, and when the range was closed to 1,000 feet the Betty broke away in a vertical power dive, smoke pouring from the starboard wing just outboard of the engine nacelle. The Betty continued its dive straight into the water, suggesting the pilot may have been killed.

The plane hit the water with a great splash and exploded, leaving only a dirty brown slick in the water. Fourteen minutes later Mellard encountered an American Carrier Task Force, the existence of which it was his mission to keep from enemy search planes. The downing of the enemy plane was a result of special line patrols flown by VB-108 and 109 for protecting forces moving toward the Marianas.

On the eleventh, Lt. Muldrow was again playing fighter pilot while searching southeast of Saipan. Port waist gunner D. J. Pollard spotted an Irving. Muldrow dove down, and 1,200 feet from the enemy plane the gunners opened fire. The Irving returned fire from a turret behind the cockpit. The Japanese gunner was not accurate but the Liberator's gunners were, and tracers began hitting the starboard engine and fuselage. The engine flared up, went out, and flared up again as more .50-caliber bullets went into it. The port engine was then hit and began smoking. Seeing he was in serious trouble, it appeared the Japanese pilot tried to make a water landing, but the Irving hit the water hard enough to rip off both wings.

Operation A-Go

Between 16 and 20 June, both squadrons vigorously sought out Japanese submarines being deployed along a picket line near Saipan. The deployment was part of Adm. Soemu Toyoda's "Operation A-Go." For the Japanese, this operation would be the defining point of the war—to stop the Americans from invading the Mariana Islands. Lt. Martin of VB-108 was the first to make contact and unsuccessfully attack a submarine on the sixteenth, but a patrol plane from VB-109 had better luck.

On the seventeenth, Lt. Bill Bridgeman had been airborne for two hours on anti-submarine patrol duty when George Murphy, in the bow turret, spotted an enemy sub cruising on the surface. It was RO-117, a 525-ton submarine with a crew of fifty-five. Bridgeman acknowledged him and started playing four-engined dive-bomber, diving toward the ocean. The sub must have seen the aircraft coming toward it and immediately began to crash dive. Bridgeman's run on the submarine was almost identical to one they had attacked on 31 March. The boat was almost submerged, with the conning tower still out of the water when Bridgeman released Mark-47 depth bombs.

Both charges hit close to the submerging boat, and immediately a large oil slick appeared after the explosions. They circled the area for many hours before another plane from the squadron relieved them, but the submarine never surfaced. After landing the crew was not given credit for sinking it. After the de-briefing, Bridgeman told the crew if they ever came across another sub he intended to run like hell in the opposite direction. Only after the war was RO-117 confirmed sunk by VB-109. Tracking of enemy submarines continued for the next few days, with pilots from both squadrons making attacks on the elusive submersibles.

The next two days saw the grand design of Operation A-Go go down in flames, as the Japanese Navy was soundly defeated at the Battle of the Philippine Sea. Nothing could impede the American conquest of the Mariana Islands and two of them would become bases for Army Air Force B-29 Superfortresses, bombers that would deliver destruction to the Japanese home islands. In fourteen months it would be here where the atomic bombs would be assembled.

VB-108 Heads Home

The final week of June saw the last missions conducted by Cdr. Renfro's VB-108, as they had fulfilled their eight-month combat

The wing section of a PB4Y-1 from VB-116 as seen today in the waters off Hawaii. ***Courtesy of Ed Robinson ©1999. Ed Robinson/Hawaiian Watercolors***

tour. A few days remained in the forward area, with patrols to be flown, and during one such flight, an enemy aircraft became the last score for VB-108; another Kate became the victim of VB-108's Lt. Wengierski on the twenty-seventh. The engagement did not last too long northeast of Truk. The rear gunner on the float plane was alert and began sending back intense machine gun fire. As the combined fire power of the Liberator's bow and top turret gunners found the range and silenced the enemy gunner the enemy plane was sent crashing in flames into the Pacific Ocean. Two days later, Lt. Harry E. Butterfield Jr. of VD-4 surprised a Betty bomber near Truk. With altitude advantage he forced the enemy plane down to the water, where his gunners shot the plane down in flames.[2]

The first week of July saw the departure of VB-108, which reportedly had been given the nickname "Tokyo Rose's Four-Engine Fighters" during the squadron's tour. The first Navy Liberator squadron to base in the Central Pacific went back to the United States for reorganization. Some months later, a number of her men would come back under the leadership of Lt.Cdr. Muldrow manning PB4Y-2 Privateers. For the new commanding officer of 108, his second tour of duty would end prematurely.

The month also saw increased photographic reconnaissance of the Marianas by VD-4. With Saipan nearly secured, American forces began preparing to land on Guam and Tinian. The Japanese on Guam mounted stiff opposition to American air power. Cdr. Clark remembers one mission over Guam in early July:

"We were out to get final landing coverage photographs for the invasion. There was terrific AA at 10,000 feet, and even as rugged as a Liberator is, we took an awful pounding. We made four runs, straight and level, over the assigned spot and got away with it."

Another VD-4 Liberator flown by Lt. Thomas N. Hatfield had to fly through the same flak conditions five times after his cameras were rendered inoperative during one run.[3]

The Blue Raiders Arrive

Back on Eniwetok, the Blue Raiders of VB-116, under the command of Donald Gumz, took over where 108 left off. The Blue Raiders was somewhat different in appearance than her sister squadrons. The nickname of the squadron reportedly came from the Japanese propagandist "Tokyo Rose," who used the term in describing the Liberator's color scheme. Their Liberators were a marked contrast to the weather-worn, olive drab bombers of 108 and 109. In contrast to their sisters, the planes of the Blue Raiders, as the name implies, sported brand new light-blue paint jobs along the upper portions of the fuselage, with a light gull gray on the underbelly. The color of pristine bombers, like her sister squadrons before her, would also begin to fade in the months to follow under the intense rays of the Pacific sun, and their skin would soon be embellished with irregular patches covering bullet and flak holes.

The new arrivals ran into a series of operational accidents after their commissioning. Indeed, the Blue Raiders lost more men and planes through operational mishaps than some squadrons had experienced during several months of combat. During February 1944, they lost one man after a spinning propeller hit him while guiding his Liberator one night at Camp Kearney. In May, Lt. Robert Duggan and his crew took off from Camp Kearney for Hawaii. An hour later he lost an engine and headed back to base. His Liberator crashed and burned while attempting an emergency landing, killing all seven on board. In June, their training in Hawaii was blemished by the loss of a plane when Lt. William Miller ditched his Liberator two miles off Maui, Hawaii. No one was killed, but the entire crew was severely injured. Operational mishaps would continue to plague the squadron throughout the remainder of the war.

Miller's Liberator was not the only heavy bomber the Navy lost in Hawaii. Eyewitnesses saw Lt. Charles J. Kovaleski's plane (32005) come out of heavy clouds on its back from 2,500 feet and crash with such force that the largest piece measured only four by ten feet. There were few identifiable remains of the unfortunate crew. Fighting a war is costly, and it does not matter to loved ones how their son, husband, or father died—the result is the same.

While accident investigators were busy trying to sort out the cause of Lt. Kovaleski's crash, preparations on Saipan were being made to conduct a very special raid on a Japanese-held island. On 14 July 1944, Iwo Jima would be raided for the first time by land-based aircraft—bombers of VB-109.

18

The Reluctant Raiders' Parting Shots
July–August 1944

Taking off from Isley Field in the late afternoon of 14 July, Cdr. Miller's *Thunder Mug* and Lt. Jobe's *Consolidated's Mistake* headed north and passed to the west of the northern Marianas at an altitude of 1,000 feet. At a point fifty miles northeast of Iwo Jima, the final approach was made at twenty-five to fifty feet off the water and the PB4Ys pulled over the hills at the northeast end of Iwo Jima just after sunset.

Enemy radar apparently failed to pick up the low-flying planes and complete surprise was effected as they approached the four by two-mile square, pear-shaped island. No enemy aircraft were airborne as the Liberators came down the length of the airfields. When the island was reached the two planes were abreast about 800 feet apart, with Jobe on Miller's port. Fire was opened immediately by all machine guns of both planes and was answered just as quickly by enemy guns around Noto Jima and Furun Yama.

Anti-aircraft fire of all types was shortly encountered, and the barrage rapidly became more intense and withering than anything experienced in the Marshalls or Carolines. The low altitude of the planes and the surprise achieved carried them through the murderous blanket of fire with only slight damage to Miller's plane. Initial strafing targets for the PB4Ys were anti-aircraft gun positions on the hills and near the fields, but fire was rapidly shifted to airfield installations, barracks, and enemy planes. Operational aircraft sighted and strafed in revetments and on the taxiway consisted of thirty to forty Zekes, Bettys, and Tonys. One Betty was blown up, and another, along with two Zekes, was left burning by the combined gunfire of the machine guns. Numerous planes were damaged and probably destroyed. Parked in line and crowded in revetments, they presented excellent targets.

At 150 feet Miller came down the west side of both airstrips and turned to starboard over the taxiway and parking areas to head for a destroyer about a mile offshore, which added to the fierce tempo of the anti-aircraft fire. As Miller began his bombing run on the destroyer at 200 feet, his gunners set ablaze a medium-size freighter to port and a coastal vessel on the starboard side; the fires were still visible and raging when the planes left the area. Several coastal vessels lying off Hiraiwa Saki were heavily strafed and left smoking, and some gunfire on a destroyer escort to starboard was silenced. Miller's run was made from the starboard quarter to the port bow of the destroyer and four 500-pound bombs were dropped.

The first two bombs fell short, but the third struck the ship at the water line and the fourth hit directly on the fantail. The bomb detonations kicked the ship forty-five degrees to starboard and explosions followed, with debris flying through the air. With bombs away, Miller began to jink and turned to port to join up again with Jobe as persistent anti-aircraft fire from the damaged destroyer followed the plane's course.

As Miller was attacking the destroyer Jobe had cleared the initial hills of the island at fifty feet, passed down the eastern edge of the upper strip over the taxi and parking areas, and along the southern edge of the lower field. Barracks and buildings were strafed, starting several fires, and planes were damaged along the strips, taxiway, and in revetments, causing

"Pappy Pearson," the commanding officer of VB/VPB-102 in the Central Pacific. ***Courtesy of Navy Squadrons 102/14 Association***

View of the seaplane base at Chichi Jima taken by carrier-based planes on 8 July 1944. ***Courtesy of the National Archives***

a number of planes to burn briskly. Three planes in the revetments—apparently carrier based, with their wings folded and parked close alongside two other planes—took continuous hits from Jobe's gunners.

Turning northwest at the southern end of the lower field and passing a boat yard, Jobe began a run on a 2,000–4,000-ton freighter about a mile offshore. Close by, a dozen or more small coastal vessels were moored close inshore to starboard of the plane's track, as well as two small tankers to port. Both of the ships were set afire by heavy and repeated strafing, as were five of the coastal vessels, and all of the vessels in the group were left smoking, although no actual flames were visible.

Spotting a larger 6,000-ton freighter about a mile beyond his target ship, Jobe broke his run on the smaller merchant ship and headed for the large freighter. A large fire from his gunners' strafing had already broken aft of the freighter and a destroyer escort farther to port was strafed in passing. Jobe's plane crossed the large merchant ship from starboard quarter to port bow with concentrated fire of all guns scoring continuous hits.

An internal explosion rocked the ship almost immediately after the plane had passed over, followed by a large fire and several smaller explosions occurring at short intervals thereafter. Jobe turned south and joined up with Miller, and the two planes headed for Ninami Iwo Jima and Saipan. On Iwo Jima five large distinct fires were burning, and as the two planes left the island behind three large explosions from oil and ammunition dumps were observed in the vicinity of the airfields.

Successful night landings were made at Saipan shortly after midnight, concluding a highly successful sneak attack. It was obvious from the number of operational aircraft and the amount of shipping clustered offshore of Iwo Jima, together with the vicious curtain of protective anti-aircraft fire thrown up from the ships, that the enemy was determined to protect the island.[1]

VB-109 Targets the Bonin Islands and Iwo Jima

Cdr. Miller led another strike against the Bonin Islands four days later, this time leading Lt.Cdr. Janeshek's Crew 10 and Lt. Bill Bridgeman's Crew 6. The author's father, Robert W. Carey, was the starboard waist gunner in Bridgeman's plane and recalled the strike:

"The formation was an extended right echelon as the planes headed northwest at altitudes of 800 to 1000 feet. Approximately 125 miles southeast of Iwo Jima the aircraft descended to 200 feet. Fifty miles northwest of Chichi Jima, I heard a change in the pitch of the engines as the Liberator began to descend to a low-level fighting altitude. I knew we were nearing the target, and as in the past said a little prayer for our safety. As I headed to my starboard waist position I began yelling, 'Okay you sons of Nippon, here we come. Let's see what you can throw at us!' My yelling had a calming effect on me as my apprehension subsided. However, most of the crew just thought I was crazy.

"As we approached Chichi Jima, the aircraft descended to fifty feet to avoid radar detection before slipping through a channel between Ani Jima and Chichi Jima, and before climbing again to clear the hills on the southern end of the

Cdr. Norman "Buzz" Miller after the first land-based strike on Iwo Jima on 14 July 1944. ***Courtesy of Thomas Delahoussaye***

island. Cdr. Miller led the formation, with Lt. Jobe 400 feet away and slightly behind the commander's plane, while our plane took up the rear some 600 feet away.

"As we cleared the hills on the northern edge of the island by some seventy-five feet shooting erupted. Japanese machine gunners on a hill above the aircraft had seen us and began firing down at the intruding aircraft. Suddenly enemy gunners on the ground below us joined in and began firing. Within seconds thick anti-aircraft fire erupted all around our plane. Rounds from 12.7 mm anti-aircraft guns began straddling our plane, along with the sound of flak hitting the aircraft. Co-pilot Ens. Lamont began shouting instructions to the gunners over the interphone to return fire. Immediately every gun on board opened up as we tried to silence the guns trying to shoot us down. Up in the bow turret, George Murphy returned fire and immediately knocked out a big 90 mm gun emplacement. In a matter of seconds the rest of the gunners on board managed to silence a few more of the gun positions before the aircraft cleared the hills and headed toward the seaplane base at Omura.

Now flying at an altitude of 150 feet, we reached the seaplane base and saw at least two dozen seaplanes of varying models sitting tied to their moorings with Japanese personnel frantically trying to get them airborne. Below us were examples of the two-seat Sasebo float bi-plane called the "Pete," the Nakajima A6M2-N single seat fighter float planes called a "Rufe," a variant of the famous Japanese "Zeke" fighter with a fixed central float and two wing-mounted stabilizing floats, and the larger twin-engine "Emily" flying boat. Every machine gun on the three Liberators opened up in unison at the seaplanes as enemy anti-aircraft guns continued to fire back in vain. In front of us, a solitary Rufe managed to get into the air for a few seconds before Miller's gunners opened fire and the enemy plane crashed into the side of a hill.

When we came into range I picked out a Pete that came into view, aimed at the gas tanks, and squeezed the trigger of the machine gun. After only firing a few rounds the plane exploded, killing a couple ground personnel with it. I then swung the gun around and achieved similar results with two more aircraft. After damaging or destroying eleven aircraft in the water we began training our fire on ground installations and fuel storage areas, leaving several buildings burning in our wake. The three Liberators headed out over the harbor and bore down on anchored merchant shipping. Gunners took aim on small coastal vessels, opened fire, and within a few seconds seven of the ships were left sinking, while several others were left on fire. While strafing the ships, Japanese anti-aircraft fire intensified and was getting much too accurate, so Mr. Bridgeman decided to get the hell out of there. Heading southward, the three PB4Y-1s reached Susaki airfield, where the targets were so plentiful it was hard to decide which one to shoot at first.

"Looking down at the airfield, I saw several aircraft parked in revetments with their ground crews frantically trying to get them airborne. I picked out one airplane, began firing, and could see tracers hitting the engine compartment. I kept firing until it burst into flames, in the process killing the ground crew around it. After firing more than one hundred rounds at the plane I decided to try what had been taught to me at Aerial Gunnery School. Picking out a second plane, I started firing at the base of the wing near the cockpit, where the fuel tank is located. Firing around fifty rounds, my tracers found their mark and the aircraft disintegrated in a flash of flame and flying debris. In front of us (some 400 feet away) Lt. Jobe targeted a large wooden aircraft hangar, released a 1,000-pound bomb, and blew it up. The enemy gunners were still firing as the three planes hauled ass out of the harbor before the enemy guns could bring any of us down.

"The three planes passed Kukuro Misaki and set course for Haha Jima, some twenty miles south. At 200 miles per hour it was not long before the Liberators came roaring single file along the western edge of the island at 200 feet, headed toward the harbor. Their comrades must have alerted the enemy on Haha Jima, as thick anti-aircraft fire greeted us as we headed toward our objectives. Flying down the western edge of the island, the Liberators bore down on shipping at Okimura and Oki Misaki. While Cdr. Miller's and Lt. Jobe's gunners were busy pummeling approximately sixteen coastal vessels, Bridgeman spotted

Repairing damage to Lt. Jobe's plane after a strike on the Bonin Islands by VB-109. ***Courtesy of George Murphy***

a 4,000-ton cargo ship in the harbor and pointed our Liberator toward it as he began his bomb run from the starboard quarter toward the port bow.

The ship's gunners must have known they were the intended target because they began to fire wildly back at the plane that was rapidly approaching. Tracers from countless enemy machine guns came whizzing past and black puffs from anti-aircraft guns filled the sky around the plane. As we neared the ship, George in the bow turret and Bensing in the top turret began shooting at the freighter before Bridgeman released three 1,000 pound bombs. I could see the bombs wobble a bit as they started on their downward plunge.

"Everything seemed to go in slow motion as I looked down and saw Japanese sailors standing on the deck looking at our plane as it passed overhead. Because our plane was flying at only 200 feet I could clearly see their mouths wide open, staring in disbelief at what they were seeing. I didn't waste any ammunition on them, knowing they would be dead within seconds. Looking down, I smiled and waved at the individuals, and one of them hesitantly waved back as the bombs hit. While the first bomb fell short, the second and third bombs entered the water ten to twenty-five feet off the ship's stern.

We were taken by surprise when the bombs detonated on impact without waiting for the four-second-delay fuse. The ship, apparently carrying ammunition, disintegrated in an explosion of fire and smoke. I watched in awe as pieces of steel from the ship came sailing past my position, some hitting the plane. The whole world seemed to blow up as the force of the explosion hurled the aircraft up some 1,000 feet.

"Before I knew it *Climbaboard* then started down toward the water. Without a doubt in any of our minds this was going to be it. 'Jesus,' I yelled, as I braced myself against the bulkhead and waited for the impending impact that was sure to come. This was a normal human reaction, for I knew damn well when the plane hit the water all of us would be killed instantly. I was terrified as the plane came down, skimming across the ocean not more than a foot below the propellers. The propellers were kicking up so much water spray it seemed to be raining. I kept looking straight ahead, positive we were going to crash any second. Seconds seemed to drag by when it finally dawned on me that Bridgeman had gained control of the aircraft. I breathed a sigh of relief. The pilot leveled the PB4Y1 out and began to climb as if nothing unexpected or extraordinary had happened. Not wanting to press our luck any longer and having expended most of our ammunition, Mr. Bridgeman headed the plane toward Saipan.

"The entire engagement over both islands had lasted only twenty minutes. As the planes flew on, the chatter over the interphone discussing what everyone had seen and taking score subsided and soon the adrenaline and excitement faded away, leaving only the noise from the aircraft's engines as we headed home. The total from the raid on the two islands was two planes destroyed, eleven probably destroyed, and fourteen damaged. One cargo ship and seven coastal vessels were sunk. Countless enemy troops had been killed and numerous buildings were set on fire. The enemy had taken one hell of a beating from VB-109."[2]

Cdr. Miller called for an additional strike against the Bonins and Iwo Jima, with each plane to carry four 1,000 pound general purpose bombs. This mission would be timed so the aircraft would take-off shortly after mid-day and arrive at Chichi Jima at dusk. Then, as with the previous mission, they would hit Haha Jima. After attacking Haha Jima, the planes would finish by hitting Iwo Jima. The crews by now had learned the islands were heavily fortified with anti-aircraft batteries manned by expert Japanese gunners. On this mission Robert Carey was ordered to man the tail gun of *Climbaboard.* The mission would have the same formation as the previous one, with Crew 6 as "tail end Charlie." He recalled:

"This mission would be the first time manning the tail turret in a combat situation. Whether this was Bridgeman or Miller's decision, I never found out. The only thing for sure was that I was to be the last man in the parade and the last one off the playing field.

"The four PB4Y-1 Liberators flew in a staggered formation, with a separation of 200 feet between the aircraft at an altitude of 2,000 feet. As each hour passed the aircraft dropped closer to the water until they were not more than ten feet above the ocean to avoid enemy radar.

"I headed toward my position and started yelling, 'Okay you mothers, we're here. We're going to kill your asses or you're going to kill ours, so let's have at it.' I knew damn well none of the enemy could hear me, but maybe one of them could read my mind.

"Through the pass the four aircraft flew, just like before, and the first Japanese to spot us was a machine gunner on top of a hill right in front of me and at about the same height as our plane. The enemy gunner started firing. His tracers seemed to have me right between the eyes, but they passed by me about a foot and a half over my head.

"I had to do something fast or else that guy was going to ruin my day before it even began. The biggest fear about being in the tail turret was about to happen. A direct hit on the seven laminations of glass on the turret would shatter it. I feared a face full of glass splinters that would disfigure me, or the loss of both eyes and the pain involved. All the enemy gunner would have to do was lower his barrel down a hair.

"I looked through the gun sight and gave a short burst from the twin fifties. The tracers from my guns faded a little to my right. I eased the turret a little to the left and gave a long burst. The rounds hit right on target and the enemy gunner quit firing.

"Meanwhile, an enemy 40 mm anti-aircraft gun had zeroed in on Jobe's plane. Louis Paulukonis, in the bow turret, took a direct hit, and a big section of the turret was blown away. Jobe was sure his gunner had been killed. Another shell hit the number three engine, then another hit the wing and landing gear, and another one hit near the belly turret. Jobe had several injured men on board and was flying a severely damaged aircraft.

"None of us in the other three planes knew how badly off Jobe's plane was as we headed toward Haha Jima. The battle over Susaki Airfield had taken only some fifteen to twenty seconds. Jobe's plane was just ahead of us, while somewhere along the trip Janeshek had fallen behind. It was pitch dark as the four planes arrived over Haha Jima. The AA was thick and accurate as we swept over the shore, bombing and strafing coastal vessels in the harbor.

"Suddenly Jobe's plane was hit again as a shell tore through the flap on the starboard wing and *Consolidated's Mistake* dropped out of formation. Jobe's voice came over the interphone, apologized to Miller for dropping out of formation, and said he was unable to continue to Iwo Jima. He jettisoned his

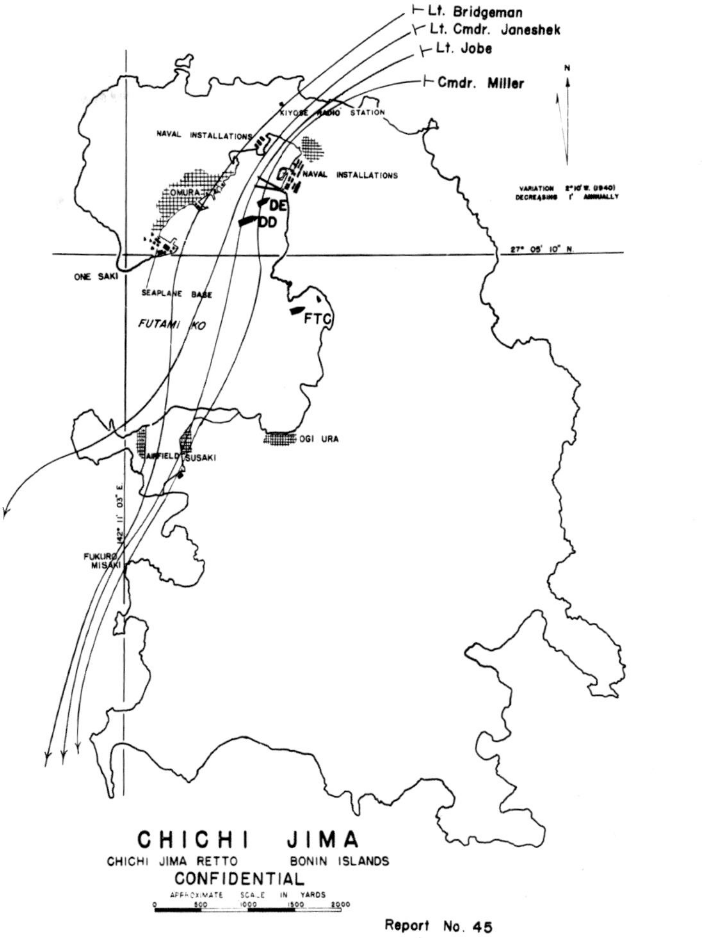

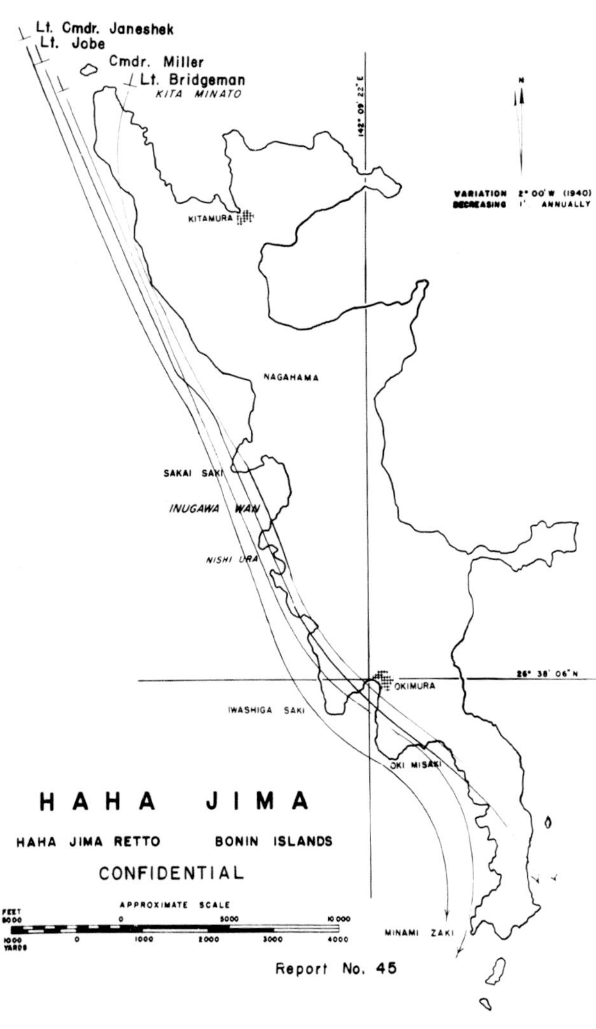

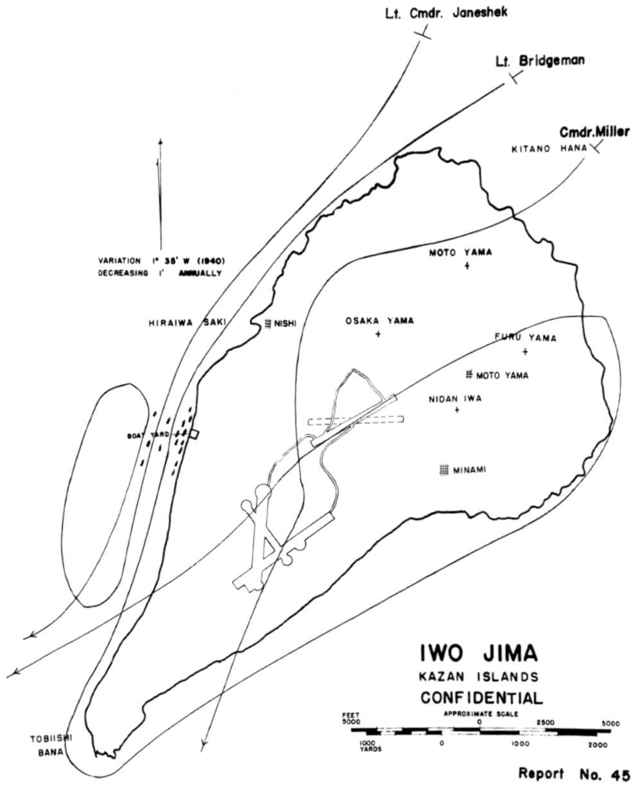

Flight tracks taken by VB-109 Liberators piloted by Cdr. Norman "Bus" Miller, Lt.Cdr. William Janeshek, and Lt. Bill Bridgeman during the attacks on Chichi Jima and Iwo Jima on 18 July 1944.
Courtesy of the National Archives

The author's father served with VB-109 and is shown at the port waist gun position. He joined the naval reserve at sixteen and became a combat veteran by the age of seventeen. ***Author's Collection***

shattered belly turret, climbed slowly to 8,500 feet, and headed the plane toward Saipan. The crews of the remaining three aircraft wished him the best of luck and prayed he would make it back the 700 miles to Saipan in his crippled plane.

"Miller, with the remaining two planes, set course for Iwo Jima. On the way to the target, the three Liberators ran into a band of thunderstorms and became separated. Each plane was on its own and continued to the target. Cdr. Miller reached Iwo Jima about ten minutes before we did, while Janeshek was still somewhere behind. We were unaware that Miller had already attacked the island and had worked it over pretty good, leaving the Japanese in an ugly humor.

"It was pretty dark and quiet when *Climbaboard* came cruising into the harbor. Matter of fact, it was too damn quiet. Looking down and to the right of the turret, I saw an enemy destroyer. The ship did not fire and neither did anyone on board the aircraft. I grabbed my mike and called the pilot. 'Mr. Bridgeman. We just flew over a destroyer. I could have damn near touched it.'

"'I know. I saw it too late to drop the bombs. I'm going to turn around and come back and get it.'

"As Bridgeman turned the plane around and headed back for the destroyer I double checked the gun sight, making sure I could see through it. Due to the darkness I turned the light down low in the sight to the point where the little dot in the center bearing the 35 mil ring and the larger 70 mil ring was barely visible. Doing this, I could still aim and not be blinded by the light inside the sight. Now satisfied, I took the controls of the turret in my hands and waited for the ship to come into view.

"Every gun on the destroyer was going to break loose when the bombs hit the water and until the four-second delay clicked off. It was going to be the job of the gunners in the aircraft to stop as many of those guns as possible.

"McDonald in the belly turret shouted, 'I see it, I see it. It's to the starboard, to the starboard.'

"Bridgeman turned the plane a little to the right. Seconds dragged by, and I began to wonder where in the hell that ship was. We should have been over it by now. Then Bridgeman shouted, 'Good God! We're over the island. Don't anybody shoot!'

Being over the island with all of those Japanese alerted and highly pissed off was not an ideal situation to be in. *Climbaboard* flew over an enemy gun position and they could clearly see the flames coming out of the exhaust from the engines under the wings. This made a beacon for them and instantly three machine guns opened fire on the plane, right on target.

"Rounds began hitting near the waist position and port wing. Within seconds we would surely be shot down. Orders or no orders, I made my mind up that I wasn't going to die without putting up a fight. I knew I would have to be quick and accurate; there was not going to be a second chance. I took aim and pressed the trigger of the twin .50-caliber guns. The tracers arched as they went down and within seconds the three enemy gun positions were silenced. No sooner had I released the trigger than three more machine guns to my left opened up and rounds began hitting the plane near the right waist position and wing. I turned the turret in their direction, took aim, and fired. Again, the tracers arched toward the ground and the machine guns quit firing. When the first three machine guns opened up every gun with varying calibers began firing toward the sky, but most of them were shooting wildly. Never in my life had I seen so many guns firing at one airplane.

"Coming over an airfield, Bridgeman released the 1,000-pound bombs over the runway, hoping the explosions would distract the enemy a little as we headed back over the harbor. As the plane headed out over the harbor numerous anchored ships began unleashing a barrage of defensive fire at the fleeing airplane.

"I sat back in the turret and was awed by the display of fireworks. I had seen many Fourth of July celebrations, but they were nothing compared to the fireworks display going

The bow turret of Lt. Joe Jobe's plane after receiving a direct hit from a Japanese 40 mm anti-aircraft shell while attacking Haha Jima, in the Bonin Islands. Gunner Louis Paulukonis would have been killed, but armor plating stopped fragments from penetrating the turret. ***Courtesy of George Murphy***

on over Iwo Jima, with red, green, and orange tracers arching across the sky as the plane cruised passed the ships and headed toward safety.

"Once *Climbaboard* was back over open water Bridgeman's voice came over the interphone, 'Who in the hell was doing that shooting back there?'

"I thought to myself, 'Oh shit, here I go back in the doghouse again.' Bridgeman sounded like he was mad as hell, and when he found out who did the shooting he would really be pissed off.

"Before I could confess my crime the voice of plane captain Ed Watts came on the interphone: 'Captain, this is Watts. Carey did the shooting, but he didn't have any choice. Those Japanese machine gunners had us zeroed in and if he hadn't killed them we wouldn't be here now.'

Bridgeman replied, 'Oh okay, good shooting.'"[3]

All four aircraft returned to Saipan, with Lt. Jobe's plane coming in last with two wounded men. VB-109 aircrews experienced highly accurate anti-aircraft fire from the Japanese on Iwo Jima and the Bonin Islands. They survived the ordeal, but another crew would not live to tell their story of attacking the Bonin Islands.

The Reluctant Raiders and Blue Raiders Hit Truk

By the end of July, Allied air activity in the Central Pacific was largely confined to mopping up operations in the Marianas, nuisance raids on the Bonins, and regular neutralizing blows at Truk. Cdr. Miller decided to take VB-116's commander on a farewell visit to Truk on a mistaken report of enemy naval vessels present. The two Liberators took off from Stickell Field and reached their objective as they covered the lagoon at fifty to 200 feet for thirty minutes. Entering the lagoon, the only shipping present were three small craft in the Dublon-Eten area of Truk and these were damaged by strafing.

After completing the bomb run, the planes were intercepted by an Oscar and four Zekes southwest of Uligar Pass. For the next thirty minutes, the Oscar and one of the Zekes pursued the bombers and periodically closed for an attack. On the last run made by the Oscar Lawrence B. Johnson, Miller's top turret gunner, and Henry F. Saligar (AOM1c), Gumz's top turret gunner, scored hits on the fighter's belly. While the two top turret gunners were busy fighting off the Oscar the Zeke made a frontal assault on the bombers, but took hits to its fuselage from Bernard R. Jaskiewicz, Miller's bow turret gunner. Making another run on the Liberators, the fighter took additional hits from Gilbert E. Downing, Gumz's tail turret gunner, and Robert Gariel, Miller's tail turret gunner. The fighters broke off their attack and the two Liberators proceeded to Ponape.

Reaching their next objective, each Liberator dropped two 1,000-pound bombs on a military headquarters building and radio station at Ponape Town and installations on Langar Island. During the run Miller's plane took accurate medium and heavy anti-aircraft fire, knocking out the hydraulic system, radio antenna, and interphone. With all bombs dropped and seeing that his plane had been damaged, Miller and Gumz left Ponape and headed back to base. Landing at Eniwetok, Miller found the brakes would not work and the plane ran off the end of the runway and into the water, smashing the nose gear and tearing off the bow turret. *Thunder Mug* was a complete loss; it was towed by a bulldozer and dumped in the boneyard.

On 29 July, Lt. Seabrook re-established VB-109's advanced echelon on Saipan, followed a day later by executive officer Lt.Cdr. Hicks, by basing temporarily at the newly completed East Field. They were joined on 1 August by Lt.Cdr. Bundy and on the third by Lt. Kasperson's Crew 13. East Field provided a 5,000-foot runway, and operations were easier, despite a difficult approach over a mountain. Officers and men were still quartered in muddy tents in the cane field, but the food was good, and a floored Japanese hen house served as squadron office and provided some additional protection from the frequent rain showers.

An order was issued that Iwo Jima and Chichi Jima be struck the evening of the fifth by Liberators of the 7th Army Air Force upon its arrival at Saipan. The night strike would follow two days of carrier strikes scheduled for the fourth and fifth in an effort to impede the enemy's ability to repair damaged air facilities and bring in new planes. However, when it became apparent the 7th AAF would not be operating from Saipan until after 4 August, the Navy Liberators of VB-109 based on Saipan assumed the mission. On the evening of the fourth four PB4Ys of VB-109 took off singly from East Field, Saipan, in adverse weather conditions to heckle Iwo Jima and Chichi Jima. The plan called for Lt.Cdrs. Hicks and Bundy to strike Iwo Jima, while Seabrook and Kasperson were to hit Chichi Jima.

Cdr. Hicks took off for Iwo Jima and flew west of the Northern Marianas to a point eighty miles Northeast of Iwo Jima. Approaching the island altitude was reduced from 1,500 to 500 feet, but the

Cdr. Donald Gumz (back row, center) was the skipper for VB/VPB-116. The squadron's tri-color aircraft were noticeably different than the standard AAF Olive drab/gull grey. *Courtesy of John H. Parker Jr.*

target was completely obscured. Rain squalls were numerous in the area, and the island was covered by thick cumulus clouds from the ground up to 20,000 feet. With almost zero visibility Hicks could not distinguish the island on the initial pass and six successive sweeps were made at 150 feet before the shoreline was dimly glimpsed. Climbing to 6,000 feet, Hicks made a bombing run from the northeast to the southwest and dropped twenty-three 100-pound bombs blindly over the center of the island. Continuing his passes at varying altitudes and from various directions, Hicks dropped ten bombs from 1,000 feet in the center of the island between the two airfields with the island faintly visible through a temporary break in the clouds. No anti-aircraft fire was received and Hicks left the area and returned to base.

Bundy took off for Iwo Jima an hour after Hicks and reached the target before Hicks. Iwo Jima was hidden in a rain squall on his initial approach and he returned to orbit Minami Iwo Jima at 300 feet until the squall had passed. Flying back to Iwo Jima, approaches were made from 500 to 2,000 feet without sighting the target.

A radar approach was made from the northwest at fifty to 100 feet and the island was crossed just north of the upper strip, the plane passing south of Osaka Yama and Moto Yama town. Thirty bombs were dropped in train from fifty feet, the first bomb being released just after the beach was crossed. No enemy fire was received until the bombs began to explode. The plane's gunners returned the awakening enemy fire, training on the revealed gun positions, but the encounter was brief due to the plane's speed.

Only moderate medium and light AA was received, but the blind protective fire of the enemy's 40 mm guns scored hits on the plane's port vertical stabilizer and the accessory section of the number two engine was struck by a round that exploded inside, severing oil lines. A 20 mm round went through the skin next to the feed box at the port waist hatch, exploding inside and starting a fire due to oxygen bottles and ruptured ammunition. Bundy climbed to 1,300 feet, feathering number two engine, lightened the plane, and returned on three engines, landing at Isley Filed ten hours later.

Lt. Seabrook took off thirty minutes after Cdr. Hicks for Chichi Jima, flying an almost direct course. The weather became increasingly poor as the plane neared the target and Chichi Jima was hidden in a rain squall on the initial approach. Turning south to Haha Jima to check his position, Seabrook flew down Haha Jima, dropping twelve bombs from 7,000 feet. Returning to the east of Chichi Jima, Seabrook approached from the northeast at 9,000 feet over Omura town and Susaki airstrip. Half the island was covered by heavy clouds, but the shoreline and a small fire on a hill north of Omura were visible. Returning from the southwest at 6,000 feet, Seabrook dropped a salvo of sixteen bombs on Omura town. No further bombs were dropped, but Seabrook continued to cross the island at varying altitudes and circled the area for an hour without any anti-aircraft fire being received.

Lt. Kasperson was the first to depart the airfield, flying PB4Y-1 *The Strip Tease* (Navy Bureau number 32263). Hicks departed twenty minutes later and passed close to Kasperson about halfway to the target. Kasperson's gunners were then test firing their guns and Hicks, thinking it was an enemy plane, began a run on them, breaking it when friendly identity was established. It was the last time anyone saw Kasperson's plane again.

An hour past his expected arrival at East Field and when radio communication had not been established with the plane, Task Force 59 organized a very comprehensive search. Within two hours a Dumbo plane of VH-1 was flying Kasperson's assumed course, two regular PBM search planes had been diverted in their regular sweep to the northwest of Saipan, Carrier Task Group 58 had been informed and their planes requested to keep lookout, and ComSubPac had been notified to advise the lifeguard submarines. The destroyer USS *Prichett* was alerted and began to zig-zag on a northerly course from Saipan.

On the sixth Hicks and Seabrook searched north and west of Chichi Jima and Iwo Jima while the two special Dumbos and the USS *Prichett* continued the search between Saipan and the Kazan Islands. The following day special searches of the Dumbo planes and the destroyer were reluctantly canceled while regular PBM searches carried on. On the eighth, a final effort was made by Cdr. Gumz and Lt. Cervone of VB-116, who searched a triangular area west of Chichi and Iwo Jima without success. The disappearance of Crew Thirteen would remain a mystery for their brethren for the next sixty years, but not for military investigators who solved the case in 1946.

Streams of phosphorous come close to a PB4Y-1 Liberator during a photographic reconnaissance and bombing mission against Truk conducted by VD-4, VB-109, and VB-116 on 6 August 1944. ***Courtesy of the National Archives***

19

The Fate of Crew Thirteen

The disappearance of VB-109's Crew Thirteen remained a mystery for the United States Navy until 1946, when a military investigation of possible war crimes by the Japanese military personnel stationed on Chichi Jima was conducted by Marine Corps investigators. Their story involves destiny and fate, where circumstance transferred some men out of the crew, while those who replaced them gave the ultimate sacrifice.

The original Crew 13 of VB-109 before departing from NAS North Island to Hawaii in late 1943. Top row (L to R): AMM3c G. L. Perkins; Ens. Norman L. Burton; Lt. J. L. Grayson; Ens. H. Bigham; and ARM3c Hugo L. Kluge. Bottom row (L to R): AMM3c Richard H. Westmoreland; AOM2c Victor B. Jones; S1c Allen K. Stinger; ARM 3c Richard D. Frye; and AOM3c William F. Schneider. Front: Mascot named "Skipper." Missing is Bobby W. Fickling, AOM3c, who apparently joined the squadron sometime between December 1943 and February 1944. Westmorland became a member of Crew 15. By June 1944, the remaining crew members were Kluge, Jones, Stinger, Frye, and Schneider. *Author's Collection*

The First Crew: August 1943–March 1944

Most of the original crew formed at NAS North Island in Summer 1943. The original crew consisted of pilot Lt. J. L. Grayson, co-pilot Ens. Norman L. Burton, and navigator Ens. H. Bigham. The enlisted crewmen were ARM3/c Hugo L. Kluge; Seaman First Class (S1/c) Allen K. Stinger, later promoted to Aviation Ordnance Mate Third Class (AOM3/c); ARM3/c Richard D. Frye; AOM3/c Victor Jones; AOM3/c William F. "Bill" Schneider; AMM3c G. L. Perkins; and AMM3/c R. H. Westmorland. Shortly after arriving at Kaneohe, Hawaii, Aviation Machinist Mate First Class (AMM1/c) Joseph W. Komorowski joined the crew, replacing G. L. Perkins as the plane captain (the equivalent of a flight engineer in the Army Air Force).

Kasperson's Crew Thirteen

Replacements of the original crew began with Ens. Warren A. Hindenlang replacing Ens. Bigham as navigator when the latter was detached on 12 March 1944. Five days later Lt. Elmer Kasperson replaced Grayson as Crew Thirteen's patrol plane commander after the latter was evacuated for unknown reasons. Hindenlang became co-pilot after Ens. Burton was detached on 29 May. Ens. Keith E. Ellis became the navigator upon Hindenlang's promotion to co-pilot. By August 1944, five members of the original enlisted crew remained—Kluge, Jones, Stinger, Frye, and Schneider—as Perkins and Westmorland were replaced by AMM2c Warren B. Simon and AOM3c Bobby W. Fickling.

The crew represented the typical American combat aircrew of the time: white and Judeo-Christian. They were Catholics, Protestants, and Jews. Their homes stretched across the US, from New York City to California and regions in between. Biographical details of some of the men are incomplete, but a general sketch of their short lives was put together by genealogical and military service documents.

Lt. Elmer Harold Kasperson hailed from Arlington, South Dakota, a town of 1,200 people in the mid-eastern section of

From a newspaper clipping showing Lt. Kasperson and the second Crew 13 after becoming the first four-engine bomber to land on Saipan. Standing (L to R): Warren B. Simon, AMM2C, mech., air gunner; Joseph W. Komorowski, AMM1C, plane captain, air gunner; Ens. Warren A. Hindenlang, co-pilot; Lt. Elmer H. Kasperson, pilot; Ens. Keith E. Ellis, navigator; and Hugo L. Kluge, ARM2C, radioman, air gunner. Kneeling (L to R): William F. Schneider, AOM2C, ordnanceman, air gunner; Victor B. Jones, AOM2C, ordnanceman, air gunner; Allen K. Stinger, AOM3C, ordnanceman, air gunner; Richard D. Frye, ARM2C, radioman, air gunner; and Bobby W. Fickling, AOM3C, ordnanceman, air gunner.

Enlisted members of Crew 13 before a flight to Saipan to become the first four-engine bomber to land on Aslito airstrip (28 June 1944). Kneeling: Hugo L. Kluge. Standing (L to R): Joseph W. Komoroski, Warren B. Simon, Richard D. Frye, Victor B. Jones, and William F. Schneider. Missing are Fickling and Stinger. *US Navy Photo via Jack Authelet*

the state. Thirty years old at the time of his death, he was a few years older than most patrol plane commanders. He was blond-haired with blue eyes, of medium build, and stood five feet nine inches—about average height for that time. Kasperson enlisted in the Navy at seventeen, serving as a radioman in the Far East. The Navy must have recognized him as a bright young man with a future in the service, as he was selected for flight training at NAS Pensacola, graduating on 8 May 1942 and commissioned as an ensign and naval aviator. He was assigned to duty with a PBY Catalina squadron in the Aleutian Islands. Afterward, he became a patrol plane commander for the PB4Y-1 and waited for assignment to a squadron, which came in March 1944.

Twenty-three-year-old co-pilot Ens. Warren A. "Hindy" Hindenlang, born in Foxboro, Massachusetts, was the only child of Florence and Arthur. His father, a machinist for the Foxboro Company, died in 1938, leaving his wife the task of raising their son and finding the means to send him to college. A scholarship and job waiting tables in the Yale University cafeteria allowed him to graduate in 1942 with a bachelor of science degree in industrial engineering. Former high school classmate Eunice Hoffman recalled him as, "Very smart, popular, and the pride and joy of his parents."[1]

Hindenlang briefly worked for the Proctor and Gamble Company, during which time he became engaged to Barbara Woodland. The day of his twenty-second birthday he enlisted in the Navy as an aviation cadet. In the September 1943 issue of *VTY* (Very Truly Yours) *Newsletter* issued by the War Services Committee he wrote an article on his childhood goal of becoming a pilot: "Ever since I was a little tot toddling around in grade school, I always thought it would be wonderful to come to Pensacola as a cadet and emerge with a pair of wings, a swell tan, and a girl resembling Heddy Lamar (sigh)."[2]

He graduated from flight training in September 1943, and thereafter navigational training in San Diego, finally joining VB-109 on 20 February 1944 as a replacement navigator in Kasperson's crew. Research failed to reveal his personal characteristics, but photographs revealed him to be a handsome young man with brown hair.

Bobby Wilton Fickling was a nineteen-year-old air gunner and the youngest member of the crew. According to his brother Tommy, he was born and raised on a farm near Portales, twenty miles from Clovis, New Mexico. As a high school student he begged his mom and dad to enlist because many of his friends were joining. His parents relented and Bobby enlisted on his seventeenth birthday on 17 November 1942. His first duty assignment was a gunner aboard a dive bomber, which it turned out was unsuited for him, as he vomited during each flight. Afterward he was transferred to VB-109 and became a part of Grayson's crew. He was wounded during an attack against Wotje on 15 February 1944.

According to Bobby's brother, Tommy Fickling, who was thirteen at the time, his mother had a complete nervous breakdown after receiving news that her eldest son was missing in action. She never recovered from the loss and became isolated, depressed, and lost in her own thoughts. She apparently destroyed any letters sent home by Bobby.[3]

Bow turret gunner William Ferguson Schneider was born in San Jose, California, but was raised on a farm in Fallon, Nevada, with his two sisters and parents Leo and Mary Schneider. His father came to Nevada from Chicago, bought a farm, and met and married Mary Ferguson, a teacher in the town. Like most farming families in the late 1920s and 1930s, they had food to eat but little money to spend on anything but basic needs. Completing high school in December 1941, he continued working on the farm until enlisting the following September at the age of twenty. Standing six feet tall with brown hair and brown eyes, he was apparently the tallest crew member.[4]

Port waist gunner Joseph W. Komorowski came from Chicago and was the eldest of two sons of Joseph and Harriet. He enlisted on 13 January 1942, and was the highest ranking enlisted man of Crew Thirteen, serving as the plane captain at age twenty-one. In a letter to his parents dated 27 February 1944, he writes about life on Apamama and makes general statements about flying missions, such as, "On one of our missions we sank a ship and I know a lot of them will never see the land of the rising sun." He ended the letter by writing, "I have hopes of getting back to the good old US for a few days sometime in August or September."[5]

Joseph W. Komorowski at the starboard waist gun position at an unknown location. Under the window is painted, "Chopper Boys" and "Ski & Clem." Ski has to be Komorowski's nickname; however, Victor Jones, in a letter to his mother, states he is the starboard waist gunner, and in none of the letters provided to the author does he refer to himself as "Clem." The only other person in the squadron with the last name Clemons served with Crew 7. *Courtesy of the Komorowski Family Collection*

This overexposed image shows Crew 13 enlisted men before the arrival of Simon and Fickling. Top row (L to R): Jones, Komorowski, Frye, and Bill. Bottom row (L to R): Stinger, "Red," Hugo, and Clem. Perhaps Red refers to Westmorland. *Courtesy of the Komoroski Family Collection*

This copy of a photograph comes from Ens. Warren A. "Hindy" Hindenlang's service record. He was a newly commissioned officer and pilot when he joined VB-109. *Courtesy of the US Navy*

A cadre of officers from VB-109 standing next to PB4Y-1 Liberator *Sky Cow* at Saipan, July 1944. Front row (L to R): Ens. Warren Hindenlang, co-pilot; Lt. (jg) Charles Tischoff, co-pilot; and Lt. Thomas Steele, air combat intelligence. Second row (L to R): Lt. (jg) Robert Conkey, co-pilot; Lt. (jg) Ernest Anderson, co-pilot; Lt. (jg) John Dooley, copilot; and Lt. (jg) Thomas Pebbles, navigator. *Courtesy of US Navy Photo via Jack Authelet*

He makes no mention that two of his crew, Bobby Fickling and Hugo Kluge, were wounded on a mission less than two weeks before.

Twenty one-year-old starboard waist gunner Victor Boyd Jones, like Lt. Kasperson, came from South Dakota, but was raised in the town of Agar, with a population of 140 according to the 1940 census. He was five feet six inches tall with brown hair and brown eyes. Jones joined the Navy on 11 January 1942, training in aviation ordnance and air gunnery. Three letters sent to his mother between April and July 1944 reveal life as a young man sent far from

Joseph Komorowski (kneeling left) and other members of VB-109 possibly on Apemama. Standing: "Oscar" Oscar Jelke, Crew 16; "DuBenny" Donald DeBruine, Crew 16; and unknown. "Clem" Roger Clemons, Crew 6, is kneeling at right. ***Courtesy of the Komorowski Family Collection***

South Dakotan Victor Lloyd Jones was twenty-one years old at the time of his death and came from a town of less than 200 people. ***Courtesy of the Falkenhagen Family Collection***

home and yearning to return one day. He must have been a religious individual because of remarks he made in a letter to his mother from April 1944:

"I was going to church Easter Eve, but they didn't have services in the evening so I missed out. Sure wish I had went in the morning, now it's the first Easter services I've missed since I can remember and I sure do feel bad about it. I guess you got you a new outfit, didn't you. A fellow sure misses them things out here; wear the same kind of clothes all the time and never seeing the gay colors. But we will be back soon, then we can enjoy them much more."[6]

His letter dated 15 June 1944 was sent from Hawaii while the crew enjoyed a fourteen-day R&R. He discusses how he forgot what trees and shade were since most of the palm trees and other fauna at the squadron's base on Eniwetok had been blasted to bits before and during the atoll's capture. He wants to lie around and do nothing but catch up on sleep, getting a tan, and drinking beer. The letter's second part shows a proud young man discussing his crew's record and him receiving a medal:

"Don't believe I told you before that I was awarded the Air Medal June 4, was given to us for attacking a Jap convoy of five ships leaving two escorts burning and the cargo ship listing badly, and also for bombing and strafing a Jap held island and doing severe damage. We done that in just the month of January. You see, we haven't altogether just been lying around."[7]

The original Crew 13's PB4Y-1 Liberator was named *Pacific Vagabond*. Victor Jones lamented the aircraft was given to another flight crew. Below the window on the left are the words "Bingham's Wigwam," named after the navigator, which places this image before 12 March 1944, when he was detached from the crew. ***Courtesy of the Komoroski Family Collection***

The last part addresses a question by his mother if he has a nickname, followed by information about the crew's aircraft:

"Some of the boys call me Washday Jones . . .the rest of the crew said I was always washing clothes, so they put it under my gun in the plane. I'm starboard waist gunner so they painted it under the hatch."[8]

He laments that their plane *Pacific Vagabond* was taken from them and how they would receive a new one. That aircraft (bureau number 32140) was renamed *Climbaboard* and was manned by Crew Six, commanded by William "Bill" Bridgeman. The aircraft Kasperson's crew received is believed to be bureau number 32263, the plane in which they flew their last mission.

He writes in a letter dated 25 July 1944—twelve days before the fatal mission—about how hot the island is, of him playing softball, and the hope of returning home. His mother received the letter after her son was classified as missing in action:

"Well Mother, things look pretty possible of me being on my way home the latter part of next month; of course I'm not banking on it too strongly, but you no [sic] how it is, every little bit helps, so I should be home the latter part of September or first of October—any how I am sure hoping so. I am hoping to get a thirty day leave when I do make it back so keep the home fires burning and the beer on ice."[9]

Little is known at the time of this work's completion about five of the crew, beginning with Keith Edwin Ellis. He was raised in Langdon, North Dakota, graduated from Langdon High School in 1938, and was the eldest of three children and the only son of Lorren and Clare Ellis. He stood five feet ten inches tall, had brown hair and brown eyes, and was twenty-four at the time of his death.

Tail turret gunner Warren Besthoff Simon enlisted on 6 October 1942, was twenty-four years old, and five feet eight inches tall, with brown hair and brown eyes. His hometown is listed as Bronx, New York, and he was the son of Harold and Lillian Simon. He joined the crew on 13 June 1944.

Radioman and air gunner Richard Dewey Frye was born and raised in Washington, DC, and was the eldest of four children—two boys and two girls—of Timothy and Dorothy

Frye. He stood five feet ten inches with brown hair and blue eyes, and enlisted, as did Simon, on 6 October 1942.

Hugo L. Kluge, radioman and air gunner, grew up in St. Louis, Missouri, as the second son of four children of John and Christian. He joined the Navy on 22 July 1944, and was the shortest member of Kasperson's crew, standing a little over five feet four inches tall. He had a stocky body with thick brownish or strawberry blond hair and blue eyes.

Belly turret gunner Allen Kressler Stinger, born in Jersey City, New Jersey, was the foster son of Ethel and Daniel Kressler Stinger. He enlisted on 8 July 1942, stood five feet six inches, had brown hair and blue eyes, and was twenty-one at the time of his death.

Shot Down

Evidence collected and interpreted by military investigators after the war raises additional questions about an incident that was apparently solved seventy years ago. The official report still stands as the final testimony of Crew Thirteen's loss.

Kasperson's late arrival at Chichi Jima on 4 August doomed he and his crew, as the Japanese were still manning their anti-aircraft batteries due to earlier strikes by Lt.Cdr. Hicks and Lt. Seabrook. According to Japanese testimony the bomber was shot down over Futami Ko and crashed near the naval barracks wreckage on the shore and in the water. Two of the crewmen survived the crash: one uninjured, who swam to shore and sat down on a pier, and the other who suffered serious injuries and died a few hours later.

The Individual Deceased Personnel Files (IDPF) of each man were created by the Department of the Army after the war. One document found in each of the crew's IDPF summarizes the sequence of events and states that seven bodies were pulled from the wreck, placed in a wooden box, and buried at sea. A second report from the testimony of Jeffrey Gilley, a resident of Chichi Jima at the time, states the aircraft wreckage, along with the remaining bodies—eight according to his testimony—was towed out to sea by the ship *Miyo Jin Maru* and left to sink. Finally, a third testimonial by Frank Washington, another eyewitness, states that one or two days after the crash eight American bodies, bloated and burned, were brought ashore and laid face down. Approximately four days after the crash the bodies, now identified as numbering nine in the testimonial, were placed in a box, and along with the aircraft wreckage were towed out to sea by the ship previously identified by Mr. Gilley and dumped. Except for the conflicting manner in which the remains were disposed of by the Japanese, there is little doubt between seven and eight of the crew were buried at sea.

According to testimonies provided by civilian and Japanese military personnel who observed the prisoner, they could not figure out whether he was an officer or enlisted man, as his clothes were burned and scorched from the crash. Eyewitnesses described the man as about five feet four inches tall with a short, round face, curly red hair, and wearing a khaki uniform. Testimony by Jeffrey Gilley stated the man was rather short, wore a wristwatch, had reddish long hair, and wore fatigues. He is also identified as a radioman, an enlisted naval rating.[10]

Therefore, there appears to be conflicting information on whether the executed individual was an officer or an enlisted radioman. The two radiomen assigned to Kasperson's crew were Richard Frye and Hugo Kluge. Frye stood five feet ten inches tall and was killed in the crash, while Kluge's height was five feet, four and ¾ inches tall, and his remains are listed as unrecoverable.

Photographs of Kluge show an individual with thick, wavy hair and a somewhat round face. His physical characteristics are strikingly similar to those reported by the Japanese. Ens. Hindenlang, from examining photographs, appears to have been a tall, slender individual who stood some five feet ten inches tall with a narrow face and brown hair.[11]

The Execution

The lone survivor was interrogated by two Japanese naval officers; following that he was tied to a tree and left there while American surface forces shelled the area. He, along with ARM2c Lloyd Richard Woellhoff, who was captured the month before, were later taken from the island's 370th Battalion guardhouse, tied to wooden stakes, and executed by bayoneting and beheading.

The origination of the order to execute the two airmen came from Lt.Gen. Tachihama, who gave the order to his senior adjutant, Capt. Seiji Higashigi; the latter gave Lt.Col. Kikuji Ito the order to carry out the execution. Ito told Sgt. Masayoshi Takano of the 307th Independent Infantry Battalion, First Mixed Brigade to select two men. Those men were Superior Pvt. Matsutaro Kido and Leading Pvt. Hisao Shimsura. Ito also instructed Capt. Seiji Higashi to select two others, Cpl. Moriki Okamoto and an unidentified private. Ito stood trial on Guam and provided answers to questions about the execution during his testimony:

"The scene of the execution was in a clearing about fifty meters from the road leading over Makayama Pass. The execution took place on a slope that sloped down from the south toward the north, and it was held in a grassy grown clearing about twenty meters square. To the east of the clearing was the dugout, about one meter deep. In front of this dugout four stakes were driven into the ground. Each prisoner was made to sit down and was tied to two of the stakes. The distance between the positions was two or three meters. After the prisoners were tied I measured off a distance for the bayoneteers so with one thrust their bayonets could pierce the chest right to the back. About twenty meters to the south of the prisoners I arranged the spectators in double ranks. The number of men was about twenty. These men had come for rifle practice, however, I brought them to the scene and made them stand in double ranks.[12]

Okamoto testified that approximately four more men were selected at the site to participate, with five men facing each prisoner. Ito walked up to each prisoner and drew two circles on their shirts—one on the chest and one on the heart—instructing four of the executioners to make one bayonet thrust to the chest to wound and the last man a thrust to the heart to kill. Each group took their turns on the prisoner in front of them. Ito, upon the last thrust to the prisoner's heart, drew his sword and beheaded both prisoners.[13]

Postwar Investigation

Marine Corps Col. Presley Rexy arrived at Chichi Jima in October 1945 to begin repatriation to Japan of approximately 20,000 Japanese military personnel based on the island. One of the first questions he asked former Japanese commanding officer Maj. Yoshitaka Horie of the 109th Division Detached Headquarters, Imperial Japanese Army, was what happened to captured American flyers. Horie replied six naval aviators had been captured: two were transferred to Japan and the others were killed during an American bombardment. Rexy did not believe the major's story and thus began an investigation which led to reports of executed American airmen and cannibalism on the island.[14]

The investigation concluded the following about Crew 13:

"The morning following the crash, 5 August 1944, the bodies of two other unidentified men were removed from the plane wreckage. These two bodies, together with the body of the unidentified crewmember who died at the naval dispensary while receiving medical attention, were buried in the old botanical gardens in the vicinity of the naval base."

The first execution Rexy substantiated was the lone survivor of Kasperson's crew and Woellhof, which took place on or around 5 August 1944. Who was the unknown crew member executed? The mystery was apparently solved through Rexy's investigation in 1946, but remained relatively unknown except for the executed man's family, which received a letter from the Navy Department that same year detailing the circumstances of his death.

Over the years those details became lost until John Luke, a former school mate of Ens. Hindenlang, rediscovered the information upon examining individuals' IDPFs. Each of the crew's IDPF includes a document stating the circumstances of the crew's loss and the execution. One document recounts, "On 5 August 1944, the survivor who is determined to be Hindenlang was bayoneted and beheaded in the Kominato area on Chichi Jima."

Luke kept the story to himself for years until he read the book *Flyboys* by James Bradley in 2003, and recognized the unknown flyer referenced by the author in the book as his friend. Thereafter, Lt. Hindenlang's story appeared in several periodicals, including *USA Today*, which ran an article, "Unknown 'flyboy' gets his eulogy," on 22 January 2004. However, the aforementioned statement conflicts with information held in a report titled "G-2 Report on Plane and Graves on Chichi Jima" written by Col. Presley Rixey, Commander of the Occupation Forces and dated 30 January 1946, which states:

"On 16 and 17 January 1946, two graves were excavated in the Kominato area. In the northern grave one vertebra was found; in the southern grave pieces of rope and pieces of a wooden stake. These men were executed."

According to the G-2 report no other graves or remains were found on that specified date. Yet another statement in Hindenlang's IDPF claims his remains were exhumed on 16 January 1946 by the United States Occupational Forces and delivered to the United States Army on Iwo Jima. They were buried in grave number 2225 as unknown individual X-81.

A week after the co-pilot's remains were reportedly excavated three sets of nearly complete skeletal remains were found buried together in the old botanical gardens on 26 January 1946. Two sets of remains were laid side-by-side, while the third was placed at the feet of the others. The report provides specific information about the remains:

Set 1: broken ribs and smashed skull
Set 2: several small holes in skull, broken leg, broken collar bone, four to five broken ribs.
Set 3: a punctured shoulder blade.

The grave also contained individual life preservers, a belt, two buckles, a corroded insignia bar, buttons, thirty-six cents in change, a finger nail file, two combs (one containing dark brown

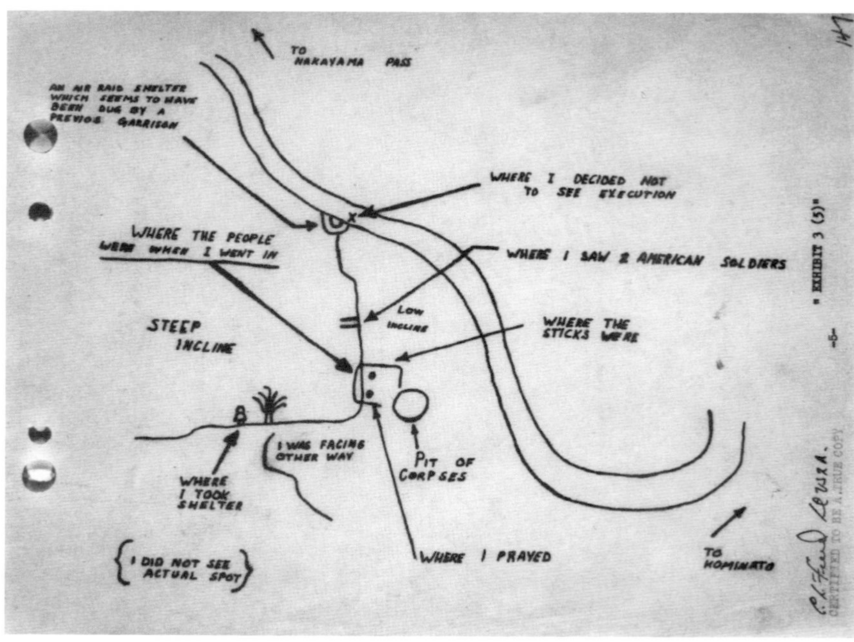

This is a copy of an illustration from an American interpreter based on an original from a Japanese soldier during the postwar investigation. It marks his location in relation to the execution of ARM2c Lloyd Richard Woellhoff and an unknown airman (Hindenlang?).

or black hair), shoes (sizes 9E, 8E, and approximately 8.5), and a corroded insignia bar of either a US Army first lieutenant or second lieutenant, or a US Navy ensign or lieutenant (jg). Ens. Keith Ellis and Hindenlang were the only two officers aboard Kasperson's plane that would have worn a single officer's bar.

Two of the three sets found in the garden were tagged X-79 and X-80, but what was the tag for the third? The remains were transported to Iwo Jima and buried at the Fourth Marine Division Cemetery in graves 2223 and 2224. Those were then reinterred three years later at Manilla. What grave marker was to the third set found in the common grave? If the sets were tagged numerically, it would lead to the possible conclusion the missing identifier is X-81 (2225).

One interesting aspect is that the remains, along with an ID bracelet of Lt. (jg) John Cavanaugh, another naval aviator whose Curtiss SB2c Helldiver was shot down on 6 August 1944, were found on 8 January 1946 and buried in grave 2226 (X-82) on Iwo Jima. The recovery of Cavanaugh's remains indicates the sequential and chronological recovery of four sets of remains consisting of 2223, 2224, 2225, and 2226.

A document from Headquarters American Graves Service PHILCOM ZONE dated 30 September states that Hindenlang's (X-81) remains were recovered together with two other sets of remains that were recommended as those of Richard Frye and Warren Simon. Hindenlang was identified through dental records, along with a size 8½ shoe, according to a document in his IDPF dated 3 January 1947. A shoe of approximately the same size was found in the grave in the botanical garden. The same document states, through dental records and a size 9E shoe, the remains of X-80 (2224) were those of Richard D. Frye. It was also reported: "The dental record of the remains now buried as Unknown X-79 (2223) is similar to the dental record of Warren B. Simon, but positive identification cannot be made due to a number of discrepancies." The determination that X-79 was Simon was later reversed in 1950.

Executions and Cannibalism

Frye's grave on Iwo Jima was between Hindenlang (X-81) to the left and unknown (X79) on the right. Cavanaugh was buried to the left of Hindenlang. Therefore, it appears that X-79, X-80, and X-81 were buried together in the same grave in the botanical garden, and their remains were found relatively intact and not cremated, as was the case of several other American flyers executed on Chichi Jima afterward.

ARM3c James Wesley Dye was shot down on 17 February 1945 and beheaded seven days later. Afterward, his liver was removed, along with flesh from the thighs, and consumed by several Japanese officers. His remains, consisting of several bones and a quantity of brown hair, were found in a grave near Yoake Radio Station. His crewmate, AOM3c Grady Alvah York, was executed on 28 February by bamboo spears and beheading while tied to a telephone pole. Two other men captured the same day as York fared no better.

Ens. Floyd Ewing Hall and his radioman, ARM3c Marvie William Mershon, were captured the same day as York when their plane was shot down. Mershon was executed first on 22 February by beheading and was buried at the Daikonzaki Army Cemetery above Omura. A day later his body was exhumed and the liver and a large portion of flesh from the thigh were removed and later eaten. Mershom was then reburied. Hall was executed on 9 March by bayonet and sword, and portions of flesh from Hall's thighs were cut off and later eaten. His body was then pushed into a bomb crater and buried approximately 300 yards from the 308th Battalion Headquarters near the Yoake Radio Station. AOM2c Glenn J. Frazier was beaten to death on or around 23 February 1945, and was also buried near battalion headquarters. The last known execution was that of 2nd Lt. Warren Earl Vaughn, USMCR, captured on 23 February 1945 and executed on 22 March by beheading. Parts of his flesh and liver were later consumed by Japanese officers.[15]

Destroying Evidence

Shigeo Ikawa, former captain in the Imperial Japanese Army, stated to Rexy that upon cessation of hostilities, Maj. Yoshitaka Horie gave him instructions to exhume, cremate, and rebury the remains in the Kominato area. Four sets of near complete remains were unearthed and cremated, taking five days to complete. The ashes were placed in an urn and reburied in the cemetery.[16]

On 13 January 1946, two shell holes containing graves were excavated near the former battalion headquarters. They unearthed in one a mechanical pencil with Frazier's name on it, along with three bones. The second grave, apparently Hall's, contained a few charred bones; the latter's was boxed up and sent to Iwo Jima and buried as number 2228 (X-83). Further investigation as reported in a document dated 30 January 1946 uncovered the aforementioned urn buried at Daikonzaki Army Cemetery above Omura, containing the ashes of three men. In 1948, the remains of Frazier, Hall, and Mershom were identified and interred together at the Sante Fe National Cemetery, New Mexico, Section N, in grave 275. The few remains of Dye found at the radio station are buried at the National Museum of the Pacific in Section N, grave 1291.

The cremated remains of York, Woellhof, Vaughn, and unknown flyer—if he wasn't Hindenlang—were not found, and their names are etched into the Tablets of the Missing at the National Memorial Cemetery of the Pacific in Hawaii. The tablets also bear the names Kasperson, Ellis, Kluge, Stinger, Simon, Jones, Komorowski, Schneider, and Fickling. Hindenlang's remains were returned to the US, cremated, and interned at Mt. Hope Cemetery in Boston, Massachusetts. Those of Frye lie buried in Plot P Row 0 Grave 407, Honolulu Memorial, in Hawaii.

The official determination is that Ens. Hindelang was executed by the Japanese, but several discrepancies remain regarding his case: the probability that he was buried with

Frye and the unknown in the botanical garden; the remains in that grave were mostly intact; and that Rexy's men recovered only a single vertebra in a grave on 13 January 1946, the day which co-pilot Hindenlang's remains were said to have been recovered. Finally, there is the improbability of the co-pilot, sitting in the cockpit, surviving uninjured in a plane crashing at over 200 miles per hour.

Eleven men went on a mission and never came back. Seven of them were buried at sea and four on Chichi Jima; three were buried together in a tropical botanical garden. The unknown flyer is now forever known as Ens. Warren Hindenlang of Boston, Massachusetts, who, like his fellow crewmen, left behind families to grieve.

Members of the Japanese Imperial Army based at Chichi Jima were charged with war crimes and stood trial between 1946 and 1949. Those not exonerated received sentences between five years in prison to the death penalty. Any allied airman held captive by the Japanese in the Central Pacific had a slim to none chance of surviving their ordeal. Two men that did survive were USAAF 2nd Lt. Louis Zamperini and his pilot, Allen "Phil" Phillips, after their B-24 bomber was ditched on 27 May 1943. They were captured and sent to Kwajalein after drifting forty-seven days in a life raft. They endured a further forty-two days of abuse and torture before being transferred to a prison camp in Japan.

20

The Reluctant Dragons Replace Miller's Reluctant Raiders August–September 1944

On the morning of the 6th, six planes from VB-109 conducted an ambitious photographic and bombing strike on Truk in conjunction with eight PB4Y-1Ps of VD-4, two F7As and one F7B of the 86th Combat Mapping Squadron, and seven PB4Ys of VB-116. The mission was coordinated with an Army bombing strike by the Eleventh Bombing Group, with the strike scheduled to begin take off an hour before the Photo strike. Weather for the mission was doubtful, so it was determined to await the report of a VB-116 search plane on the weather to Truk, thus causing a delay of an hour.

The formation encountered severe weather during the outward trek requiring flying on instruments and the Army strike force abandoned the mission and returned to Eniwetok while the navy bomber continued towards the target. The planes climbed to a cruising altitude of 8,000 feet and proceeded toward the target.

The weather from Eniwetok to Minto Reef was largely flown on instruments, and it became difficult for formation flying. The Army bombing strike was called off, and they returned to Eniwetok because of bad weather. At Minto Reef, the weather became clear and a climb to 20,500 feet was begun. The sky began to clear as the formation approached Truk and the planes began a gradual dive from 20,500 to 19,500 feet for the photo runs. Scattered clouds over the target did not prevent obtaining good vertical coverage of all the main areas except Dublon by VD-4 as the photographic run commenced. The formation began dropping their bombs on targets falling on the flight lines of the photo runs. VD-4 scored 60 hits on the islands of Moen, Dublon, Eten, Param, Tol, and Ulalu. Barracks and an airstrip on Param Island, shore installations on Dublon town and Eten airfield, and dock installations on Tol Island were bombed and left on fire by VB-109. Dublon Town, barracks on Moen, and buildings on the northwest tip of Tol Island and Tol Canal were hit by

Pictured is Crew 15 of VB-109, who were aboard a PB4Y-1 when the plane suffered engine failure on takeoff from Camp Kearny, California, for a flight to NAS Kaneohe, Thailand. It crashed into a mess hall, killing the crew and many others on the ground. Ens. John H. Parker Jr. of Crew 8 was a friend of the navigator, R. R. Rastelli, who told Parker many times he would not survive his tour with -116. ***Courtesy of John H. Parker Jr.***

Sky Cow **of VB-109. She was damaged beyond repair on 21 July 1944.** ***Courtesy of Oden Sheppard***

VB-116. As the formation completed its bombing run, it came under fighter attack.

One fighter between Fefan Island and South Pass within the atoll attacked Lieutenant Clark. Two fighters were observed flying on the port wing slightly above him out of gun range. One fighter slightly ahead and above flipped over on his back, made a frontal pass, and then passed under to the starboard side. Harold E. Mittendorf in the belly turret fired 200 rounds at the plane and scored hits on the fuselage and wing. The fighter then went into a dive but pulled out, apparently under control before going into a cloud. Two fighters dropping three phosphorous bombs attacked Lieutenant O'Brien. One fighter made a run above at the bomber, and the bombs were released in a glide at 500 feet above and burst near the tail of the Liberator.

A section of six bombers led by Lieutenant Richard F. Mather bore the brunt of some 12 enemy fighters while proceeding over Param Island towards the northwestern tip of Dublon Island. One fighter made a run on Mather with phosphorous bombs, then pulled up on the starboard side and retired. A second fighter attacked from 1,000 feet above Mather's plane where he did a half roll, a split recovery, and dropped a bomb in a glide run.

Northwest of Tol Island one fighter made a high overhead run out of the sun from 7 o'clock, scoring three 20mm hits on Mather's plane. The gunners did not observe the fighter out of the sun until it was too late for defensive action. One shell hit the horizontal stabilizer on the starboard side, while another hit the port wing just aft of the number two engine and forward of the leading edge of the flaps, tearing a large hole in the wing. A third shell entered the engine through the cowl flap opening and exploded in the air duct to the oil cooler. The explosion blew shrapnel through the inboard side of the engine and pierced the fuselage in the radio compartment in six places, as well as the forward bomb bay, severing the throttle control cable to the engine.

Immediately upon being hit, the pilot feathered the engine, and without a supply of oxygen at 20,000 feet, the plane captain, Kenneth Gaddis (AMM1c), began the transfer of fuel, which prevented a fire. For his action, Gaddis was given a flag promotion to Chief Petty Officer by Vice Admiral Hoover.[85] One fighter closed on the tail and one from below, but broke away before coming to close range. Even after the Liberators left Truk, one persistent fighter followed this section for 55 minutes before finally giving up.

Six fighters consisting of Zekes and Hamps attacked the second division. Lieutenant Tuttle's gunners scored hits on one fighter. One fighter started an attack at the same level as the bomber, closed to 1500 feet, and then turned to starboard. His gunners reported hits on this fighter, which made a snap roll, then went into a dive straight down before being lost in cloud.

Two Zekes intercepted the bombers just outside Truk Reef. One fighter made a run on Lieutenant Graves' plane, reaching a position immediately beneath the bomb bay doors,

Award ceremony for the men of VB-109 taken at Stickell Field, Eniwetok Atoll. ***Courtesy of the National Archives***

at which point the enemy fighter skidded to port. The port waist gunner, W.T. Logam, opened fire, scoring hits on the fuselage forward of the wings. Black smoke began pouring from the cowling, followed by flame. The enemy fighter went into a spin before it disappeared into a cloud. A Zeke attacked Lieutenant Anderson's plane next. His port waist gunner fired 75-100 rounds into the engine and wing roots. Black smoke began pouring out of the cowling and the starboard wing root, and the fighter went into a steep dive, disappearing in the clouds below. The remaining fighters lost their taste for battle and left the bombers alone.

Back on Saipan, the advanced echelon of VB-109 celebrated the first anniversary of the squadron's existence with a barbecue consisting of roasted pig. Members of Commander Hicks' crew had captured the pig. Just before the festivities, the animal escaped, but not for long. War often brings out contradictory actions by men, who can kill each other without much thought, but find it inhumane to act upon a basic instinct, such as slaughtering an animal. Only one man in the crew, Roger Clemons, had the inclination to butcher the animal for the celebration.

A tragic accident involving a crew from VB-116 escalated into the largest loss of naval aircraft from non-enemy action of the war. On the night of 9 August, Lieutenant Anderson pushed the throttles forward in his heavily loaded Liberator and went down the rolling runway on Eniwetok. He was not used to it, especially at night, and did not believe he had enough room to take off. Thinking the Liberator's wheels were still on the ground, he cut the throttles. He was wrong—the aircraft was airborne. Losing power, he drifted into carrier planes that were parked along the side. The plane hit the first rows of parked planes, carrying away tips of folded wings and canopies before crashing 50 yards past the end of the runway. The Liberator began to burn, with flames reaching other aircraft. The heat detonated nine 500-pound bombs on board Anderson's plane, and the ensuing inferno consumed the Liberator and 106 carrier planes. Ten men on board the bomber were killed, along with several others on the ground. The cataclysm of a fully loaded bomber crashing was so great that parts of bodies were hurled hundreds of yards across the island. The only survivor from Anderson's crew was Ensign O.B. Tully, who managed to crawl out of the burning wreck with third-degree burns all over his body; the injuries were too severe, and he died a week later.[1]

Even as plans were being confirmed for 109's movement to Tinian, the Reluctant Dragons of VB-102, now under the command of Lieutenant Commander G. Russell Pearson, began arriving at Eniwetok for their second tour of duty and to relieve Miller's Reluctant Raiders. For Commander Miller the war was over, but VB-109 would return to the Pacific some eight months later under the command of George Hicks and outfitted with PB4Y-2 Privateers. In 1946, Commander Norman "Buzz" Miller, the "One-man Task Force," would contract an illness that he would not be successful in battling, and die at the age of 38. Other personnel from the squadron would never see the end of the war and would be lost on future missions. Even after the war, aircraft accidents would take the lives of a few more men, including J.F. Bundy, who was killed in 1950.

21

Above Angry Seas
The Men and Missions of PB4Y-1 Liberator and PB4Y-2 Privateer Squadrons

The Reluctant Dragons' second appearance in the Pacific was marked by operational losses back in California and Hawaii. On 30 May, there was a mid-air collision over California. Four Liberators of the squadron were flying over Mt. Palomar when a fighter from VF-36 dove straight down through the formation. Lt. (jg) Luke Sauder's Liberator was hit, shearing ten feet off a wing. The bomber and the fighter spiraled down and crashed, killing all eleven men on the PB4Y-1 and the fighter pilot.[1]

The squadron suffered another tragedy on 6 June, when a Liberator from VB-117 crashed into a storehouse at Camp Kearny. Lt. (jg) John Golden of 117 took off without proper clearance and headed into heavy overcast. For a few minutes the plane came in and out of the clouds, and at one point went into a steep dive before the pilot recovered from less than one hundred feet above the ground. The Liberator re-entered the clouds, only to come back down again in a stall. A couple crews were standing outside for the morning roll call when the incident occurred. Three men from VB-102 recall that morning. Dick Halverson was sleeping in his barracks:

"Our new plane came in, and we were supposed to unload it first thing in the morning. Somehow I overslept. Harry Harrison, our new crew chief, left for breakfast with Hornbeck and Smith (the crew's two radiomen). He yelled back to me, 'See you down there.' They unloaded the plane and went to the supply shack. After eating breakfast I knew the stuff from the plane was supposed to go to the supply shack, so I headed that way. Here comes a PB4Y-1 out of low-hanging clouds, perpendicular to the runway, heading for the hangars. It looked as if he was coming in for a landing."

Donald Quinn was in front of the supply shack, standing in formation for the morning roll call: "I estimated the ceiling was about 500 feet. The fellow that was mustering us had time to call out just a few names when we heard a roar of engines and saw the plane burst out of the overcast heading straight for us."

Halverson continued: "He tried to turn away. His wing tip hit the ground and the plane plowed into the supply shack. Harrison, Hornbeck, and Smith were in there. We visited Harrison and Hornbeck in the hospital. They were comatose and terribly burned. Smith was slightly injured. Harrison and Hornbeck died within a week. Smith quit flying."

The crash killed some twenty-two men, six belonging to VB-102. The plane's fuselage broke in half behind the bomb bay. Only three of the Liberator's crew, who were in the rear section, survived. Carl McDermit remembers the crash scene: "When we could approach the wreckage, I walked over to the scene and recognized one of the plane's crewmen sitting on his parachute in an apparent daze. I asked him if he was OK. 'Yes,' he replied. 'How did you get out of the plane?'

"'I have no idea.'"[2]

The Squadron Patch for VB/VPB-102

The three Liberator crewmen who survived the accident were AMM3c Walter P. Gorton, AOM3c James M. Worthington, and S1c Cleo E. Jarrett. A board of inquiry could not determine if the Liberator suffered a mechanical failure prior to the crash. The incident destroyed most of VB-102's equipment so deployment was delayed for a couple weeks.

The arrival of the Reluctant Dragons on Tinian coincided with the rainy season, with rain falling nearly every single day and soon turning dirt into mud. Living accommodations for the next couple months were tents with coral floors. When it rained the floor turned into goo that covered men and materials. There were still Japanese holdouts on the island, and they were known to attempt sabotage, or occasionally enter the air base to steal food.

The first missions for Pearson's squadron were single-plane strikes on bypassed Wake and Ponape on 19 August, with Lt. Stiles hitting the former, while Lt. T. R. Clark took on Cdr. "Bus" Miller's favorite punching bag. Successful anti-shipping sweeps continued, with Lts. W. B. Oliver and W. M. Miller of VB-116 attacking two small cargo ships 150 miles northwest of Marcus Island. The little ships put up a fight and managed to knock out an engine on one of the Liberators. On the twenty-second, two planes from 102 were sent to Isley Field, Saipan, to begin anti-shipping sweeps in the Bonins. The Reluctant Dragons would quickly find out how dangerous those islands could be for low flying bombers.

A day later, Lts. Clark and J. M. Welsh of VB-102 took their two Liberators from Isley Field on a special anti-shipping strike in the Bonin Islands. Their search proved fruitless at Iwo Jima and Haha Jima, but ten miles west of Chichi Jima they sighted a convoy consisting of five ships. The two PB4Y-1s approached the targets ten feet off the water when Welsh recognized two of the ships as destroyers. Welsh called Clark and asked him if he saw the warships, but there was no reply from the other pilot. Both planes climbed to one hundred feet as they neared 500 yards, with Clark leading the attack on the largest transport while Welsh picked out another.

The convoy was taken by surprise and did not open fire until the Liberators' bow and top turrets began firing. Clark turned and pickled off four 500-pound bombs. One was a direct hit and the ship began burning. Welsh's four bombs were direct hits that broke the ship in two. Clark's path took him past the two destroyers that were spaced 1,000 yards apart.

Clark's plane received crippling damage from the vessels, and with one engine smoking his voice came over the interphone, calmly announcing, "So long fellows." Whether he was talking to his crew, Welsh, or both will never be known. The Liberator hit the water and exploded with such force that there could not have been any survivors. Welsh withdrew and headed home to tell the squadron they had lost one of their own.

September proved to be a month of long patrols, with ten search sectors covering 800 to 1,000 miles. The month also proved an operational nightmare for VB-102 when two of their aircraft were destroyed in take-off accidents; fortunately there were no personnel injuries. For Lt. (jg) F. J. Lencioni, a bulldozer and its driver decided to cross the runway just as Lencioni was cruising down the runway, trying to take off. The two hit, knocking the front nose gear off, the starboard tire blew out, and the fuselage was ripped from the forward bomb bay doors past the starboard waist hatch. The Liberator became airborne, and fortunately the skillful pilot turned the plane, came back around, and made a successful crash landing.

The Squadron Patch for VB/VPB-116

On the first, 116's Lt. J. F. Gammell encountered a convoy of small ships near the Bonins. In contrast to the convoys discovered and attacked during previous months by PB4Y squadrons, which consisted of small vessels weighing less than 500 tons, this one had 1,500-ton and 700-ton freighters and three small trawlers. Gammell's men manned their positions as the pilot headed for the largest target.

As the Liberator approached at 200 feet the ships began evasive action and began sending up intense machine gun fire. From 150 feet Gammell pickled off three 250-pound depth bombs. The first bomb hit the ship's deck and detonated, while the other two hit the water and exploded alongside the vessel. As the Liberator turned away to attack one of the

Wreckage of Luke Sauder's VB-102 Liberator taken in May 1944. ***Courtesy of Navy Squadrons 102/14 Association***

trawlers the tail turret gunner saw the freighter turn over on its side and sink. Gammell's gunners strafed the three trawlers, inflicting serious damage to all of them. As the Liberator headed for the second freighter the crew saw two F6Fs attacking it. One fighter scored a direct hit with a 100-pound bomb as Gammell approached to join the attack. The ship was strafed and was left sinking after the Liberator's gunners had expended all their ammunition.

By late Summer and early Fall 1944, the Japanese merchant fleet in the Central Pacific was mainly down to small coastal freighters weighing less than 500 tons, and it was a significant site to see anything larger than that. Most of the shipping was now situated in the Bonin Islands, with the Japanese trying to reinforce Iwo Jima from the larger base at Chi Chi Jima.

Lt. H. T. Klovstad of the Blue Raiders was searching this area when he encountered two enemy aircraft. A Nell and a Tess were spotted headed for Iwo Jima when the Liberator caught up to them. In the ten-minute aerial battle, the top and bow turrets sent a deadly stream of .50-cailiber machine gun fire into a hapless Tess, which plummeted to the sea in flames.

Five days later Lt. Johnson of the Reluctant Dragons took off in the pre-dawn hours from North Field and headed toward Iwo Jima to check it out. On the outbound leg of his 1,000-mile sector he could see some activity on the island, which five months later would be the site of one of the bloodiest battles of the war. Five hours later Johnson headed back home; it had been a routine patrol.

On the return leg Johnson was some sixty miles northwest of Iwo Jima when he spotted a single ship. The ship saw the Liberator coming in and turned broadside. The Liberator's gunners held their fire until they were one hundred yards away, then all guns opened up on the bridge. Coming in at fifty feet, Johnson pulled up and pickled off two bombs just as he crossed the starboard side of the ship. Even before the bombs hit the tanker's crew began abandoning ship by launching lifeboats and climbing down the ship's side with ladders and ropes.

The first bomb detonated underneath the bow, blowing it off completely and taking one of the loaded lifeboats with it. The ship stopped dead and began going down by the bow. The second lifeboat, carrying two dozen men, became a target and was strafed. Johnson came back around and his gunners

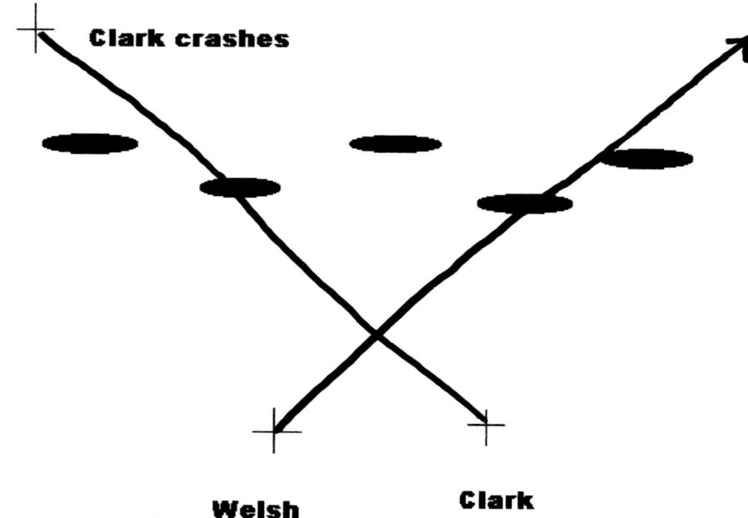

Attack by VB-102 aircraft on 23 August 1944

continued to pour rounds into the bridge, which began to burn. A large puff of steam began rising 200 feet into the air. The ship was now afire from stem to stern, yet Johnson's gunners continued firing at the ship's waterline. The ship was left burning, with many of her crew dead and floating in the water.

The Japanese were serious about strengthening the Bonin and Volcano Islands, with increasing convoy activity located by the two squadrons. On the fifteenth, Lt. (jg) Mott was nearing the end of an uneventful patrol when a convoy consisting of two destroyers and two merchant ships was spotted. The formidable guns on the ships precluded any attempt at hitting the freighters so Mott continued. Not long after two LSMs were spotted sixty miles off Iwo Jima.

Preparing for an attack on the lead ship Mott instructed his bow gunner to rake the target, while the port and belly turrets were instructed to provide suppressing fire on the second LSM. The pilot dove down to 200 feet and headed toward the target, and that is when all hell broke loose.

Both ships began sending up a thick blanket of anti-aircraft fire, from 12.7 mm machine gun fire to four-inch cannons. Just as he was about to release a string of 100-pound bombs Mott's starboard waist gunner came over the interphone, "Being attacked by fighters from 4 o'clock." Mott heard the sound of the waist gun firing and then the tail gunner opened up. On the water in front of the Liberator splashes of 20 mm and 7.7 mm rounds began appearing. A Zeke had come in to interrupt the attack on the shipping.

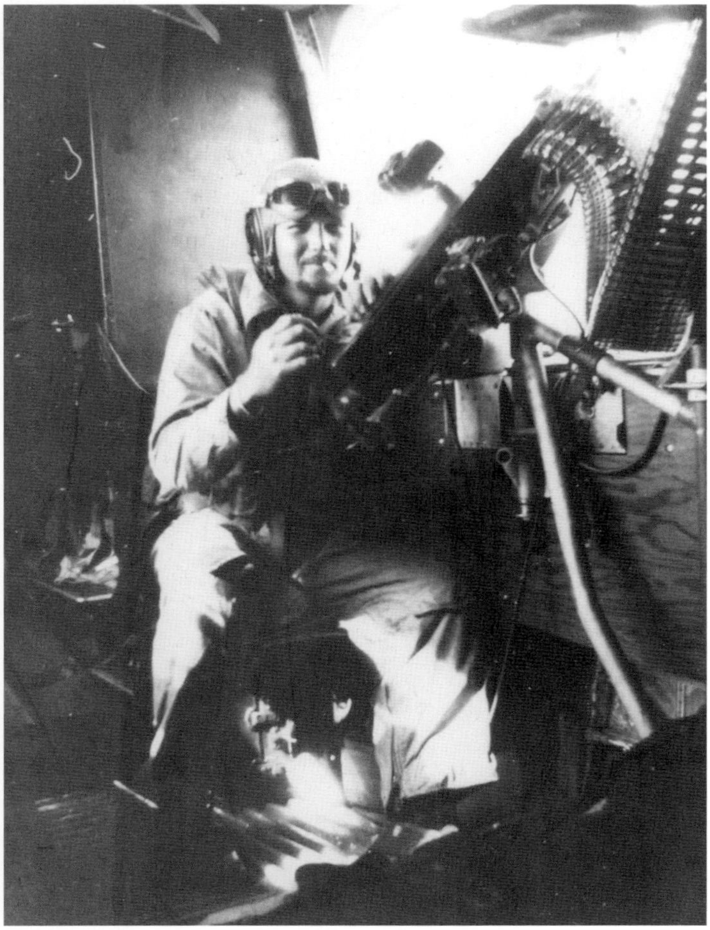

The battle lasted less than five minutes. Mott turned the bomber into the attacking fighter. The top and port waist gunners riddled the Zeke at the wing roots and fuselage. R. C. Johnson (AMM2c), in the top turret, saw his tracers piercing the Zeke's fuselage. The fighter began streaming black smoke and the plane pulled up to 300 feet, the pilot bailed out, and the Zeke nosed over and crashed 300 yards from where the pilot had landed in the water. Mott circled the parachute floating on the water; there was no sign of the pilot.

The following day another Blue Raider led by Lt. L. D. Sullivan engaged a Betty and the bow turret gunner, R. O. Schroeder (AOMB2c), shot it down. This was followed on the twenty-second by D. Torrence (AOMB3c), the bow gunner for Lt. (jg) P. W. Guika of VB-102, who shot down another Betty in the Bonins.

An unidentified member of VB-116 manning his waist gun position is sporting a non-regulation mustache and goatee circa July–September 1944. Several images the author came across have crewmen sporting full beards. ***Courtesy of Ed Beasley***

22

Pacific Operations
October 1944–September 1945

The Mariana Campaign was over and the next campaign to seize Iwo Jima was months away. In the interim USN Liberator squadrons continued striking by-passed islands in the Caroline and Marshall Islands. Even photographic reconnaissance missions, except those of Iwo Jima, grew fewer and less important.

VD-4, which had provided extensive coverage of the Marianas, had by September been reduced to training flights. For Lt.Cdr. Clark and VD-4 the war was all but over, and they would be relieved by VD-5 early in December. In the interim, Pearson and Gumz's boys kept pounding the Japanese when they could.

The close of the Marianas Campaign was a turning point of the war and marked a resting period for the opposing sides. Now that Saipan and Tinian were secured the Army Air Force could hit the Japanese mainland with B-29s. Not since the Doolittle Raid in April 1942 had Japan been subjected to American bombing. From September 1944 until the end of the war the Japanese people would feel the brunt of American strategic bombing, but the military might of the Japanese was still a potent threat to be conquered.

The island hopping campaign across the South and Central Pacific had ended, and Gen. MacArthur's triumphant return to the Philippines was just over the horizon. The last eleven months of the war would be the bloodiest, with the United States and her allies pitted against an enemy who did not want to relinquish its hold on the territories it had gained two years before. American, Australian, and British forces had to fight their way through the Philippines, Borneo, Iwo Jima, and Okinawa before victory could be achieved. Playing an often underlooked role in the drama would be Navy Liberator and Privateer squadrons, whose designation would change from Navy Bombing Squadron (VB) to Navy Patrol and Bombing Squadron (VPB) on October 1, 1944.

Squadrons such as VD-4 and -5 would continue their mission of supplying photographed images of future landing sites, while their sister squadrons continued with sixteen-hour patrols ferreting out Japanese naval forces, merchant shipping, and hitting enemy held territory.

By the dawn of 1945, some Navy land-based squadrons would have a new aircraft—named the PB4Y-2 Privateer—at their disposal to hunt down enemy shipping and land targets, and for a few select ones an air-to-ground guided missile would be added to the ordnance of bombs and bullets.

During the last year of the war veteran squadrons 104, 106, 108, 109, and 111 would return to combat, teaming up with new squadrons 117, 118, 119, 121, 123, and 124. In the final days of the war VPB-120 and 122 would arrive in Alaska. As these squadrons began hunting near Japan combat tactics would change in the months ahead, with the majority of Navy Liberator and Privateer squadrons abandoning the concept of one-plane armed reconnaissance for a two-plane approach. Many more aircraft and their crews would pay the ultimate sacrifice in the war against Imperial Japan. The history of United States Navy Liberator and Privateer operations in the Pacific continues in *Above an Angry Sea.*

Appendix A: Comic Books Pay Tribute

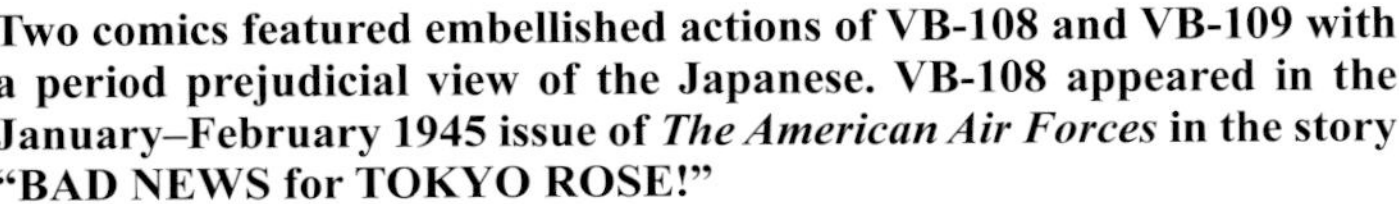
Two comics featured embellished actions of VB-108 and VB-109 with a period prejudicial view of the Japanese. VB-108 appeared in the January–February 1945 issue of *The American Air Forces* in the story "BAD NEWS for TOKYO ROSE!"

The same issue of *The American Air Forces* has a story on AOM1c Walter H. Brugge titled, "He Trucked on Down. . . ." Brugge was aboard aircraft bureau number 32100, piloted by Lt. Richard H. Rice of VB-108, when a truck occupied by seven Marines drove in front of the plane taking off on 21 March 1944. Two of the vehicle's occupants were killed and four were injured.

The September 1945 issue of *Real Life Comics* featured Cdr. "Bus" Miller, ace of the Reluctant Raiders. This is a fictional account of VB-109's strike against Japanese shipping in the Marshall Islands. The squadron was sometimes referred to as Miller's Raiders. *Author's Collection*

THE FOLLOWING MARCH...
WHAT'S BUZZIN' AT PONAPE, SKIPPER?
REAL JAPANESE GRAB-BAG! WE OUGHT TO FIND EVERYTHING THERE BUT FUJIYAMA!
ABOARD A JAMMED JAP TRANSPORT...
AGAIN, LIBERATOR ...BUT REGRETTABLY OUT OF RANGE!
COWARDLY DOGS! IF THEY WERE CLOSER... I WOULD PERSONALLY MAN GUN!
Suddenly... YARD BY YARD...
THEY COME NOW! YOU HAVE HONOR OF FIRST SHOT, YES?
THINK PERHAPS HAVE MISPLACED EYEGLASSES! KINDLY EXCUSE... I LOOK FOR THEM!
HIYA, JAPSON?
AS COMMANDER MILLER SWERVED THE "THUNDER MUG"...
WAIST GUNNERS... QUIT READING FROM "YANK" OVER THE INTERCOM! THERE'S A BIG FREIGHTER WALLOWING AROUND THE LAGOON!
I SAID YOU COULDN'T CLIP OFF THE CAPTAIN'S EPAULETS, JOHNSON!
RATS! I THOUGHT YOU SAID HIS CIGARETTE!

SOME WEEKS LATER... OVER ETON ANCHORAGE...
THERE'S A GOOD TEN THOUSAND TONS FOR DAVY JONES'S SCRAP PILE, BUS!
WE'LL HAVE TO BRUSH OFF THE DESTROYER... NOT ENOUGH BOMBS!
BAM!
BUT FOR THE CRUISER... A LALLAPALOOZER!
POM! POM! POM!
IN A DIVE TO MASTHEAD HEIGHT...
BOOM!
IN MAY... DURING A SURPRISE RAID ON THE SECRET JAP BASE OF PULUWAT...
WUP! PICKED UP A FEW THIS TIME, BUS!
BLAM!
SO DID I, JIMMY... BUT WE'RE GETTING THE "THUNDER MUG" HOME!
"HOME" LAY ACROSS EIGHT HUNDRED MILES OF HOSTILE SEA... BUT MILLER MADE IT!
IT'S BUS! BROTHER ...WHAT THIS NAVY NEEDS IS A FEW MORE SQUADRONS LIKE HIM!
ATTACKING CONTINUALLY WITHIN TWO HOURS OF TOKIO... COMMANDER MILLER'S "RELUCTANT RAIDERS" CAME THROUGH WITHOUT THE LOSS OF A SINGLE PLANE!

Appendix B: Personnel Losses Including Killed in the Line of Duty February 1943–September 1944

VP-51/VB-101 (February 1943 to August 1943)
Killed In Action
14 February 1943
Herman R. Abbott, AMM3c
Ernest F. Adams, AMM3c
Frank E. Atkins, AOM2c
Jay D. Bacon Jr., Lieutenant
William Barber, ARM2c
Frank L. Betz, ARM1c
Stuart T. Cooper, Lieutenant
Harold A. Elliott, Ensign
William C. Fowler, AP1c
Howard Goldstein, AOM2c
Jessie L. Henderson, AMM1c
Bernard T. Hussey, AMM1c
Edmund J. Kolazyk, Ensign
A.T. Montgomery, AMM2c
Otis E. Nelson, ARM2c
Norman L. North, AMM2c
Herman T. Sauter, ARM3c
Andrew E. Sheek, AOM3c
John M. Walker, AMM2c
Oscar K. Ward, AMM2c
Roy R. Wells, AMM3c
Joseph H. Zattera, AOM3c

5 March 1943
Frank M. Fisler, Lieutenant
William R. Gallagher, Ensign
Wallace T. Jones Lieutenant
Robert P. Combs, Ensign
Lawrence W. Alvord, AMM2c
Lee Baldwin, ARM3c
James J. Curry, AMM2c
Raymond L. Flower, AMM1c
Paul J. Patterson, AMM2c
Talmadge H. Power, ARM1c
Benjamin Rogozinski
Walter S. Slachter, AOM2c

5 March 1943
Howard J. May, Lieutenant (jg)
Donald H. Lehman, Ensign
Charles E. Heintzelman, Ensign
Joseph F. Winters, Ensign
Fernando P. Spadoni, AMM1c
Arthur Valhusky, AMM2c
Hulin O. Moore, ARM3c
John J. Colby, AOM2c
Anthony N. Cortese, AOM2c
Gerald T. Grant, ARM1c
William E. Webber, AMM2c
George C. Wilson, ARM2c
22 August 1944
William T. Van Meter, AOM1C

Killed in the Line of Duty
1 January 1944
Philip A. Nelson, Lieutenant
Richard C. Fette, Ensign
Ralph C. Runels, Ensign
Harlan W. Barnes, AMM2c
Jack H. Ring, S1c
Thomas F. Bastinsen, AOM3c
Jerome W. Knight Jr., ARM3c
Harry W. Walker, AMM2c
Samuel E. Pugh, ARM2c
Donald Q. Williams, AMM2c
Alex J. Brown, S1c

VB-102 (April 1943 to November 1943)
Personnel killed after 1 October 1944 are not included.
3 July 1943
W. J. Bartek

6 July 1943
Henry F. Watson, AMM2c
Bruce Van Voorhis, Lieutenant Commander
Jack O. Traub, Lieutenant (jg)
George C. Stephens, AMM1c
John Renner, ACRM
Herschel A. Oelhert, Lieutenant (jg)
Charles A. Martinelli, AMM2c
Charles D. Linzmeyer, ACOM
Donald B. Clogston, AOM2c
Frederick C. Barker Jr., AMM3c

17 July 1943
Duane L. Beaman, Ensign
Eric B. Bolling, ARM2c
Clarence C. Dodson, AMM2c
John H. Harr, AMM2c
Alvin P. Harrow, AMM2c
John B. Haskett, Lieutenant (jg)
Merle W. Hinshaw, AMM2c
Kenneth R. Johnson, Lieutenant
D.H. Lehman
Henry F. Lohmeier, AOM3c
Donald H. Siley, Lieutenant (Passenger)
Lloyd R. Morgan, ARM2c
Norman M. Ostroff

23 August 1944
Thomas R. Clark, Lieutenant
Garland L. Crandall, AOMB2c
Robert C. Hays, ARM2c
John P. Madsen, Ensign
Winston S. Powel, AOM
Melvin A. Roehs, ARM3c
William Saylor, S1c
William D. Schultz, Ensign
Raymond A. Schwartz, AMM1c
John J. Thomas, AMM3c
Harry Todor, S1c

Killed in the Line of Duty
6 April 1943
John B. Adams, Ensign
Herbert S. Bonn, Lieutenant
Ralph D. Boswell, AMM2c
Ronald D. Brown, ARM2c
Cameron L. Collier, Ensign
Jock G. Hart, AMM3c
Joseph B. Leonard, AOM3c
Raymond O. Marchand, ARM3c

30 May 1944: Killed during training for second tour.
Donald L. Atkins, AOM3c
Clinton T. Baker, AMM3c
William Cordell, S2c
Clinton F. McKinstry, AMM3c
Carlton B. Rowland, AMM2c
Luke Sauder, Lieutenant (jg)
Robert I. Searight, S1c
Thomas R. Shannon, AOMB2c
Raymond L. Shovelton, ARM3c

6 June 1944
V.P. Hornbeck
Edward R. Lamberton, ACOM
Jack M. Smith, AOM3c
Lawrence Dodge, AOMTC2c
J. Golden (unknown rating)
Lawrence Harrison, AMM2c

VB-104 (August 1943 to March 1944)
15 November 1943
N.M. Honey, Lieutenant (jg)
Leonard E. Swanson, Ensign
Leslie Watt, Ensign
William F. Beard, AMM3c
Gerald I. Conover, AMM2c
William E. Gwaltney Jr., AMM1c
Donald E. Johnson, AOM2c
John P. Kvaratius, AOM2c
Robert O. Leishman, AMM2c
Benjamin E. Snuffer, ARM2c

8 January 1944
H.E. Dvorachek, Lieutenant
H.E. Campbell, Lieutenant (jg)
P.D. Riley, Lieutenant (jg)
H.O. Jeska, AMM2c
J.C. Bennet, ARM2c
G.W. Masters, AMM2c
J.A. Griskiewicz, ARM2c
H.W. Jones, AMM2c
B.H. Keogan, AOM2c
W.F. Hagendoorn, AMM2c
L.F. Green, AOM3c

7 March 1944
W.D. Searls, Lieutenant (jg)
H.S. Joslyn, Lieutenant (jg)
R.P. Therrien, Ensign
E.O. Emory, ACMM
R.J. Plank, ARM1c
F.P. Browning, AMM2c
D.E. Nelson, ARM2c
J.E. Page, AMM2c
L.J. Verret, AOM2c
A.L. Duranti, ARM2c
R.J. Roller, AMM1
L. Boucher, ARM3c

9 March 1944
A.E. Anderson, Lieutenant (jg)
M.O. Andrews, Lieutenant (jg)
D.E. Pate, AMM1c
W.B. King, ARM1c
M.M. Weinschenk, AOM1c
E.B. Healy, AOM3c
R.E. Flack, AMM2c
J.M. Nichols, AMM2c
D. Solari, ARM2c
H.W. Pierson, AMM2c

Killed in the line of duty
6 June 1944
Edward Guy Woodward, AMM3c
Henry Ignatius Ladowski, ARM3c
John Daniel Fuller, AMM3c
Killed when a PB4Y-1 from VB-117 crashed at Camp Kearney while squadron trained for second tour.

VB-106 (October 1943 to May 1944)
20 October 1943
Samuel I. Patella, Lieutenant
Richard H. Wood, Ensign
John C. MacKay, Ensign
John G. Walden, Jr., AMM3c
Argus W. Story, Jr. AOM3c
Donald D. Dickey, AMM3c
Itley D. Winn, ART1c
O. Atkinson, AMM3c
Lloyd E. Hume, AMM3c
William E. Lexlow, AMM3c

1 May 1944
A.L Seaman, Lieutenant
A.H. Saviko, Lieutenant (jg)
R.L. Egger, ARM1c
B.C. Mankus, AMM2c
I.L. Nilson, AOM1c
J.E. Brown Jr., AMM2c

23 May 1944
E.S. Thompson, AMM1c

27 May 1944
E.T. Morrison, Lieutenant
Marvin Hayek, Ensign
Mark Cross, ARM2c

Killed in Line of Duty
25 December 1943
William S. Snead, Ensign
Lynus N. Briggs, AMM3c
James S. Welch, AOM2c
Dennis J. Paquette, AMM3c

22 March 1944
Richard J. O'Donnell, Lieutenant

VB-108 (October 1943 to July 1944)
13 December
John J. McCormick Jr., Lieutenant Commander
Richard S. McClung, Ensign
Darrell D. Whitmore, Ensign
John F. Ilkovich, AOM3c
Santiago A. Lopez, ARM2c
Jas E. Morgan, AMM3c
Robert W. Nelson, ACOMA
Lonnie Powell, ACRMP
Lonnie H. Ziesemer, AOM3c
John A. Zillis Jr., AMM1c

18 December 1943
John H. Stickell, Lieutenant

29 December 1943
Vernon E. Niebruegge, Lieutenant
Lewis E. Hastings, Ensign
Donald G. Hardin, Ensign
Max O. Perry, AMM2c
Arthur N. Borgaard, AMM2c
Alvin B. Carnahan, ARM2c
Donald D. Olson, ARM2c
William J. Guidera, AOM2c
Robert E. Heidy, AMM3c
Wilbur F. Jolly, AMM3c

3 March 1944
John B. Blattner, AOM2c

VB-109 (December 1943 to August 1944)

13 January 1944
Samuel E. Coleman, Lieutenant
Leroy A. Shreiner, Lieutenant (jg)
Leslie E. Fontaine, Ensign
Louis E. Sandidge Jr., AMM1c
Sterling T. Brown, AMM2c
James T. Heasley, AOM2c
Truman Steele, AOM2c
Harry F. Donovan, ARM2c
Daniel J. Dujak, ARM2c
Lou C. Petrick, S1c
John E. Tusha, S1c

13 February 1944
John H. Herron, Lieutenant (jg)
Charles M. Henderson, Lieutenant (jg)
Nelson T. O'Bryan, Ensign
Robert J. Bennington, AMM1c
Benjamin W. Anderson, AOM(T)1c
Raymond W. Devlin, ARM2c
Clarence H. Ziehlke, AMM3c
Paul J. Graham, AOM3c
Richard C. Vancitters, AOM3c
Aern R. Durgin, S2c

5 August 1944
Elmer H. Kasperson, Lieutenant
Warren A. Hindenland, Ensign
Keith E. Ellis, Ensign
Joseph W. Komorowski, AMM1c
Warren B. Simon, AMM2c
Richard D. Frye, ARM2c
Hugo L. Kluge, ARM2c
William F. Schneider, AOM2c
Victor B. Jones, AOM2c
Allen K. Stinger, AOM3c
Bobby W. Fickling, AOM3c

5 June 1944
Hale D. Fisher, AMM1c

VB-115 (March to November 1944)

Killed in Action
22 April 1944
William R. Doerr, Lieutenant
Harold E. Barrett, Ensign
Bernard L. Johnson, Chief Aviation Pilot (CAP)
Steve C. Burkhart Jr., S1c
Rocco C. Capobianco, ARM3c
Reno A. Chiste, AOM2c
Robert F. Holman, ARM2c
John J. Marrapodi, AMM2c
John W. Meggison Jr., AMM3c
Thomas F. Reed, AOM3c
Russell E. Hill, SSGT (USAAF)

20 May 1944
Killed in the Line of Duty
Steven B. Pitt, Lieutenant (jg)
Philip F. Reese, Ensign
Charles R. Marquois, Ensign
Robert Casselman
Thomas W. Miller, AOMM
Howard S. Hasbrook, AOMB1c
Basil E. Whitney, AOM2c
Elmer E. Bowman, ARM2c
Andrew J. Jelak, AMM2c
John F. Sturtevant, AMM3c
James F. Steele Jr., AMM2c
Tino M. Flores, AOM3c

VB-116 (July 1944 to August 1945)
Does not include personnel killed after 1 October 1944.

Killed in the Line of Duty
23 February 1944
George W. Wolfe, AMM2c. Plane Captain struck by propeller at night while guiding Liberator at Camp Kearney, California.

26 May 1944
Robert E. Duggan, Lieutenant
Roberto R. Rastelli, Ensign
Harvey G. Tassano, AMM2c
James L. Carmichael, AMM3c
John T. Watts, ARM1c
Roy V. Payton, ARM3c
G.R. Voegley

9 August 1944
R.C. Anderson, Lieutenant
T. M. Pettit, Ensign
O.R. Tully, Ensign. Died of injuries on 15 August 1944.
L. Johnson, AMM1c
H.A. Heper, S1c
J.W. Chalmers, ARM1c
A.F. Burkhartmeyer, ARM3c
J.D. Rothwell, AOM2c
A.A. Van Winkle, S1c
G.A. Ehinger, AOM3c

VD-1 (April 1943 to August 1944)
Douglas Brown, Ensign

VD-3 (October 1943 to May 1944 and June to August 1945)

Killed in Action
5 January 1944
Larren M. Allen, Lieutenant
Billy J. Buchanan, PHOM1c
Peter T. Chester, Lieutenant
Kirk E. Crowe, S1c
Raymond A. Dandoy, AMM2c
Rano Dellassanta, AOM2c
Robert D. Derosa, PHOM1c
Reed G. Held, Lieutenant
Gosta H. Johnson, ARM1c
Laurence J. McDonald, PHOM2c
Gail Miller, AOM2c
Harold C. Peterson, Ensign
William I. Walsh, AMM2c

Killed in the Line of Duty
26 May 1943
Walter F. Martin, Ensign
C.A. Rethers, Lieutenant
Killed in crash of SNJ-4 Bureau Number 09864 at Naval Air Station, San Diego.

7 July 1943
Alfred Wilstam, Lieutenant Commander
Charles J. Kovaleski, Lieutenant
Gerald T. Kearns, Lieutenant (jg)
William H. Roemer, Ensign
Cecil E. Mathews, AMM1c
Richard F. Coan, ARM1c
Joseph A. Kezich, AOM2c
Paul R. Cochran, AMM3c
Karl W. Ruess, PhoM1c
Dave Bergman, ARM3c
Walter A. Thomas, PhoM3c

Appendix C: Squadron Combat Records February 1943–November 1944

VB/VPB-102 and 116 are not included. These figures are estimates based upon squadron records and ***Japanese Naval and Merchant Shipping Losses During World War II by All Causes.***

VB-101 (February-August 1943)
Accurate assessment of this squadron's record was unavailable.
Bombing Attacks: 11?
Ships Attacked: 12?
Planes Destroyed:?
Planes Attacked:?

VB-102 (April-November 1943)
Planes Destroyed: 16
Planes Attacked: 75 (No data on number damaged)
Ships Attacked: 43
Ships Sunk: 5 (No data on actual number sunk)
Bombing Attacks: 59

VB-104 (August 1943-March 1944)
Ships Sunk: 28
Ships Damaged: 24
Planes Destroyed: 14
Planes Damaged: 5
Probable: 11
Bombing Attacks: 72
Aircraft Lost by All Causes: 7

VB-106 (October 1943-June 1944)
Ships Sunk: 43
Ships Damaged: 54
Planes Destroyed: 20
Planes Damaged: 31

VB-108 (November-July 1944)
Ships Sunk: 20
Ships Damaged: 22
Planes Destroyed: 20
Planes Damaged: 13
Bombing Attacks: 65
Strafing: 40

VB-109 (December 1943-August 1944)
Ships Sunk: 43
Ships Damaged: 91
Planes Destroyed: 24
Planes Damaged: 44
Probable: 26
Bombing Attacks: 200
Strafing: 152
Aircraft Lost by All Causes: 7

VB/VPB-115 (March-November 1944)
Ships Sunk: 46
Ships Damaged: 44
Probable: 9
Planes Destroyed: 35
Planes Damaged: 12
Probable: 5
Bombing and Strafing Attacks: 28
Aircraft Lost by All Causes: 7

Appendix D: Listing of Known PB4Y-1 Liberators Assigned to Pacific-based Squadrons February 1943–August 1945

Some squadrons transferred aircraft and thus are noted.
Bureau Numbers 31936 to 32335 B-24Ds

BUREAU NUMBER	SQUADRON(S)	NAME	REMARKS
31939:	VB-101		
31941:	VB-101		
31946:	VB-108/122/123		
31947:	VB-101		Lost in Action 3 March 1943
31948:	VB-101		Lost in Action 14 February 1943
31950:	VB-101		Lost in Action 3 March 1943
31951:	VB-101/VD-5		
31952:	VB-101		
31953:	VB-101/VD-5/VPB-121		
31954:	VB-101/115/VPB-120		
31955:	VB-102		
31959:	VMB-154/VB-108/VPB-123/122		
31960:	VB-101		
31970:	VB-101		Lost in Action 14 February 1943
31972:	VB-102/VB-115/VPB-120		
31975:	VB-102/106	*Stoop-N-Droop It*	
31976:	VD-1/VB-102	*Spirit of 76*	
31980:	VD-1		Operational Loss 7/43
31981:	VD-1/VB-102		Operational Loss 2/10/44
31982:	VD-1	*Satan's Wagon*	
31984:	VB-101/VPB-117		
31986:	VD-3		Scrapped in Stillwater, Oklahoma
31987:	VD-3/VD-5		
31989:	VB-102		Operational Loss 4/7/43
31990:	VB-102/VPB-109		Scrapped in Stillwater Oklahoma
31992:	VB-102		Lost in Action 7/7/43
31995:	VD-1/VB-102	*Hell's Angels*	Operational Loss 2/14/44

BUREAU NUMBER	SQUADRON(S)	NAME	REMARKS
31996:	VD-1/VB-102		
31997:	VD-1		Operational Loss 9/19/43
31998:	VPB-122/124		Possibly with VD-1 under *Butch*
32003:	VD-3/VPB-119		
32005:	VD-3		Operational Loss 7/7/43
32006:	VD-3/VD-5		
32007:	VD-3/VB-115/VPB-120		
32008:	VD-3		
32009:	VB-102/104/108/122	*America's Playground*	
32010:	VB-102		
32011:	VD-3		
32012:	VB-101/102/104	*Jungle Fever*	Operational Loss 11/15/43
32016:	VB-102		Operational Loss 2/26/43
32019:	VD-3		Lost in Action 1/4/44
32069:	VB-102	*The Schooner*	Lost in Action 9 March 1943
32073:	VB-104/VPB-117	*Pistol Packin' Mama*	Operational Loss 6/6/44
32074:	VB-104	*Donald's Duck*	Operational Loss 1/29/44
32077:	VB-104	*Vulnerable Virgin*	Lost in Action 1/8/44
32078:	VB-106/115/120		
32079:	VB-104	*Wata Honey*	Lost in Action 3/7/44
32080:	VB-104/115/120	*Unapproachable*	
32081:	VB-104/VPB-118	*Whit's Shits*	
32084:	VB-106/ VPB-118		
32085:	VB-106		Operational Loss 2/10/44
32087:	VB-106	*Fatso*	
32091:	VB-106	*Mitzi-Bishi*	
32092:	VB-106		Operational Loss 12/25/43
32093:	VB-106		Operational Loss 12/15/43
32094:	VB-106/115/120		
32097:	VPB-122		
32098:	VB-108/VD-3/122/123	*Sugar*	
32099:	VB-108		Lost in Action 12/12/43
32100:	VB-108		Operational Loss 3/21/44
32102:	VB-106		Operational Loss 10/20/43
32103:	VB-108	*Flying Dutchman*	
32104:	VD-4		
32105:	VB-108/106/VD-4	*Pistol Packin' Mama*	
32106:	VB-108/VD-1/VD-4	*Wabbit Twacks*	Scrapped in Stillwater, Oklahoma
32108:	VB-109	*Thundermug*	Crashed on landing 06/44
32109:	VB-108/VD-1/VD-4	*Little Joe*	
32113:	VD-3/VMB-254		
32114:	VB-106		
32115:	VD-4/VB-115		Operational Loss 5/17/44

Listing of Known PB4Y-1 Liberators Assigned to Pacific-based Squadrons

BUREAU NUMBER	SQUADRON(S)	NAME	REMARKS
32116:	VB-108/VPB-124/VD-4	*Nippo Nippin' Kitten*	
32119:	VD-4	*Overexposed*	
32120:	VB-108	*Virgin Sturgeon*	
32121:	VB-109	*Sky Cow* and *Big Cow*	Operational Loss 7/21/44
32122:	VD-4	*Sleepy Time Gal*	
32123:	VB-108		Operational Loss 11/18/44
32124:	VB-106/108	*Nobody's Baby*	
32125:	VB-108/VD-1/VD-4	*Nucky No No Maru*	
32128:	VD-4		
32130:	VB-109	*The Stork*	Scrapped in Stillwater, Oklahoma
32131:	VB-109	*Consolidated's Mistake*	
32132:	VPB-121		
32136:	VB-109	*Our Baby*	Destroyed by enemy bombing 01/03/44 Operational Loss
32137:	VB-109	*Helldorado*	
32138:	VB-108/109		
32139:	VB-109		Lost in Action 1/13/44
32140:	VB-109/122/123	*Climbaboard*	
32141:	VB-109		Operational Loss 1/44
32142:	VB-108/VPB-119	*Lady Luck*	
32143:	VD-4	*Witchcraft*	
32145:	VB-109	*Urge Me*	
32146:	VB-101		Operational loss 2/17/44
32148:	VB-109	*Flying Circus*	
32149:	VB-109/VD-1/VD-4	*Available Jones*	
32150:	VB-115		Lost in Action 6/5/44
32152:	VB-106/VPB-109		Scrapped in Stillwater, Oklahoma
32154:	VB-106/VPB-109		Scrapped in Stillwater, Oklahoma
32155:	VB-108/VPB-119	*Hells's Belle*	
32156:	VPB-102/VPB-122		Scrapped in Stillwater, Oklahoma
32157:	VD-4/VPB-102/VD-4		
32158:	VB-108	*Dinah II*	Scrapped in Stillwater, Oklahoma
32159:	VB-115		Operational Loss 5/20/44
32162:	VB-115		
32163:	VB-101		Operational Loss 1/20/44
32164:	VD-4		
32165:	VPB-101		
32166:	VPB-101		
32168:	VB-115		
32169:	VB-115?	*Loose Livin II*	
32170:	VB-115		Operational Loss 4/20/44
32171:	VB-106		Operational Loss 5/28/44
32172:	VB-106		Lost in Action 4/6/44
32174:	VD-1		Operational Loss 5/30/44

BUREAU NUMBER	SQUADRON(S)	NAME	REMARKS
32175:	VB-106	*Mark*	Lost in Action 5/1/44
32176:	VB-115		
32177:	VB-115		Lost in Action 6/5/4
32178:	VB-115		
32182:	VB-115	*Snuffy's Mischief Maker*	
32215:	VB-115		Operational Loss 5/15/44
32216:	VPB-101		
32119:	VB-106		Operational Loss 3/22/44
32220:	VB-115		
32221:	VPB-115/116?	*Rita's Rebel*	
32222:	VB-115		Lost in Action 4/22/44
32225:	VB-115		
32228:	VPB-101/VPB-111		
32229:	VD-1		
32231:	VD-1		
32238:	VB-106/115	*Chick's Chick*	
32240:	VD-1	*Little Jo*	Operational Loss 4/30/44
32241:	VB-109	*Sugar Queen*	
32243:	VB-106/115	*Bales Baby*	Operational Loss 10/26/44
32247:	VPB-116		
32260:	VPB-101		Operational Loss 11/25/44
32263:	VB-109		Lost in Action 8/5/44
32264:	VD-4		
32265:			
32266:	VPB-101		Lost in Action on 10/25/44
32267:	VD-1	*Little Green Apples*	
32269:	VPB-104		Lost in Action 10/25/44
32272:	VPB-101		
32273:	VB-115		
32274:	VB-115		May have been *Snuffy's Mischief Maker II*
32275:	VPB-101		
32276:	VPB-101	*Comair Wolfpac II*	
32277:	VPB-101		
32278:	VB-101		Operational Loss 5/6/44
32279:	VPB-101		
32280:	VPB-101		Lost in Action 10/19/44
32283:	VB-115	*Snuffy's Mischief Maker*	
32284:	VD-4		
32887:	VD-1		
32998:	VPB-115		
32299:	VPB-101		
32300:	VB-116		Operational Loss 5/26/44
32301:	VPB-115		

Listing of Known PB4Y-1 Liberators Assigned to Pacific-based Squadrons

BUREAU NUMBER	SQUADRON(S)	NAME	REMARKS
32302:	VPB-115/VPB-101	*Loose Livin*	
32304:	VPB-115		
32305:	VPB-116		
32306:	VPB-116		
32307:	VB-116		
32308:	VB-116		
32309:	VB-116		
32310:	VB-116		
32311:	VD-1		Scrapped in Stillwater, Oklahoma
32312:	VD-1		
32313:	VD-1		
32314:	VD-1/VPB-122		Scrapped in Stillwater, Oklahoma
32316:	VPB-102		
32317:	VPB-102		
32318:	VPB-102		
32319:	VPB-102		Operational Loss 9/9/44
32320:	VPB-102		
32321:	VPB-102		
32322:	VPB-102		Operational Loss 9/8/44
32323:	VPB-102	*Easy Maid*	Lost in Action 8/23/44
32324:	VPB-102		
32325:	VPB-102		Loss 3/3/45
32326:	VPB-102		Loss 3/3/45
32327:	VPB-116		
32328:	VPB-106		Operational Loss 12/19/44
32329:	VPB-111		
32330:	VPB-111		
32331:	VPB-111		
32332:	VPB-111		
32333:	VPB-102		

Bureau Numbers 38733 to 38979 B-24Js

38733:	VPB-111	*Chief's Filly* or *Modest Miss*	
38734:	VPB-116	*Dazy May*	
38735:	VPB-117		
38736:	VPB-117		
38737:	VPB-117		
38738:	VPB-117		
38739:	VPB-117		Operational Loss 8/9/44
38740:	VPB-117		
38741:	VPB-117		Operational Loss 2/17/45
38742:	VPB-117		
38743:	VPB-117/119		

BUREAU NUMBER	SQUADRON(S)	NAME	REMARKS
38744:	VPB-117		
38745:	VPB-111/117		
38746:	VPB-111/106	*Doc's Delight*	
38747:	VPB-111	*Too Hot To Handle*	
38749:	VPB-111	*Three Dreams and a Drink*	
38750:	VPB-111	*The Snooper*	
38754:	VPB-104		Operational Loss 1/7/45
38755:	VPB-116	*Peace Feeler*	
38756:	VD-5		
38757:	VPB-117		
38758:	VPB-117		
38759:	VPB-117	*Ready, Willing, and Able*	
38760:	VPB-117		Lost in Action 11/12/44
38761:	VPB-117/104		
38762:	VD-5		
38764:	VD-5		
38766:	VPB-116/102	*Lady Lib*	Operational Loss 8/9/44
38767:	VPB-102		
38768:	VPB-116		
38769:	VPB-116		Operational Loss 6/26/44
38773:	VPB-117		
38774:	VPB-117?	*The Frumious Bandersnatch* (sp)	
38776:	VPB-116		Lost in Action 10/11/44
38777:	VPB-116	*Sleepy Time Gal*	
38779:	VB-109/116		
38780:	VPB-116		
38781:	VD-5		
38783:	VPB-102	*No Strain II*	
38788:	VD-5		
38789:	VPB-104		
38791:	VPB-102		
38792:	VPB-102		Loss 3/10/45
38794:	VPB-102		Operational Loss 4/1/45
38795:	VPB-104		
38799:	VPB-116		
38800:	VPB-116	*Tin Yan Ty Foon*?	
38801:	VPB-104		
38802:	VD-5		Loss 5/22/45
38803:	VPB-116		Loss 4/13/45
38804:	VPB-102		
38805:	VD-5		Loss 5/22/45
38806:	VPB-104		

Listing of Known PB4Y-1 Liberators Assigned to Pacific-based Squadrons

BUREAU NUMBER	SQUADRON(S)	NAME	REMARKS
38807:	VPB-104		Operational Loss 1/24/45
38808:	VD-5		
38809:	VPB-104/119		
38812:	VD-5		
38813:	VPB-104		
38814:	VPB-104		
38815:	VD-5		Loss 3/6/45
38816:	VPB-104		
38817:	VD-3		
38818:	VD-3		
38819:	VPB-116/102		Loss 4/17/45
38820:	VPB-116		
38821:	VD-3		
38822:	VPB-111		
38823:	VPB-117		Operational Loss 5/12/44
38827:	VD-3		
38828:	VPB-102		Loss 3/27/45
38829:	VB-115/101		
38830:	VD-3		
38831:	VD-3		
38832:	VD-1		
38833:	VPB-117/111		
38836:	VPB-111	*Little Snatch*	
38834:	VPB-104	*Here She Is Again*	
38835:	VPB-104		
38836:	VPB-111		
38840:	VPB-101		Operational Loss 1/15/45
38843:	VPB-102	*Lil Effie* (previous name "Boss Burten's Nightmare")	Operational Loss 5/26/45
38844:	VPB-116		Loss 4/11/45
38845:	VPB-116		Loss 4/14/45
38846:	VPB-117		
38847:	VPB-101/117		
38848:	VPB-101		
38849:	VPB-104		Operational Loss 12/30/44
38852:	VPB-101/104/117		
38853:	VPB-116/117/121	*Low Blow*	
38854:	VPB-116		Loss 5/18/45
38855:	VPB-116		Loss 7/28/45
38856:	VPB-101/104		
38857:	VPB-102		Loss 5/9/45
38858:	VPB-116		Loss 7/28/45

BUREAU NUMBER	SQUADRON(S)	NAME	REMARKS
38859:	VPB-104		
38860:	VPB-116		Loss
38861:	VPB-117		
38862:	VPB-116		
38863:	VPB-117		Operational Loss 5/14/45
38867:	VPB-102		Loss 3/23/45
38868:	VPB-116		Loss 7/28/45
38869:	VPB-104		Operational Loss 5/13/45
38870:	VPB-104		Operational Loss 5/13/45
38871:	VPB-102		Loss 4/23/45
38872:	VPB-101		
38873:	VPB-116		Operational Loss 4/2/45
38874:	VPB-104		
38875:	VPB-104		
38876:	VPB-104		Lost in Action 1/11/45
38880:	VPB-102		
38882:	VPB-111/117		Operational Loss 7/4/45
38883:	VPB-117		
38889:	VPB-104		
38890:	VPB-104		
38891:	VPB-101/117		Operational Loss 2/23/45
38892:	VPB-111	*Lady Luck*	
38893:	VPB-123		Operational Loss 4/6/45
38894:	VD-1		
38895:	VPB-111	*Mucalone*	
38896:	VPB-117	*Lucky Puss*	Operational loss on 4/18/45
38897:	VPB-111		
38898:	VPB-101/117		
38899:	VD-3/VD-l		
38900:	VPB-111		Operational Loss 1/10/45
38901:	VPB-111	"Slidin Home"	
38904:	VD-3		
38905:	VPB-102		Loss 6/10/45
38906:	VPB-111	"Reputation Cloudy"	
38908:	VD-3		
38913:	VPB-111	"Rugged Beloved"	
38914:	VPB-116		Operational Loss 1/12/45
38915:	VPB-116		Loss 7/28/45
38916:	VPB-102		
38917:	VPB-104/111		
38918:	VPB-102		Loss 7/2/45
38920:	VPB-102		Loss 8/11/45
38922:	VPB-116		Loss 7/28/45

Listing of Known PB4Y-1 Liberators Assigned to Pacific-based Squadrons

BUREAU NUMBER	SQUADRON(S)	NAME	REMARKS
38923:	VPB-116	"Easy Maid"	
38924:	VPB-104		
38925:	VPB-117		
38926:	VPB-101/104		
38927:	VPB-104		Operational Loss 12/12/44
38932:	VPB-102		Operational Loss 5/9/45
38933:	VPB-104		Operational Loss 3/45
38934:	VPB-117		Operational Loss 6/33/45
38935:	VPB-102		Operational Loss 7/10/45
38939:	VPB-102		
38940:	VPB-111		
38942:	VPB-111		
38943:	VPB-102		
38944:	VPB-116		
38945:	VPB-111		Operational Loss on 7/5/45
38946:	VPB-117		
38951:	VPB-111		
38953:	VPB-116		
38954:	VD-5		
38955:	VD-1/VPB-108		
38956:	VD-4		
38957:	VPB-111		
38958:	VD-4		
38959:	VPB-102		
38960:	VPB-116	"Worrybird"	
38961:	VPB-117		
38962:	VPB-102		
38963:	VPB-117		
38964:	VPB-102		
38965:	VPB-102		Loss 7/30/45
38970:	VPB-117		Scrapped in Stillwater, Oklahoma
38971:	VPB-111/119		
38972:	VPB-104		Operational Loss 1/17/45
38973:	VPB-104		
38974:	VPB-101/104		
38975:	VPB-102		
38976:	VPB-111		Operational Loss 6/20/45
38977:	VPB-116/VD-5		
38978:	VPB-117		
38979:	VPB-111/104		

BUREAU NUMBER	SQUADRON(S)	NAME	REMARKS
Bureau Numbers 46725 to 46737 B-24Ls			
46725:	VPB-104		Operational Loss 7/9/45
46726:	VPB-111		
46728:	VD-1		
46729:	VPB-104		
46730:	VPB-104		Operational Loss 8/1/45
46731:	VPB-102		
43746:	VPB-104		
46737:	VD-4		
Bureau Numbers 63915 to 63991 B-24Ds			
63813:	VPB-104		Operational Loss 1/2/45
Bureau Numbers 65287 to 65396 B-24L and M			
65298:	VD-5		
65299:	VD-1	Rovin' Redhead"	
65320:	VD-5		
65327:	VD-5		
65328:	VD-5		
65338:	VD-5		
65339:	VD-5		
65341:	VD-5		
65385:	Possibly VD-1	"Brown Baggers Retreat"	
Bureau Numbers 90462 to 90483 B-24Ms			
90471:	VPB-102		Operational Loss 8/10/45
90478:	VPB-116		Loss 5/18/45
90479:	VPB-116		
90482:	VPB-104		Loss 6/29/45

Bibliography

Government Documents

Aircraft Accident Reports, Roll 25. Naval Aviation Safety Center. Navy Historical Center, Washington, DC.

After Action Reports and War Diaries from various squadrons available through the National Archives and Records Administration at College Park, Maryland.

Air Force Combat Units of World War II. Washington, DC. US Government Printing Office, 1961.

Japanese Naval and Merchant Shipping Losses During World War II by all Causes. Joint-Navy Assessment Committee, 1947.

Air Intelligence Group, Divison of Naval Intelligence, Office of the Chief of Naval Operations, Navy Department, Washington, DC. Interview of Lt. Commander Gordon Fowler, USN: Ten months as the Executive Officer and Commanding Officer of VB-102. OPNAV-16-V-#E36, 14 March 1944.

Air Intelligence Group, Divison of Naval Intelligence, Office of the Chief of Naval Operations, Navy Department, Washington, DC. Interview of Lt. Commander J. T. Hayward, USN: From October 1943 to June 1944 Commanding Officer of VB-106, Operating in the Central, South, and Southwest Pacific OPNAV-16-V-#E117, 23 June 1944.

CinCPac-CinCpoa Confidential Serial SE-260900 dated 26 October 1945 and Dispatches from and to commanding officer USS *Thornhill* (DE-195).

Individual Deceased Personnel Files of: Elmer H. Kasperson, Warren A. Hindenlang, Keith E. Ellis, Joseph W. Komorowski, Warren B. Simon, Richard D. Frye, Hugo L. Kluge, William F. Schbeider, Victor B. Jones, Allen K. Stinger, and Bobby W. Fickling. Department of the Army: US Army Human Resources Command.

Memorandum from Commanding Officer, No. 100 Squadron, RAAF, Townsville to Headquarters, No. 5. B.P.S.O, RAAF, Milne Bay. Confirming Memorandum Loss Beaufort A-9-255-Flying Officer J. C. Davis dated 18 July 1943. RAAF Aircraft Lost Report Index Card dated 12/7/43 with handwritten updates to 12/7/47.

US Naval Aviation in the Pacific. Office of the Chief of Naval Operations. US Navy, 1947.

Naval Aviation Combat Statistics: World War II. Air Branch, Office of Naval Intelligence, Office of the Chief of Naval Operations. Navy Department. OPNAV-P-23V No. A129. 17 June 1946.

WWII JAG Case Files, Pacific-Navy. JAG Docket No. 154578. Transcripts of Case No. 33, The Trail of Yoshio Tachibana et al., August 15–October 4, 1946. War Crimes Trial of Tachibana, Yoshio et al. 1946.

Published Sources

Arnold, Rhodes. *The B-24/PB4Y in Combat: The World's Greatest Bomber*. Reserve, New Mexico: Pima Paisano Publications.

Birdsall, Steve. *Log of the Liberators*. Garden City, New York: Doubleday & Company, 1973.

Boyd, Karl and Akihiko Yoshida. *The Japanese Submarine Force and World War II*. Annapolis, Maryland: Naval Institute Press, 1995.

Carey, Alan C. *The Reluctant Raiders: The Story of United States Navy Bombing Squadron VB/VPB-109 in World War II*. Atglen, PA: Schiffer Publishing, 1999.

Carey, Robert W., with Alan C. Carey. *Junior: The Tales of a Teenage Waist Gunner in the Pacific*. Merriam Press, 2002.

Casey Louis S. and John Batchelor. *The Illustrated History of Seaplanes & Flying Boats*. New York, New York: Exeter Books, 1980.

Dawes, Gavan. *Prisoners of the Japanese*. New York, New York. William Morrow and Company, 1994.

Frank, Richard B. *Guadalcanal: The Definitive Account of the Landmark Battle*. New York, New York: Random House, 1990.

Friedman, Norman. *U.S. Naval Weapons*. Naval Institute Press.

Furey, Charles. *Going Back: A Navy Airman in the Pacific War*. Naval Institute Press: Annapolis, Maryland. 1997.

Green, William and Gordon Swanborough. *The Complete Book of Fighters: An Illustrated Encyclopedia of Every Fighter Aircraft built and Flown*. New York, New York. Smithmark Publishers, Inc., 1994.

Hata, Ikuhiko and Yasuho Izawa. Translated by Don Cyril Gorham. *Japanese Naval Aces and Fighter Units in World War II*. Annapolis, Maryland: Naval Institute Press, 1989.

Hearn, Chester. *Sorties Into Hell: The Hidden War on Chichi Jima*. Guilford, Connecticut: The Lyons Press, 2005.

Ito, Masanori. *The End of the Imperial Japanese Navy*. New York: Mackadden-Bartell, 1962.

Johnson, Frederick A. *Bombers in Blue*. Tacoma, Washington: Bomber Books, 1979.

Mason, Francis S. *The Illustrated Encyclopedia of Major Aircraft of World War II*. New York, New York. Crescent Books, 1983.

Miller, Norman M., and Hugh B. Cave. *I Took the Sky Road*. New York, New York: Dodd, Mead & Company, 1945.

Morison, Samuel Eliot. *History of United States Naval Operations in World War II. Breaking the Bismarcks Barrier*. Vol. VI. Little, Brown and Company, 1950.

Morison, Samuel Eliot. History of United States Naval Operations in World War II. *Aleutians, Gilberts and Marshalls*. Vol. VII, Boston, Mass: Little, Brown and Company, 1990.

Morison, Samuel Eliot. *History of United States Naval Operations in World War II. New Guinea and the Marianas*. Vol. VIII. Boston, Mass: Little, Brown and Company, 1981.

Stevens, Paul F. *Low Level Liberators*. El Cajon, CA: Whitmar Electronic Press, 1997.

Thompson, Henry J. *The Buccaneers of Harry Sears: The History of Navy Bombing Squadron 104*. Coronado, CA: Charlie Horse Books, 1997.

Tillman, Barrett. *Corsair: The F4U in WWII and Korea*. Annapolis: Maryland. Naval Institute Press, 1978 reprinted in 1987.

Wolpert, Robert L. *The Story of One Eleven*. Emerson, NJ: Emerson Quality Press, Inc., 1990.

Woodbury, David O. *Builders for Battle*. New York, NY: E.P. Dutton and Company Inc., 1946.

Periodicals

Jack Authelet. Author of a Memorial Day 2004 article appearing in the *Foxboro Reporter* newspaper.

Non-Published Sources

Scott, Harlan G. United States Bombing Squadron One Hundred Eight (Tokyo Rose's Four Engine Fighters).

Thoman, Louise T, Editor. US Navy Squadrons VP-14, VB-102, VPB-102: A Chronicle—1938 to 1994, 1998.

VB-106 Tour Book.

Personal Correspondence and Digital Recordings

Downing of a Betty by Robert E. Jacques (VB-102) and contributed by his nephew Frank Ziberna.

Letters from Victor Boyd Jones letters to his family.

Letters from Commander William A. Moffitt Jr., to Lafayette L. Baldwin the father of Lee Baldwin.

Letters from Lee Baldwin to his Family.

Letters from Joseph Komoroski to his family.

Navy Flightlog book of Frank Betz.

Notes written by Jack W. Cook in his flight log book.

Digital Audio Recordings of Allen Morgan by his son Joseph Morgan.

Digital Audio Recordings of Robert W. Carey by personnel from the Armed Forces Retirement Home, Biloxi, Mississippi. 2003.

Digital Written Version of, "In Memorial of William Ferguson Schneider." by nephew Dan C. Dwyer. September 9, 2004.

Endnotes

Introduction

[1] Steve Birdsall *Log of the Liberators: An Illustrated History of the B-24* (Garden City, NY: Doubleday), 128

[2] Frederick A. Johnson, *Bombers in Blue* (Tacoma, WA: Bomber Books), 1.

Chapter One

[1] From a letter titled, *The Non-Pilot Navigators, The VB-106 Agitators, and the Terrible Thirteen*, by Howard Ells with corroboration by Art Hacker. The Navy had established a system where three naval aviators would be assigned to a patrol plane flight crew. Patrol Plane Commanders (PPC), Patrol Plane First Pilot (PP1P), and Patrol Plane Second Pilot (PP2P-actually the Navigator). Because of a shortage of naval aviators, the Chief of Naval Personnel established a new policy. This policy established a non-pilot navigator position on the flight crew. This was a one-year tour of duty overseas and volunteers would be returned to the United States for primary flight training. Some squadrons, such as VB-106, found this system an irritation because combat-trained navigators would leave the squadron as soon as their replacements arrived.

[2] Andy Halaz as told to Dianne Hunter.

[3] Samual Elliot Morison, *Breaking the Bismarcks Barrier (22 July 1943-1 May 1944)* (Boston, MA: Little, Brown and Company).

[4] Richard B. Frank, *Guadalcanal: The Definitive Account of the Landmark Battle* (New York, NY: Random House).

[5] Louise C. Thoman, US Navy Squadrons VP-14, VB-102, VPB-102: A Chronicle-1938 to 1994).

[6] Flight log book of Frank Betz from the Betz Family Collection.

[7] Tillman, Barrett. *The F4U in World War II and Korea*, 30.

[8] Morison, 97.

[9] Letter by Lee Baldwin to his sister Lillie Ann Flora (Baldwin).

[10] Ibid.

[11] Remembrances by George H.G. Webster.

[12] Copy of a letter to Mr. Baldwin's father from Commander Moffett courtesy of Mrs. Lillie Ann Flora.

[13] Letter to the author from Lillie Ann Flora (Baldwin) dated 9 February 2016.

[14] Louise C. Thoman, US Navy Squadrons VP-14, VB-102, VPB-102.

Chapter Two

[1] Morison, 139–42.

[2] Ibid. 147–55.

[3] Ibid. 160–75.

[4] Japanese units identified by Kamada.

[5] Louis Thoman.

[6] Morison, 180–91.

[7] Kamada.

[8] Memorandum from Commanding Officer, No. 100 Squadron, RAAF, Townsville to Headquarters, No. 5. B.P.S.O, RAAF, Milne Bay. Confirming Memorandum Loss Beaufort A-9-255-Flying Officer J. C. Davis dated 18 July 1943. Aircraft Lost Report Index Card dated 12/7/43 with handwritten updates to 12/7/47.

Chapter Three

[1] H. Peter Kooy, One Against Seven, *Foundation Magazine*, Spring 1994, 62–67.

[2] H. J. Thompson, *The Buccaneers of Harry Sears*, (El Cajon, CA: WhitMar Electronic Press).

[3] Thompson, 118–22.

[4] 96–98.

[5] Ibid.

[6] Ibid.

[7] Ibid.

[8] 114–115.

Chapter Four

[1] Thompson.
[2] Ibid. 118–22.
[3] Thompson, 127–29.
[4] Sears, 113–114.
[5] Ibid, 116–117.
[6] Kamada.
[7] Downing of a Betty by Robert E. Jacques (VB-102) and contributed by his nephew Frank Ziberna.
[8] Thompson, 127–29.
[9] Ibid, 137–38.
[10] Ibid, 140–147.

Chapter Five

[1] Thompson, 149–51.
[2] Interview of Lt. Commander Fowler, Air Intelligence Group.
[3] Interview of J. T. Hayward, Air Intelligence Group.
[4] Nate Hodge as told to the author.
[5] Medals awarded fifty years later. Four enlisted crewmen from VB-109, including the author's late father, were awarded two Distinguished Flying Crosses and nine Air Medals in 1997.
[6] Thompson, 153–54.
[7] Ibid.
[8] Ibid, 158.

Chapter Six

[1] Thompson, 171–73.
[2] Ibid. 165–168.
[3] Morison, 323.
[4] Ibid.
[5] Thompson, 193.
[6] Nate Hodge as told to the author.
[7] Ibid.

Chapter Seven

[1] Interview J. T. Hayward, Air Intelligence Group.
[2] Letter from Howard Ells with information provided by Art Hacker.
[3] Letter from Howard Ells with information provided by Art Hacker.
[4] Morison, 412–19, 432–448.
[5] Thompson, 234–37.
[6] Ibid. 240–242.
[7] Ibid. 254–55.
[8] Ibid.
[9] Ibid. 258–59.
[10] Ibid.
[11] Ibid.

Chapter Eight

[1] Letter from Rex Hardy to the author.
[2] The 17th Weather Squadron news letter provided by James F. Van Dyne.
[3] Going Back: A Navy Airman in the Pacific War, 156-57

Chapter Nine

[1] Letter from Rex Hardy.
[2] *Going Back: A Navy Airman in the Pacific War*, 156–57.

Chapter Ten

[1] Morison, 257–78.
[2] Ibid. 132–40.

Chapter Eleven

[1] Tape recordings of Allen C. Morgan by his son Joseph Morgan.
[2] Ibid.
[3] Morison, *Aleutians, Gilberts, and the Marshalls* (Boston, MA: Little, Brown and Company), 76.
[4] Letter to the author from Paul Hardy.

Chapter Twelve

[1] Recordings of Allen C. Morgan.
[2] See: Harlan Scott, *United States Navy Bombing Squadron One Hundred Eight (Tokyo Rose's Four Engine Fighters)*; CinCPac-CinCpoa Confidential Serial SE-260900 dated 26 October 1945; Dispatches from and to commanding officer U.S.S. *Thornhill* (DE-195); Allied Translator and Interpretation Section South West Pacific Area: Research Report No. 65 (Suppl No. 1), 29 Mar 1945.
[3] Japanese Naval and Merchant Shipping Losses during World War II by all Causes, Joint-Assessment Assessment Committee, 1947.

Chapter Thirteen

[1] Andy Halaz as told to Dianne Hunter.
[2] Morison, 214–15.
[3] Alan C. Carey, *The Reluctant Raiders: The Story of United States Navy Bombing Squadron VB/VPB-109 in World War II* (Atglen, PA: Schiffer Publishing, Ltd).
[4] Carey.

Chapter Fourteen

[1] Carey, 36.

Chapter Fifteen

[1] Morison, 315–332.
[2] Ibid.
[3] Ibid.
[4] Carey, The Reluctant Raiders.
[5] Morison, 310–14.

Endnotes

Chapter Sixteen

[1] Audio taped interview of Robert W. Carey Sr. by Soldiers and Sailors Home.

[2] A letter from a crewman on him being relieved of duty with a VB flight crew.

[3] Squadron press release courtesy of T. W. McCarthy.

[4] This is a very controversial statement, as an official report states Cdr. Miller piloted the plane back to base. See also Norman M. Miller and Hugh B. Cave, *I Took the Sky Road* (New York, NY: Dodd, Mead, & Company), 154–160, and *The Reluctant Raiders*, 73–77.

[5] The statement stating that both pilots were incapacitated was provided to this author orally by one of the crew members now deceased.

Chapter Seventeen

[1] Carey.

[2] T.W. McCarthy.

[3] Ibid.

Chapter Eighteen

[1] Miller and Cave, 167-177.

[2] Interview of Robert W. Carey Sr.

[3] Ibid.

Chapter Nineteen

[1] An article in the *Foxboro Reporter* about Memorial Day 2004 by Jack Authelet.

[2] Ibid.

[3] Phone interview of Tommy Fickling by the author.

[4] Dwyer, In Memory of William Fergusan Schneider.

[5] Letter from Joseph W. Komorowski to his family.

[6] Letter from Victor Jones to his mother.

[7] Ibid.

[8] Ibid.

[9] Ibid.

[10] A well-researched book on Japanese atrocities on ChiChi Jima is Chester Hearn's *Sorties Into Hell: The Hidden War on Chichi Jima*. The unknown flyer is referenced as a radioman and describes his physical characteristics, 90–93.

[11] Hearn, 92.

[12] Transcripts of Case No. 33, The Trail of Yoshio Tachibana et al.

[13] Hearn, 96–97

[14] Ibid, 36.

[15] Ibid, 152–53.

[16] Ibid, 134.

Chapter Twenty

[1] The Combat Diary and After Action Report of VPB-116.

Chapter Twenty-One

[1] Louis C. Thoman.

[2] Thoman.

Notes